T0358369

The **Rise** and **Fall** of Global Austerity

E Ray Canterbery

Florida State University, USA

The Rise and Fall of Global Austerity

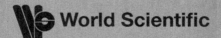 World Scientific

NEW JERSEY · LONDON · SINGAPORE · BEIJING · SHANGHAI · HONG KONG · TAIPEI · CHENNAI

Published by

World Scientific Publishing Co. Pte. Ltd.
5 Toh Tuck Link, Singapore 596224
USA office: 27 Warren Street, Suite 401-402, Hackensack, NJ 07601
UK office: 57 Shelton Street, Covent Garden, London WC2H 9HE

Library of Congress Cataloging-in-Publication Data
Canterbery, E. Ray.
 The rise and fall of global austerity / by E. Ray Canterbery (Florida State University, USA).
  pages cm
  ISBN 978-9814603485
 1. Global Financial Crisis, 2008–2009. 2. Recessions--History--21st century. 3. Economic
policy--21st century. I. Title.
  HB37172008 C363 2015
  330.9'0511--dc23

                                    2014011431

British Library Cataloguing-in-Publication Data
A catalogue record for this book is available from the British Library.

Photo by Allison Harden

Copyright © 2015 by World Scientific Publishing Co. Pte. Ltd.

All rights reserved. This book, or parts thereof, may not be reproduced in any form or by any means, electronic or mechanical, including photocopying, recording or any information storage and retrieval system now known or to be invented, without written permission from the publisher.

For photocopying of material in this volume, please pay a copying fee through the Copyright Clearance Center, Inc., 222 Rosewood Drive, Danvers, MA 01923, USA. In this case permission to photocopy is not required from the publisher.

In-house Editors: Dipasri Sardar/Chye Shu Wen/Rajni Gamage

Typeset by Stallion Press
Email: enquiries@stallionpress.com

Printed in Singapore

To the Keynesians and Post Keynesians who got it right

Also by E. Ray Canterbery

Harry S. Truman: The Economics of a Populist President
The Global Great Recession
Alan Greenspan: The Oracle Behind the Curtain
F. Scott Fitzgerald: Under the Influence (with Thomas Birch)
The Making of Economics (four editions)
A Brief History of Economics (two editions)
Wall Street Capitalism: The Theory of the Bondholding Class
Black Box Inc. (a novel)
The Literate Economist
Economics on a New Frontier
Foreign Exchange, Capital Flows and Monetary Policy
The President's Council of Economic Advisers

Contents

About the Author

Photo by
Allison Harden

A former Professor of Economics at Florida State University, E. Ray Canterbery is one of the most respected economists of his generation. In 2003 John Kenneth Galbraith, who knew both Michal Kalecki and John Maynard Keynes, called Canterbery, "the best." He conducted research as a Truman Scholar in 2004, which led to his recent book, *Harry S. Truman: The Economics of a Populist President* (2014). Canterbery is the author of many acclaimed books (and articles), including *The Global Great Recession*, the tour de force *Wall Street Capitalism*, biographies of *Alan Greenspan* and of *F. Scott Fitzgerald* (co-authored with Thomas Birch), the classic, *The Making of Economics*, and the best-selling *A Brief History of Economics*, many of which are available in several languages. He returns to his global concerns with *The Rise and Fall of Global Austerity*. He served as President of the Eastern Economics Association in 1986–1987 and of the International Trade and Finance Association in 1997–1998.

In January 1996, Prentice-Hall, Inc. selected Canterbery for their Hall of Fame Economist Baseball Cards for "significant contributions to the economics discipline," including the development of one of the first complete mathematical theories of foreign exchange, a new theory of the labor market and of personal incomes (vita theory), which later was integrated into international trade theory.

The international Biography Centre in Cambridge, England includes Canterbery among 500 persons worldwide in its *Living Legends* (2002), among 2000 scholars worldwide in its *Outstanding Scholars in the 21st Century,* among *One Thousand Great Intellectuals* (2003), among *2000 Outstanding People* (2003) worldwide, and among *1000 Great Americans* (2003). The American Biographical Institute includes Canterbery in its *Great Minds of the 21st Century* (2002) and *American Biography* (2003). He is also listed in selected issues of Marquis *Who's Who in the World* and *Who's Who in America,* as well as other biographical sources.

Introduction

A usterity is a 17th century noun, which has new-found popularity. It was the most researched term of 2010. It has three layers of definitions. In no case is it a pleasant term. In the first instance it refers to severity or plainness, severity of discipline, regime, expression, or design. In the second layer of meaning it is an economy measure: a saving, economy, or act of self-denial, especially in respect of something regarded as a luxury. It invokes the idea of self-flagellation at the personal level. Still, not forgetting about the notion of self-denial, we will be concerned mostly with the third layer of meaning. Austerity is enforced, thrift: thrift imposed as government policy, with restricted access to or availability of consumer goods. With regard to public policy, it has a broader meaning with broader implications, the outcomes including poverty and ill-health. In a period of slow recovery from the Great Recession, should we really be worried about austerity?

We begin our story in 2010, the year when austerity became a famous 21st century term. The global economy was slowly beginning to hum in January 2010, clawing its way out of the depths of the Great Recession. Two Harvard economists, Carmen Reinhart and Ken Rogoff, at that time published a brief paper with a simplistic conclusion: Too much debt stifles economic growth.[1] They claimed to show that debt episodes throughout the 20th century led to years — sometimes decades — of stagnation. To be exact, the study

---

[1]The paper was titled "Growth in a Time of Debt." Later, it was summarized and "updated" in *Bloomberg Business Week*, "When Debt Stifles Growth," July 14, 2011, available on the Internet.

"found relatively little association between public liabilities and growth for debt levels of less than 90% of GDP. But burdens above 90% are associated with 1% lower median growth. Their results are based on a data set of public debt covering 44 countries for up to 200 years."[2]

The study was a bombshell heard round the world, or at least from Washington to Brussels. The 90% rule was ignored, and the broader conclusion accepted wholeheartedly. In the short run, it was one of the influential papers in history. Suddenly, ending federal budget deficits became more important than ending a recession. As luck would have it, for at least the next three years, austerity was the catchword of the day. There was a headlong rush to slash spending among many countries, including especially, the United States. The 90% rule was surpassed during the Great Recession. Had the researchers been anywhere but Harvard, they perhaps would have been ignored.

Illus. I.1:   Austerity as the only answer.

---

[2] *Ibid.*, p. 2.

It was not until April 15, 2013 that the Reinhart–Rogoff paper could be dismissed as rubbish. Two researchers at the University of Massachusetts published a paper that closely examined the Reinhart and Rogoff database. R & R's data contained data from 20 countries that filled lines 30–49 on the spreadsheet, but the formula that calculated the results relied on lines 30–44. It was the Excel error heard round the world. The second paper changed everything, but political opinions.

To understand why what should have been a dry academic debate became a cause to celebrate, we need to return to that moment in January 2010. While the Great Recession was "officially" over way back in June 2009, the reality for working Americans remained bleak. The unemployment rate was around 10%, at depression levels. A broader unemployment measure that includes discouraged job seekers and those forced to accept part-time work was near 17%. GDP was limping along at about 2% a year. Real wage growth was negative. Contrary to classical economic theory, falling real wages were accompanied by high unemployment.

The overall problem has been explained elsewhere. The housing bubble had burst. Banks were hanging tough with great losses on their housing-related security issues. They had to sell assets to remain solvent. However, when everyone sells all at once, and nobody wants to buy, falling prices require ever more asset sales, producing in turn ever steeper price drops and further asset sales. It is a vicious cycle that transformed an ordinary recession into a banking crisis recession.[3]

With recovery so weak that a faint pulse is all that could be heard, another round of economic stimulus seemed to be in order. But the political world had something else in mind, namely austerity. Republicans had voted against President Obama's first stimulus bill almost unanimously. There was little reason to think they would be any more receptive to a second Obama round. (The first stimulus bill by the George Bush Administration was anemic in comparison.)

---

[3]See E. Ray Canterbery, *The Global Great Recession* (New Jersey, London, and Singapore: World Scientific Publishing Co., 2011).

Worse, there was other opposition. In the fall of 2009, with the economy still on life support, there was internal disagreement within the White House about whether to push for more injections or rather to turn toward the country's mounting deficits. The federal deficits were a natural consequence of falling incomes during the Great Recession. For reasons both political (reality) and ideological (in part coming from the public), Obama decided to give the federal deficits priority. As he said in his 2010 State of the Union address, "Since families across the country are tightening their belts," the federal government should do the same. The Herbert Hoover of the Great Depression could have written this line.

Hoover notwithstanding, during hard times, most economists are Keynesians. Most economists said that fiscal stimulus was appropriate at this time. Only the lunatic fringe argued otherwise. Nobel Prize winners Paul Krugman and Joseph E. Stiglitz were quick to publish books stating emphatically the case for Keynes and his interpreters.[4] Stiglitz prophetically contended that the dominance of believers in immediate austerity or "Austerians" were already well established by the spring of 2010.[5] I joined the Nobel choir, contending that the Great Recession had never really ended, and more fiscal stimulus was needed.[6]

The problem was so simple, it is difficult to understand why it was missed by most economists. The housing bubble had burst, and commercial banks were struck with enormous losses on their housing-related securities. They needed to sell assets to remain solvent, but which assets and when. If everyone wants to sell all at once, then nobody wants to buy, the result is falling prices for goods and assets. Such declines require ever more asset sales, which in turn means ever steeper price drops and more asset sales. It was a non-virtuous

---

[4] See Paul Krugman, *End this Depression Now!* (New York and London: W.W. Norton & Company, 2012) and Joseph E. Stiglitz, *Freefall* (New York & London: W.W. Norton & Company, 2010).

[5] Stiglitz, *ibid.*, p. 189.

[6] See E. Ray Canterbery, *The Global Great Recession, op. cit.*, especially, pp. xii–xiv, 315–334.

cycle that was to transform an ordinary recession into something far worse — a financial crisis recession.

In an earlier (more accurate) work by Reinhart and Rogoff, red flags were raised for a different reason: the title, *This Time is Different,* bristles with irony.[7] Reinhart and Rogoff found that while quick government action might rescue failing financial institutions, the broader recessions brought on by the financial crises last a very long time. Five years is not unusual. What is always needed is for the federal government to apply the same urgency to saving the economy that it did in rescuing the banks. As noted elsewhere, in the U.S. bank bailouts and emergency cash injections by the Federal Reserve saved the banks.[8] Properly taken, *This Time is Different* was an early warning for what was to come and the needed response. The general economic problem was similar to the banking system.

Everyone wanting to save, and no one wanting to borrow or spend is a recipe for a long-lasting disaster. Earlier, it was described by John Maynard Keynes as the paradox of thrift. While it is a virtue for individuals to save money, in the macroeconomy it brings the economy to a grinding halt because everyone stops spending at once. Factories are closed, workers are laid off, and unemployment rockets upward. It is what happened during the Great Depression. The remedy, insufficient though it was, was embedded in the New Deal.

The lesson learned is that we cannot count on the private economy through rising consumption and investment to right the economic ship. The waters are too turbulent for that. In 2010, there was still a need for a second major Obama stimulus. Instead, what we got were weak half-measures, though in the right direction. To be fair, the President was faced with implacable Republican opposition. If the truth be known, there also was opposition in his own party. The opposition invoked the theory, such as it was, of austerity. To Keynesians the Obama Administration had it exactly

---

[7] Carmen M. Reinhart and Kenneth S. Rogoff, *This Time is Different: Eight Centuries of Financial Folly* (Princeton and Oxford: Princeton University Press, 2009). The book is favorably cited by Canterbery, *ibid.*

[8] See Canterbery, *op. cit.* The details are provided here.

backward. But it wasn't just Keynesians. Only a few die-hard econo-mists were saying that the federal deficit was crowding out private investment and public consumption. Most economists said that deficit spending was appropriate at a time that was *not* different.

Anyway, Keynes around the world was beside the point. The little paper by Reinhart and Rogoff carried the day. Fiscal policy for the next three years was set in concrete. The Reinhart–Rogoff conclu-sions were headlined in newspapers around the world. Cited by columnists, they also testified before Congress. Moreover, the head of the European Union's commission on economic policy used their findings to justify sharp spending cuts designed to reduce govern-ment debt in Greece, Italy, and Spain. Austerity became the world's theme song.

In the U.S., deficit hawks were all singing the same song. Future Vice Presidential nominee Paul Ryan warned that a debt level above 90% "intensifies the risk of a debt-fueled economic crisis." Republicans never saw a debt wagon that they didn't want to jump on. Scared Democrats went along. "We're past the danger zone," Sen. Kent Conrad (D.N.D.), Head of the Senate Budget Committee, intoned at the time. The consequences for the U.S. were set.

Budget deals in 2010 and 2011 reduced the deficit by $760 bil-lion. An Obama compromise in August 2011 to resolve a debt ceiling crisis and government shutdown, produced about $1.1 trillion in spending cuts along with the promise of more from a congressional super-committee. At the end of 2012, the fiscal-cliff showdown resulted in $850 billion in tax increases and spending cuts. Then, in the ides of March, sequestration cuts came in, to the tune of another $1.2 trillion. As a whole, these measures cut the deficit by $3.9 trillion over the next 10 years. This excludes cuts in unemployment benefits and the elimination of stimulus measures like the payroll tax holiday. Compared with like periods of post-recession fiscal policy, this was unprecedented. After every other recent recession, government spending continued during the recovery.

This country, like most, cannot depend on deficit spending by state and local governments for stimulus, for statutes require their budgets be balanced. So *total* government spending peaked in the second quarter of 2010 and then started falling, and falling some more. Between the publication of Reinhart and Rogoff's little paper and 2013, government spending at all levels — state, local, and federal combined — declined 7%.

This new austerity did not go entirely unnoticed. There were plenty who warned that austerity was strangling the recovery in its infancy. All one needed to do was look at history. Recovery was underway during the first New Deal, until fear of inflation raised its ugly head. Then FDR prematurely cut spending in 1937, guaranteeing that the recession become the Great Depression. After 2008, austerity in Europe crippled the recovery there and kept unemployment at amazingly high levels in Greece, Portugal, Spain, Ireland, and other countries. Ben Bernanke, a student of the Great Depression, all but begged Congress not to sabotage the recovery with foolish spending cuts. He responded to the fiscal malpractice by following the easiest monetary policy in history. Few recognized that sometimes debt is simply debt. Moreover, faster growth can reduce debt in the long run.

A lethargic economy causes the obvious short-run problems — people out of work, wages stagnant, and houses foreclosed, but it also causes permanent damage in the future. When people are out of work for a year or two, nobody wants to hire them and they end up out of the labor force for good and bad. Cyclical unemployment of the normal kind turns into permanent, structural unemployment.

Spain may provide the worst example with unemployment reaching depression levels of 27%. Policymakers there swore on some defunct economist's bible that austerity was the route to redemption. Some one-tenth of the country had been without work for more than two years. Among the young, the unemployment rate was 57%. That is, more than half of the youth of Spain was out of work. The data for Greece is just as bad, and only slightly less catastrophic in Ireland, Italy, and Portugal. Austerity was taking its toll in Europe.

But let us return to the U.S., the world's largest economy and the keystone to the global system. What has been the cost of austerity at this juncture? Extrapolating from Congressional Budget

Office estimates, a rough guess is that austerity has cut economic growth by about 2 percentage points — about half the total growth we might normally expect following a recession. This is the halving of economic growth predicted by Reinhart and Rogoff for running up the national debt above 90%, but we got this from *not* running up the debt. As a result, we are unlikely to return to full capacity utilization and full employment until around 2017.

We have a sustained output gap, the difference between actual GDP and potential full capacity GDP. If we had spent more, we would have had more jobs, higher wages, healthier retirement accounts, and, ironically, but predictably, a shrinking deficit due to higher tax revenues and lower spending on welfare programs for the poor. Our obsession with austerity has damaged us in more subtle ways, as well. With real interest rates actually negative much of the time, the federal government could have spent money and then paid it back with less than what we borrowed in the first place. We had a once-in-a-generation opportunity to repair our decaying infrastructure at bargain prices — more roads, bridges, airports, rail lines, local transit, electrical grids, gas pipelines, internet backbones, and more. Not only would such projects employ more workers short-term, the increased public productivity would lead to higher rates of economic growth over the long run. Sooner, rather than later, we will have to pay the price for this higher maintenance. Worse, we missed the opportunity to pull this off on the cheap. Moreover, the rate of return on public investment is higher than on private investment.

Besides slow growth and parsimony in public investment, our obsession with austerity hurts in other ways. Austerity can kill people because it goes beyond self-denial, to imposed denial of social benefits. During the Great Depression, states that implemented New Deal programs most quickly saw significant declines in infectious diseases, child mortality, and suicides. Similar findings apply to the Asian financial crisis of 1998, and the current Great Recession. Austerity programs were life-threatening for the poor and the unemployed. And many were unemployed and poor because of austerity policies. Those whose health remains unaffected by austerity are the rich.

With such transparent problems, why does austerity often carry the day? Surely Reinhart and Rogoff are not entirely to blame for Washington's desire to ignore Econ 101 and instead commit America to a self-defeating war on the deficit and government debt. Not only was theirs just another paper, it was deeply, hopelessly flawed. Part of the answer, we will discover, is found in ideology. Another part is found in politics. Among Republicans, for instance, austerity provides a needed excuse for cutting social spending that they have never approved of in the first instance. Besides, they did not want a growing economy for President Obama to campaign on in 2012.

There is still more to it than this. Many think of economics as a morality tale. When we have been on a binge, we need to pay the piper. Others rely on folk wisdom. When times are bad, it is natural for households to tighten their belts. What is the decent thing to do for the households is not necessarily to be recommended to the government. After all, the proper role of the Federal government is to be countercyclical. When households and businesses are all cutting back at once, Congress needs to be the spender of last resort, thus to keep the economy from falling even further into recession. Folklore does not translate into good public policy.

Then, too, there is the matter of simple self-interest. Plenty of people have something to gain from austerity. The banks and pension funds and other creditors are hostile to the risk of deficit-fueled inflation eating away at the value of their assets, even if it means tolerating a long recession. And, they always believe that deficit-spending leads to hyper-inflation irrespective of the conditions in the economy. Among the fans of austerity polities are those of the finance industry. Austerity nicely diverts attention away from the market excesses that caused the banking crisis in the first place. And, again, inflation is the enemy of Wall Street, which again associates inflation with public debt.

In short, Reinhart and Rogoff were pushing on an unlocked door, or even a door ajar. How nice it was to be able to say that the pursuit of austerity was motivated not by polities or self-interest, but by a virtuous desire for economic growth. The 90% paper provided a red-line for that view.

We should not neglect the role of the top 1%, which jumped on the austerity bandwagon. Their assets are growing, their taxes are low, and their jobs are safe. It is the balance of society that is paying a high price in the form of slow growth, high unemployment, and stagnant wages for years to come. The poor and middle class has been remarkably sanguine about their fate. Those who run the world nonetheless may well ponder how long that is going to last.

No introduction to austerity would be complete without reference to the great Reaganomics experiment and its sister counterpart of Thatcherism in England. In the early 1980s, Reaganomics was implemented as a combination of supply-side economics and tight monetary policy. The intention was to balance the budget, end the growth of federal debt, and dismantle the welfare net. The theory behind supply-side economics was the old idea of trickle-down economics. By slashing taxes of the rich, investment would grow and the

Illus. I.2:   Reaganomics.

benefits would trickle down to the rich. The austerity came in the way of ending programs aimed at aiding the poor and the unemployed. It was Robin Hood in reverse; money taken from the poor would benefit the rich. This economic perversion caused the greatest downturn since the Great Depression with unemployment reaching 12%. The sister program in England had similar results. Still, to this day, Reaganomics is looked up to as the paradigm for fiscal austerity.

1

A Brief History of Austerity

Ideas, even bad ones, have intellectual origins. Austerity is not exceptional in this regard. Such good breeding gives such ideas respectability long after their usefulness has passed. The story of austerity begins with John Locke, one of England's most renowned philosophers. Along with austerity is a list of bad ideas handed down by Locke. Locke's writings were essential propaganda for the emerging merchant classes that were slowly taking power away from British aristocratic elites. His was a part of a movement that culminated in the Glorious Revolution of 1688 that unseated the king and empowered the rising merchant class.

John Locke: The Ultimate Defense of Private Property Rights

Locke was more than that: he was an economic revolutionary. Legitimate rule lay in individual property rights, required for economic liberalism and the separation of the state from the market. Capitalism as we know it today could not exist without this idea. Locke's vision is displayed in his *Second Treatise of Government* (1690). The separation of state and the market place requires several things. Income and wealth inequality must be naturalized, the private ownership of land must be legitimated, there must be an emergence of labor markets, and money must be depoliticized. Through it all, the individual is pitted against the state. In this are the beginnings of austerity's intellectual force.

Since the market did not exist, Locke had to imagine it. How is it possible for "God, who hath given the world to men in common" to allow the unequal, if not unlimited, accumulation of wealth?[1] To Locke, property resides in us all, in our persons, but it is only important because it resides with our labor. When we work on something, such as land, the laboring makes it our own. Thus, "whatsoever then he removes out of the state [of] nature . . . [and] mixed his labor with . . . [he] thereby makes it his property."[2] Taking a portion of land in this way does not deplete it because of its abundance. Thus, property does not require a vote to apportion it because it is infinite. You have to wonder where economists got the idea of scarcity.

The only argument against the accumulation of property is spoilage, having so much that you cannot store it properly. This is why if we did not have money, we would have to invent it. Actually, the device called money was invented out of necessity. Money can be stored indefinitely without fear of spoilage. It is the greatest invention since . . . you know. Money also enables the creation of a labor market because hired labor requires money wage payments. Workers can store money and swap it for consumer goods. Conveniently, contends Locke, "men have agreed to a disproportionate and unequal possession of the earth . . . by . . . voluntary consent [they have] found out a way how a man may fairly possess more land than he can fairly use the product of, by receiving, . . . the overplus of gold and silver, which may be hoarded up without injury too anyone."[3] Convenient indeed: Liberal economists never let us forget this argument favoring benign inequality.

It is inequitable and therefore good that markets in land, labor, and capital are created unequally. It was the project of the propertied class. These new institutions must be protected from capitalism's nemesis, the state.

And, so, Locke creates the imaginary state. The legislature is limited to the public good of the society, defined as freedom from intervention by government into private affairs, especially concerning

---

[1] John Locke, *Second Treatise on Civil Government* (Indianapolis, IN: Hackett, 1996), p. 28 [1690].
[2] *Ibid.*, p. 27.
[3] *Ibid.*, p. 50.

property, unless citizens consent to it. Taxes can be levied but only with the consent of the people. Taxation without representation is a just cause for rebellion by the people.

For Locke, there is an unfortunate side-effect from the use of money. Money enables individuals and states to buy time; to incur debt. Recall that Locke is making these arguments in 17th century England, where public debt is the debt of kings, kings who invoke rights given by God (and the church) to appropriate the property of others willy-nilly. Hereby hangs a liberal dilemma. It is similar to the argument sometimes made by men about women: "You cannot live with them, cannot live without them." The same can be said for money. The state: cannot live with it, cannot live without it, does not want to pay for it. The narrowest of state business *requires* the expenditure of money. The expenditure of money over time inevitably leads to debt. Debt is to be avoided. Austerity is born.

David Hume, Money, and Debt

Locke's are narrow foundations, but bricks can be laid on narrow foundations. The intellectual bricks of the Scottish enlightenment are laid by Adam Smith and David Hume. We first consider Hume. Hume is still remembered today for the idea that a monetary stimulus can in the short run stimulate economic activity but in the long run must either show up as inflation or dissipate without effecting real variables. This is the centerpiece of his essay "On Money." It remains a cornerstone of contemporary macroeconomic theory of the liberal variety. Hume also writes much about "public credit" or what we know as government debt.[4]

Like Locke, Hume sees money as an instrument, as "nothing but the representation of labor and commodities . . . a method of rating or estimating them."[5] Money defines wages and prices.

---

[4]The discussion of Locke and Hume follows closely that of Mark Blyth, *Austerity: The History of a Dangerous Idea* (New York: Oxford University Press, 2013), pp. 104–109. For much more on the history of austerity, see this excellent book.

[5]David Hume, Of Money, in *Essays, Moral, Political, and Literary* (Library of Economics and Liberty), p. 1 [1742]. http://www.econlib.org/library/LFBooks/Hume/hmMPL.32.html#Part II, Essay IX, OF PUBLIC CREDIT.

Contrary to Locke, money does not relate to spoilage; rather, money follows trade, which places Locke's merchant classes, and not the state, at the center of everything. For Hume, merchants are the catalyst for trade and the creators of wealth. They are the most useful race of men; they are to be admired and served. Thus, "it is necessary, and reasonable, that a considerable part of the commodities and labor [produced] should belong to the merchant, to whom, in great measure, they are owing."[6] Only merchants can expand industry and by increasing frugality, give command of that industry to particular members of society, namely members of the merchant class.

Make no mistake about it. Public debt, to Hume, is bad. His arguments against debt are used to this day. The problem with public debt is that it has no limit, no limit until the interest payments on the debt become crushing. Debt will always be abused. Worse, the issuance of public debt diverts funds away from industry; there is a crowding out effect. Worse still, when issuance of debt eventually hits a ceiling, governments will sell more of it to foreigners, which will give foreign governments power over us. Then, liberty is undone.

This sounds all too familiar. Northern European criticism of the budget policies of Greece and Italy was that debt is politically easier than taxation. The Obama stimulus was criticized as government debt crowding out private investments. Quantitative easing was criticized for driving up prices, even though the price level was stable. "China owns the USA" was the fear of foreigners owning the U.S. The fact is that foreigners hold less than one-third of outstanding U.S. Debt. As for Hume, he predicted the demise of Great Britain due to excessive debt issuance just at the moment that Great Britain was about to dominate the world for a century. The truth is that facts seldom triumph over good liberal ideology, and when it comes to that, we must turn to Adam Smith.

---

[6]Steven G. Medema and Warren J. Samuels, *The History of Economic Thought: A Reader* (New York: Routledge), p. 142.

Adam Smith: In Defense of Markets

Adam Smith was Hume's more famous contemporary. He too was troubled by the problem of public debt. While Hume had no solution to the problem of debt, Smith claimed to solve it. He embraced the principal of austerity, otherwise known as the parsimony of the Scots. Smith's notion of austerity is close to its modern incarnation. Personal frugality and parsimony is the engine of capitalist growth. Undermine this, and capitalism collapses. To fully understand Smith's position, we need to know his view of banking.[7]

Banking is all about having confidence in the banker. Given confidence in the banker's paper money, the banker will be able to lend out more in paper than he keeps in reserve in gold to cover his withdrawals. Today, we call this "fractional reserve banking." It is magical. Like Hume, Smith sees money as being unable to affect real variables in the long run, which means that adding paper money to the economy will not lead to economic growth. Rather, the key to growth is the inherent frugality of the Scots — their parsimony. The Scots would rather buy investment goods than foreign wines. Thus, the act of saving drives investment, not consumption. Then, the wealth of the nation is its total income. Once wages are paid out of this income, what is left is profits. Profits are then reinvested in the economy via merchants' savings. Today this is called supply-side economics, and it was the passion of President Ronald Reagan. This idea behind austerity has moral force to this day, especially among Republicans and the rich.

What could go wrong? What could upset this natural desire to save and invest? The answer is easy money, which is what credit markets (debt) offer. By perverting the sensibility of saving into lending of the government, "great nations are ... impoverished by ... public prodigality and misconduct."[8] Lest there be any misunderstanding: The market can do no wrong, it is all the fault of government.

---

[7]Much of the following is based on E. Ray Canterbery, *A Brief History of Economics*, 2nd Edition (Singapore, New Jersey, London: World Scientific Publishing, 2011), Chapter 3.
[8]Adam Smith, *An Inquiry into the Nature and Causes of the Wealth of Nations* (Indianapolis, IN: Hackett, 1996) [1776], p. 64.

Smith is painfully aware of another thing: the market cannot exist without the state. The state is necessary to supply external defense, internal justice, and even the training and education of workers. And, he readily admits, wherever there is property there is great inequality. The acquisition of valuable and extensive property necessarily requires the establishment of civil government. A civil government is required for the security of property and is instituted "for the defense of the rich against the poor, or to those who have some property against those who have none at all."[9] Once again, we have the liberal dilemma. You cannot live with the state, and one cannot live without it, but worse, you must pay for it, and that is what undermines capitalism itself. To pay for it requires the issuance of debt.

How do we pay for the state? Smith begins by favoring progressive taxation. This implies that the rich carry more of the tax burden than the poor. However, Smith downplays progressivity, and recommends consumption taxes on luxuries — anything above the bare essentials as the best way to fund the state. Consumption taxes are perhaps the most regressive form of tax. Still, a consumption tax on non-essentials will not suffice to fund the state. Thus, government debt enters the picture.

Great states are filled with merchants who have lots of cash and can lend to the government. Easy money undermines the incentive to save by both the merchant class and the state and undermines the state's incentive to tax. More debt is issued. Eventually, this strategy hits a ceiling, a debt ceiling, and taxes are then imposed for the sole purpose of paying the interest on the debt. The only possible option left to the government is to default upon the debt it owes.

There are distributional consequences. Lenders will be paid in devalued coin to stave off the inevitable sovereign default. As a consequence of this inflationary financing, the fortunes and hence, the ability to invest via saving will be destroyed. The easy money offered by purchasing government debt subverts parsimony, the engine of economic growth. For this reason, government debt must be

---

[9] *Ibid.*, p. 181.

resisted: Austerity, in the form of parsimony, must be embraced. Austerity's genesis is found in the pathological fear of government debt that sits at the heart of economic liberalism. Government debt perverts savers, distracts merchants, and ruins accumulated wealth. Liberalism must limit the state at all costs.

Today, Smith's moral critique of debt is as familiar as Hume's economic one. Saving is a virtue, spending is a vice. Austerity as we know it today, an active policy of budget cutting and deflation, may not be readily apparent in the history of early economic thought. But the conditions of its appearance — parsimony, frugality, morality, and a pathological fear of the consequences of government debt — lie deep within economic liberalism's fossil record from its inception.

In the bustling world of commerce at the edge of the early Industrial Revolution, Smith was the right scholar for the time. It was too much to expect religion to cover all the alleged sins of the rapidly expanding merchant class, and the merchants needed a new economic philosophy. The merchants and the rising manufacturing class seized on those ideas from Smith that provided justification for a growing economy in which money facilitates the efficient market exchange of goods and services. Adam Smith is remembered not for his intent, but rather for the social uses to which a distillation of his ideas was put. Ever since, Smith' ideas have been put into service by commercial interests.

There is still more to Smith. Historically, self-interest has been as unpopular as money lenders. In Smith's *Wealth of Nations*, the individual pursuit of self-interest in a two-way exchange economy guarantees social harmony. In his economic behavior, an individual neither intends to promote the public interest nor knows that he is promoting it. He intends only to provide for his own security. Smith famously wrote, "It is not from the benevolence of the butcher, the brewer, or the baker, that we expect our dinner, but from their regard to their own interest." Such self-interest and economic self-reliance were perfectly natural, grounded in "the desire of bettering our condition," which "comes with us from the womb, and never leaves us until we go into the grave."

Economic self-interest is morally beneficial, too: "I have never known much good done," says Smith "by those who affected to trade for the public good." But the self-interested action of one person is "good" only if it is limited by the self-interested actions of others. Free to pursue self-interest, the individual has no need for government.

We must not neglect the roles of natural law and private property. By the mid-18th century, most educated people believed that God did not control people and events personally but only indirectly, by means of laws at work in nature. Isaac Newton's story of God creating the universe as a self-propelled machine gave a more lasting spin to the virtue of self-interested individualism. After all, what harm can one worker or one manufacturer do to the rest of society as long as the outcomes will always be determined by natural law? This view was bolstered in politics by the aforementioned John Locke (1632–1704), who claimed that natural laws and natural rights existed prior to governments. Never mind empathy; persons need be responsible only to themselves.

Besides justifying ungoverned individualism, this Newtonian–Lockean world view also vindicated private property. Private thrift and prudence by individuals were now rewarded on earth, and sufficient savings would lead to the ownership of private property. And if one had accumulated a great amount of private property, it must have been the machine's will. Once property was accumulated, its protection was a natural right because it belonged to the one who produced it. Accumulation became virtuous. Saving and accumulation of capital assured economic growth. Parsimony and its implied austerity was next to Godliness.

Smith distilled Locke's natural rights argument in favor of the private property and its protection until it was 86% proof. Government was to be feared because it alone could strip persons of their private property and hence, also deprive individuals of their liberty. The sanctity of private property became another justification for a *laissez-faire* economic policy.

Smith transformed the virtues of natural law into the requisites of what later would be called capitalism (by Karl Marx). Profits are "good" because they provide the incentive for master manufacturer's savings.[10] In every manufacturer beats the heart of a Scotsman. Capital accumulation is "good" because its technological results create a division of labor, which in turn enhances productivity and the expansion of international trade. Without privately owned property, the master could not assemble the means to build and equip factories and provide employment for themselves and a wages fund for others. All this was best for society and therefore, should proceed naturally, without any governmental restrictions.

Let there be no mistake about it; Smith was a radical in his time. The rulers saw no advantage in a decentralized economic system in which the government's role was replaced by the "natural order." The French Revolution followed *The Wealth of Nations* by 13 years, and many English people found in Smith's doctrines of freedom and his criticism of public policies, a subversive spirit like that which lit the fires of the French revolt.

Within Smith's system nonetheless was a liberal dilemma. Though he strongly opposed intervention in the market mechanism, Smith certainly was not opposed to all governmental activity. In general, he favored government provision of military security, the administration of justice, and privately unprofitable public works and institutions. When we turn to specifics, the list runs to 15 items, among which are the government's right to impose tariffs to counter tariffs, to punish business fraud, to regulate banking, to provide post offices, highways, harbors, bridges and canals, and so on. Even so, only if private domestic markets were unfettered would the consumer continue to reign as king. For the same reason, Smith also opposed monopolization of the production of a commodity by one producer. Yet, on balance, Smith considered the civilizing effects of commerce to be a blessing worth defending

---

[10] Smith wrote at a time when "manufacturers" were primarily identified with the half-entrepreneur, half-merchant of the domestic handicraft system. He used the terms master, manufacturer, and master manufacturer interchangeably. Master denoted both the craft skills of the manufacturer and the master–worker managerial relation.

against the medieval and mercantilist forms of social organization. But, even the smallest of governments requires funding, and funding requires some combination of taxation and debt. These in turn would threaten austerity.

David Ricardo on Taxes and Debt

Smith was only the beginning of classical economics. Nineteenth-century liberal economists built upon the foundations laid by Locke, Hume, and Smith. They both replicated and amplified the "can't live with it, can't live without if, don't want to pay for it" problem of the state that haunts economic liberalism. Among the new liberals, David Ricardo sat firmly on the "can't live with it" side of the fence when it came to the state. Ricardo imagined a highly competitive economy of small firms in which initially high profits accruing to those first to enter a market converged to a very low average rate of profit as more people joined in and technology was diffused throughout an industry. At this low profit point, capital and labor would exit the market, searching out new areas of profit, thus starting the investment cycle all over again.

What of the state? There was no positive role for the state in Ricardo's vision. Mainly, any attempt by the state to intervene to cushion market adjustments was doomed. Attempts to "amend the condition of the poor — instead of making the poor rich ..., makes the rich poor."[11] The proper role of the state is to teach the poor the value of independence rather than to alter the distributions of the market. Property is to be protected, but the distribution of property is to remain intact. Locke too remains intact.

Ricardo did not always hold sway. The state's role was changing throughout the 19th century. Nationalism and state building demanded a far more interventionist state than envisaged even by Smith. The success of capitalism brought forth a variety of social movements that demanded political representation, economic compensation, and

---

[11] David Ricardo, *Principles of Political Economy and Taxation* (New York: Prometheus Books, 1996) [1817], p. 73.

social protection, all of which cost money and threatened the distribution of private property in favor of the rich.

Enter Charles Dickens

The factory system was not all milk and honey. One of the worst abuses of the early factories was the exploitation of women and children, who were prized as valuable and obedient workers, especially in the spinning and printing factories. The number of adult males working in such factories was relatively small. Women and children had the fewest civil liberties and were least able to make effective protests against brutal working conditions. Disciplined easily, they worked for little compensation. The works of Charles Dickens (1812–1870) offered memorable descriptions of life among the working classes and industrialists. Dickens himself was yanked from school at age 12 and put to work with other boys pasting labels on blacking bottles, an experience bitterly recounted in the autobiographical *David Copperfield* (1849–1850). In *Oliver Twist* (1937–1938), Dickens presents an attack on the workhouse and slum conditions as seen through the nightmarish experiences of an innocent young boy. In *Dombey and Son* (1846–1848) one can see the growing power of industry as opposed to the waning power of mercantile interests. Dickens's most vivid picture of industrial society comes later in *Hard Times* (1854), combining a moral fable with realistic social analysis in the depiction of Coketown, Dickens prototypical industrial town.

Dickens breathes life into Ricardo's starkly abstract income classes: Thomas Gradgrind, a retired merchant; Stephen Blackpool, a worker; and Josiah Bounderby, the factory owner. Gradgrind, a caricature — but not too broad — of the calculating Ricardian, to whom everything is cut and dried. Dickens's contempt for classical economics is shown by his naming two Gradgrind children, Adam Smith and Malthus.

The lives of Charles Dickens and of John Stuart Mill (1806–1873), the last great economist of the classical school, overlapped. The coincidence, if that is what it is, is filled with an irony that does not end at Dickens' edge. Initially devoted to the ideas of

Smith, Ricardo, Jeremy Bentham, and his father, J. S. Mill parted company with their ideas on the relation of production and the income distribution. To the great distress of the orthodoxy, J. S. Mill attempted to separate the science of production from the distribution of its rewards.

John Stuart Mill: At the End of the Classical Line

Mill's great summary of classical economics, *Principles of Political Economy* (1848), was the leading textbook in its field for more than 40 years. The book is a survey of all the ideas of Smith, Thomas Malthus and Ricardo, but it arrives at a happier ending because of Mill's own discoveries. His most important and controversial discovery was the separation of distribution from production. Its popularity is related in part to the apparent improvements in the economic conditions that began to be real for workers in the 1860s, which justify the book's optimistic tone. The book's success made him the dominant economist of his age and altered the classical economic school during Mill's lifetime.

Like Smith and Ricardo, Mill thought that the industrialist's rate of profit would continue to fall and even agreed with Ricardo's explanation — inevitably rising foods costs in the face of a growing population. Although he also envisioned a stationary state for the economy, at this point Mill began to part company with his famous predecessors. Smith and Ricardo saw the stationary state as undesirable; Mill saw it as the crowning achievement of economic progress. And, unlike his predecessors, Mill emphasized the importance of a more equal distribution of income, a concept not unrelated to the stationary state.

Though Mill valued material accumulation, he also directed humans towards striving for higher goals. In Britain, he thought, the desire for wealth need not be taught, but rather the use of wealth and an appreciation of the objects and desire that wealth could not purchase. As he put it, "Every real improvement in the character of the English, whether it consists in giving them aspirations, or only a juster estimate of the value of their present objects of desire, must necessarily moderate the ardor of their devotion in the pursuit of wealth."[12]

Once Britain had achieved a sufficiently high level of wealth, Mill saw no reason for a continued growth in production, as long as population growth was limited. And proper education of the masses, according to Mill, would check the birth rate. He did not want the laws of production repealed; he simply wanted the division of labor and capital accumulation to take the economy to a high plateau, the rarefied air of the stationary state in which production ceased to grow. To Mill, the stationary state was a blissful, pastoral existence in which justice in the distribution of income and wealth ranked above relentless accumulation.

In Mill, we see the first crack in the veneer of austerity. Rather, there is a higher purpose in production of goods and services. His separatism of the science of production from the rules governing distribution rests on a distinction between natural law and custom. In Mill's view, the laws of scarcity and diminishing returns derive from nature just as much as the laws of gravity and of the expansion of gases. But although the factors of production must be combined according to scientific principles, the distribution of that production and income from it is a social issue and its rules, customary.

To Mill, the distribution of income obeys the laws and customs of society. Even what a person has produced by his individual toil, unaided by anyone, he cannot keep, unless society allows him to. Where Ricardo saw the necessity of allowing natural price changes to keep the landlord from garnering all income, Mill could envision a law that would evict the landlord from his "own" land.

Whatever the relation of rich to poor, if society did not like what it saw, it had only to alter those conditions. Society could — if it had the will — expropriate, redistribute, tax, subsidize, and generally raise havoc with the distribution of income initially decided by the economic machine. The state could tax away the inheritances of the rich and prevent the landed gentry from gaining Ricardian rents.

---

[12]John Stuart Mill, *Principles of Political Economy*, ed. J. M. Robson (Toronto: University of Toronto Press, 1965), Vol. 2 [1819], p. 105.

The associations of workers such as the Grand National would end factory control by the master manufacturers. Through modest reforms such as these, benign evolution would preempt the need for revolution.

These were the beginnings of austerity, but there is much more. Though the ideology and politics are there, the economics was not complete. We will go on to see how austerity became the basis for expansionary economics, as odd as that may seem.

2

Expansionary Austerity in the 21st Century

The Austrian School

In the late 19th century, Austrian economics emerged in the Austro–Hungarian Empire from the debate over the role the state might play in fostering economic development following Germany's state-led growth spurt. Initially, the key figure was Carl Menger, one of the first so-called marginalist economists, who saw economic value as a question of subjective utility and relative prices, rather than as a function of costs of production. Most important for austerity's purposes, he was also dead set against the state being involved in helping capitalism along the way.

An academic generation later, Menger's students contested the increasing interventionism of the liberal state from Austrian premises. To Ludwig Von Mises, Friedrich Hayek, along with Joseph Schumpeter, the Austrian émigré voice in the U.S., the free market has a long-run evolutionary structure that government intervention can only harm. The Austrian school rejected the state as having any positive or necessary role in the economy. First ignored and then defeated in Europe, Austrian ideas survived in America, where their popularity has ebbed and flowed for nearly a century. Battered down and beaten by the Keynesian revolution after World War II, Austrian ideas never quite disappeared from the American scene. They staged a stunning comeback in the 1970s when Hayek won the Nobel Prize in economics and provided a popular justification for Reagan's supply-side policies, but they disappeared again until a financial crisis brought them back to the fore. What they said about banks explains the reemergence of Austrianism.

Austrian Boom and Bust

The Austrians never saw the economy as smooth, except in the long-run. Money was seen as the evil force that could upset the economy. Since banks create money, banks had to be involved. This is contrary to what economists generally thought. From the 1930s on, money was seen in pretty much the same way that Hume saw it 200 years before, as short-run stimulative, long-run neutral, and potentially inflationary. Money changes neither preferences nor possibilities. Money is credit, and one person's debt is another person's income.

This placid world of the economists blew up with the 2008 financial crisis. The Austrians, as we will see, seemed to describe the crisis perfectly. However, its aftermath, and what to do about it was a different matter entirely. In the 1920s, Hayek and Mises drew attention to the idea that banks make money from the extension of credit. Each bank has the incentive to expand credit beyond its base reserves to stay in business against more aggressive banks and to capture market share. The central bank encourages over-expansion as the backstop of the financial system with its infinite liquidity. These forces provide an expansion of credit beyond what real savings would allow and lowers the interest rate on loans. The extension of credit signals to entrepreneurs that the real cost of capital has fallen, and thus they can undertake new projects, financed through cheap credit, that hitherto they would not have found profitable. This leads to an expansion of aggregate borrowing and a weakening of the desire to save. Astute, thrifty, and prudent in free-market conditions, entrepreneurs become reckless, debt-gulping dupes once the banks hand out mountains of cheap money.

Entrepreneurs hire more people and buy more materials, which pushes up prices and wages. This short-term monetary stimulus shows up as rising prices, especially asset prices, which encourages more borrowing. Bond prices rise and interest rates fall. Meanwhile, the underlying economy is unchanged. More money chasing fewer goods means inflation. Banks extend more credit, lower interest rates further, and generally kick the can down the road.

The banks are their own worst enemies. They pump up the credit bubble further still while diverting capital away from the market. Everyone's balance sheet collapses and all this malinvestment must generate even greater returns. In the face of inflation, the banks start to raise interest rates at the same time their ability to generate new credit shrinks. But the demand for credit to keep the bubble inflated accelerates. When the general public realizes that the asset growth is just monetary inflation and not a rise in real values, the bubble pops, the panic begins, assets are dumped, balance sheets implode, and the economy craters.

All this calls for austerity measures. As people realize that the crisis and ensuring period of recession are a culmination of unjustified investment brought about by cheap credit, a flight into real values begins. The economy adapts to losses by curtailing consumption. Squandered savings need to be rebuilt, which means less consumption. Banks must realize their losses to begin the process of recovery, which means austerity. Neither bankers nor consumers should be bailed out. After all, the problem was caused by intervention into the market, the lowering of interest rates via the expansion of credit beyond that which real savings could produce. It would be wrong to do more of the same. Government intervention would simply prolong the recession.

When there is a financial bust, there are four ways to adjust: inflate, deflate, devalue, or default. The right thing to do, according to the Austrians, is predicable. Deflation, cutting wages and prices so the economy can adjust to real values is the answer. Governments do not like this because it causes unemployment and instability. Governments prefer devaluation, if they have their own exchange rate, or inflation, or both, as the way to pass the costs onto creditors to pay for the mistakes of debtors. Devaluation makes the home currency cheap to foreigners, encouraging exports, and discouraging imports. An improving trade balance adds to GDP. As to the banks, let the banks fail and then restart the system. If the real economy does not right itself, it is because unions are keeping wages too high.

The Austrian school provided an American pied-à-terre for a more austere liberal argument. The state is to be abolished once and for all as the only way to save ourselves from boom and bust cycles.

Schumpeter's Theory of Capitalist Motion

Joseph Alois Schumpeter (1883–1950) was born in the year of John Maynard Keynes's birth and of Karl Marx's death. The ideas of this second-generation Austrian who considered himself superior to John Maynard Keynes and who had an ego the match of Ayn Rand's will provide a surprise ending to the Austrian story. Earlier, other Austrians had defined the psychology that underlies the theory of capital and entrepreneurship, where entrepreneurs outperform the masses in mental power and energy. Generally, the neo-Austrian's insight into entrepreneurship sees such humans as not only calculating agents but also as keenly alert to opportunities "just around the corner." Still, these agents seem more cunning than productive, more opportunistic than constructive.[1]

Schumpeter's entrepreneur has more substance. Schumpeter elevated the role of capitalism's entrepreneur to the highest plane — to be the central force in capitalistic development. Despite this, he came to the same gloomy conclusion as Karl Marx, namely, that capitalism was doomed. Unlike Marx, Schumpeter decried the self-destructive tendencies inherent in capitalism but nonetheless envisioned it being superseded by a workable socialism.

No doubt Schumpeter's grief was more over the euthanasia of the business entrepreneur than that of capitalism itself, even though there was nothing wrong with capitalism that reincarnation would not cure. The neo-Austrians, who have inherited the Austrians' mantel, have kept Schumpeter at a respectful distance, perhaps because of the volatile mixture of his respect for Marx and his pessimism regarding the future of capitalism.

---

[1]The following is derived from E. Ray Canterbery, *A Brief History of Economics*, 2nd Edition (Singapore, New Jersey, London: World Scientific Publishing, 2011), Chapter 13.

Vienna has been described as one of the most pleasant places on Earth during the closing year of the Hapsburg epoch of the Austro–Hungarian Empire, at least for those as properly endowed and trained as Schumpeter. To this day Vienna remains charming. To the end, Schumpeter remained outwardly the cultivated, autocratic, egocentric Austrian gentleman of the old school who found from 1914 on, little evidence of progress in civilization.

In Schumpeter's theory of capitalism, the entrepreneur is the agent of economic change — a grander, more dramatic figure than the persona usually described by the Austrians. As an innovator, the entrepreneur does much more than take advantage of price movements, the entrepreneur creates entire industries. This heroic figure seems more like the knight of chivalry. Such a romantic figure comes even closer to the grim, domineering man of action — the Roark, Rearden, and Galt invented by Ayn Rand and stereotyped by actor Gary Cooper.

In *Atlas Shrugged*, Ayn Rand describes the first pouring of Rearden Metal, a new alloy much harder than steel:

> He stood leaning against a column, watching, the [red] glare cut a moment's wedge across his eyes, which had the color and quality of pale blue ice — then across the black web of the metal column and the ash-blond strands of his hair — then across the belt of his trenchcoat and pockets where he held his hands. His body was tall and gaunt; he had always been too tall for those around him .... He was Hank Rearden.[2]

Rearden is the entrepreneur, literally the Man of Steel, Schumpeter's Superman. Schumpeter, however, would have described his hero as a man much shorter, more like himself.

The heroic task of Schumpeter's superhero is to ignite an industry that keeps capitalism on a generally upward path for a half century. Schumpeter did not deny other cycles; there was an inventory cycle of short duration, an investment cycle in which the

---

[2]Ayn Rand, *Atlas Shrugged* (New York: Random House, 1957), p. 28.

pendulum swung back and forth for a 7- to 11-year duration, and a long wave sparked by breakthrough inventions like the steamship, locomotive, or automobile. To Schumpeter, the cycles within cycles of capitalism, each unhappily reaching their respective bottom at the same time during the period 1929–1933, explained the Great Depression.[3] The three cycles reaching their nadirs could explain much of the debacle of the 1930s. The recession beginning in August 1929 looked like the result of accumulated and unsold inventories; as Keynes discovered, business investment collapsed during the 1930s; and the once innovative automobile industry had become a mature industry, ending a long wave.

Robert Heilbroner, a student in one of Schumpeter's classes at Harvard, suggests, however, that Schumpeter was ambivalent toward the Great depression. "After removing his long cloak with a flourish, [Schumpeter] told us in heavily accented English: 'Chentlemen, a depression is for capitalism like a good cold douche' — a statement whose shock value lay not only in the unthinkable sentiment that the Depression had its uses, but in the fact that very few of us knew that a douche was the Europeans' term for a shower."[4] What was happening to industry during a depression was, to Schumpeter, "creative destruction," which is a good thing.

In Schumpeter's beginning of the cycle, there is no depression, though there is stagnation. In this stationary condition of "Walrasian equilibrium," there is no extraordinary opportunity for profits; only a circular flow of economic activity takes place, and the system merely reproduces itself. The extraordinary person, the entrepreneur, daringly raids the circular flow and diverts labor and land to investment. Since savings are inadequate for such ventures, the entrepreneur must be provided credit created by the bankers as the capitalists.

Since only the more enterprising and venturesome persons act, innovations appear in "swarms." The innovations include setting up new production functions, techniques, organizational forms, and

---

[3] See Joseph A. Schumpeter, *Business Cycles* (New York: McGraw-Hill, 1939).
[4] Robert Heilbroner, "His Secret Life," *The New York Review of Books*, May 14, 1992, p. 27.

products. Even though they stand above the reluctant crowd, the heroic entrepreneur creates favorable conditions for other, less venturesome businesspersons to follow. These activities bring growth to the circular flow as well as rents (super-profits) to the temporary monopolists, the entrepreneurial elite. This glowing business prosperity is enhanced by the creation and expenditure of new incomes.

The boom, however, limits itself as, paradoxically, innovations contribute to the downswing. The competition of new products with old ones causes business losses even as rising pries deter investment. Entrepreneurs use the proceeds of the sale of their new products to repay indebtedness and, in this way, bring deflation. The depression results from the slow process of adaptation to innovation and from this secondary deflation. When adaptation to the innovations is complete, deflation ends and Walrasian equilibrium is restored.

In equilibrium, a time when all vital signs are stable, there is little cause for capitalism to suffer cardiac arrest. Left to itself, capitalism even has "trickle-down" benefits — Schumpeter told his students at Harvard how "The capitalist achievement does not typically consist in providing more silk stockings for queens but in bringing them within the reach of factory girls for steadily decreasing amounts of effort."[5] The presence of innovations helps to explain why new industries with new products for the masses emerge and old ones — with great reluctance and stubborn resistance — die.

It is industrial concentration — the rise of big, stubborn, and bureaucratic business — that weakens capitalism. The early monopoly of the individual, venturesome entrepreneur who makes the breakthrough and corners the market is always acceptable to society. However, the maturing of an industry into a gigantic monopoly generates the political and social attitudes that ultimately destroy it. Andrew Carnegie (like Rearden in *Atlas Shrugged*) was a majestic figure, but the U.S. Steel Corporation casts a foreboding shadow of death across the face of capitalism. The growth of giant business deprives capitalism of its individual and wonderfully gifted entrepreneurs even as it makes itself vulnerable to political and social assault.

---

[5] *Ibid.*, p. 27.

The bourgeois eventually would attack private property with as much force as it once used against popes and kings.

In contrast, for the other neo-Austrians, private property prevails — as it does for Ayn Rand. In *Atlas Shrugged*, John Galt gives the longest speech (60 pages) ever made in celebration of the victory of private property over collectivism.

But in Schumpeter, even though New Deal nostrums could sustain "capitalism in the oxygen tent": by artificial means — paralyzed in those actions that had guaranteed past glories — the inevitable beneficiary of capitalism's fatal disease was socialism. Socialism would work because it would be run by the same elite that ran capitalism. Whereas most neo-Austrianism wears blinders to giant business, Schumpeter's singular prophecy for capitalism is Marx's denouement; like the Biblical whale that saved Jonah, capitalism is swallowed by the state in order to save it.

Since Schumpeter has a theory of the business cycle, one might suppose that he would favor state intervention. He does not. The entrepreneur displaces any need for government. Moreover, when capitalism finally goes belly up, the entrepreneur runs the government. And so, like the other neo-Austrians, Schumpeter does not favor government intervention even during a Great Depression. Thus, he continues that Locke–Hume–Smith tradition.

We next consider some real-world experiences with expansionary austerity. We began with the Japanese case, move onto the French, the Danish, and the Irish, and then consider the expansionary fiscal contraction in the 1980s under the REBLL (Romania, Estonia, Bulgaria, Latvia, and Lithuania) Alliance.

Japanese Austerity and Military Expansion, 1921–1937

While in a near permanent slump, Japanese banking elites and the Bank of Japan sought a swift return to the gold standard after abandoning it in 1917. As background, the real rate of economic growth in 1922 was −2.7%, −4.6% in 1923 and −2.9% in 1925. The nation was heavily import dependent. Foreign trade was its lifeline. Arrayed against the bankers were farming, labor, and business interests.

Complicating this debate, the two dominant political parties, the Seiyukai and the Kenseikai, both wanted to go back on gold, but could not agree on the conditions under which that should happen. In any case, in July 1928 the public was told that to rejoin gold people must endure the pain as in dietary surgery, shrink first and expand later. Thus lay the ground for austerity.[6]

Junnosuke Inoue, the finance minister, conducted a propaganda campaign to clinch the case for gold. In this, Inoue said, "We cannot avoid fiscal tightening and liquidation at least once in the process," and so "the surest way is to go straight towards the repeal of the gold embargo . . . since we cannot avoid some pain . . . and sacrifice anyway."[7] Inoue traveled across the country arguing his case, asking the people to be prepared to tighten their belts in an already austere economic environment. He got his wish and Japan rejoined the gold standard in January 1930, just when the rest of the world's economy was contracting. The consequence was the *Showa Depression*, the greatest peacetime collapse in economic activity in Japan's history. Japan's growth rate fell to −9.7% in 1930 and −9.5% in 1931, while the Yen rose about 7% against the dollar. As one could predict, demand in the U.S. and elsewhere for Japanese manufactures fell as the Yen appreciation and the general collapse of the economy strangled trade. Average Japanese household income fell sharply from 1929 to 1931. Meanwhile, the state kept public spending in check throughout the 1920s, rising modestly over the course of the decade. The military took the brunt of this shrinkage in real terms. Inoue's party's 1930 election slogan was "economy, disarmament, purification of politics, reform of China policy, and removal of the gold embargo" which amplified the austerity crusade.

---

[6]Much of the following is based on Mark Blyth, *Austerity* (Oxford: Oxford University Press, 2013), pp. 137–228.

[7]Junnosuke Inoue, "The Repeal of the Gold Embargo: An Appeal to All the Nation," quoted in Hamada and Noguchi, "Role of Preconceived Ideas," p. 17. See Koichi Hamada and Asahi Noguchi, "The Role of Preconceived Ideas in Macroeconomic Policy: Japan's Expediences in Two Deflationary Episodes" Economic Growth Center, Yale University, Discussion Paper Number 908, New Haven, CT, March 2005.

The austerity accelerated through monetary and fiscal measures. Interest rates were raised into the teeth of the depression and government spending was cut by almost 20% from an already low level. In early 1931, there was an attempt to cut army and navy budgets still more. In October 1931, a plot by the army to overthrow the government was uncovered. The government resigned.

The new government was quite different. The Seiyukai party, now in power, appointed a new finance minister. Takahashi Korekiyo left the gold standard as quickly as possible and then cut the discount rate on commercial bills from 5.57% in early 1932 to 3.65% in July 1934. He dramatically increased the money supply and instituted capital controls to stop its flight abroad. Furthermore, he instructed the Bank of Japan to underwrite long-term government bond issues. On the fiscal front, government spending increased by an initial 34%, and by the end of 1932 it totaled an extra 10% of GDP. Prices rose, debt burdens fell, and the Japanese economy rocketed out of the depression, growing 4% a year in real terms each year between 1932 and 1936. The rest of the world was deflating and remained on gold standard. The Japanese success was remarkable.

Austerity was bad even for the health of its practitioners. Still campaigning for a return to the gold standard, Inoue was assassinated in 1932. Later that year, a leading bank director and Takahashi's prime minister were also assassinated. Worse, a decade of austerity had convinced the Japanese military that they were at war with the entire civilian political elite. In 1936 Takahashi was murdered, along with several other political figures, in another aborted coup. When war was declared on China in 1937, financial prudence in Japan was also killed.

Needless to say, expansionary austerity did not work in Japan. Rather, it created the worst depression in Japanese history, provoked assassinations, and empowered the military which brought us Pearl Harbor. Japanese austerity was bad for the health of the U.S. Navy; 2402 American soldiers were killed. In the Pacific War that followed, 111,606 more Americans died. And, there were self-inflicted wounds; 17,400,000 Japanese soldiers died in the Pacific. Expansionary austerity was deadly. The private economy tanked; the military economy boomed. Surely, this is not what Schumpeter meant by creative destruction.

French Austerity Policies, 1919–1939

French culture is quite different from the Japanese. The French are pleasure-seekers and value leisure. Compared with the Japanese, they are much less disciplined. During the 1920s and 1930s, jazz was influential. Jazz is notable for the universal appeal it has held in France and beyond — appealing to rich and poor, black and white, and everyone in between. New Orleans, as a city steeped in French history and influence, is an example of the successful intermingling of jazz with French culture, but in France also, jazz has deep roots.

Songstress Josephine Baker fled from the U.S. to France because of racism, where she quickly rose to popularity. Baker was not alone, she and other musicians, such as saxophonist Coleman Hawkins and

Illus. 2.1: Josephine Baker dancing the Charleston, 1926.

Source: *Wikipedia*, the free encyclopedia.

Illus. 2.2:   Louis Armstrong.
Source: *Wikipedia*, the free encyclopedia.

Louis Armstrong emigrated to France that welcomed the musical form even under the shadow of the German occupation. Jazz influenced art. Henri Matisse is one of the most prominent examples of the direct influence of jazz music on French art. Matisse created work commissioned by the publisher of *Verve* magazine, a publication that appeared in both French and English. Other artists, such as Pablo Picasso, Paul Poiret and Erie, created work that was strongly influenced by jazz. The Art Deco Movement flourished in France during the 1920s and bears hallmark influences of jazz culture as well. Jazz gave America and France a common heritage. And, it is not accidental that F. Scott Fitzgerald, who coined the name Jazz Age in America, lived and wrote in Paris and on the Riviera.[8]

At first blush, France does not seem to be fertile ground for austerity. Still, we find austerity policies in vogue during 1919–1939.

---

[8]For much more on Fitzgerald and the Jazz Age, see E. Ray Canterbery and Thomas D. Birch, *F. Scott Fitzgerald: Under the Influence* (St. Paul, MN: Paragon House, 2006).

After World War I the French relied for a large portion of their budget on German reparations. When these payments were not forthcoming, the resulting budget deficits had to be met with higher interest rates to attract capital. One might have thought that tax increases were in order, but France was a deeply divided society that could not agree on whom to tax.

The political right sought to raise excise and consumption taxes on everyone else, while the political left wanted to tax only the right's income and wealth. In protecting the right, whenever it looked like the left might win an election, the Bank of France refused to roll over Treasury bills; that is the short-term debt instruments funding the government, thereby forcing the authorities to print money. By 1924, after several rounds of stoking inflation this way, the right came to power and as expected raised taxes on the left's constituents. The left won the next election the same year but was unable to shift the burden back. As a result, deficits ballooned. In time, the left government resigned and in 1926 a rightist government under Raymond Poincare' raised enough taxes to close the budget shortfall. In response to this balancing of the budget and reduction in inflation, investors bought francs. This enabled France to go back on the gold standard in 1926 and 1930; the economy stabilized and gold inflows increased, augmented by high interest rates, such that the newspaper *Le Figaro* proclaimed France should "rejoice in our timid yet prosperous economy as opposed to the presumptuousness and decadent economy of the Anglo–Saxon races."

This, of course, was nationalistic nonsense, hubris at its worst. Next came the U.S.-bound capital flight, the Wall Street Crash, and the central European liquidity crunch to slam into the French economy at great speed. The gross national product fell 7% and industrial production fell 13% by 1932. With the desire to stay on gold when everyone else was deserting it meant that France could only deflate as everyone else reflated.

France was saved to some extent. The depression tree fell mainly on capital expenditures and investment rather than consumption. But France could only take so much deflation, when reflation was needed. However, reflating on the gold standard was going to produce capital flight, especially if the monetary authority did not cooperate. Reflation required the support of the Bank of France, which was not about to cooperate.

Central banks often confuse their own interests with the national interest. The Bank of France was not exceptional in this regard. While it was the fiscal agent of the French Treasury, it was also a private institution with 40,000 shareholders whose 200 largest share-holders, often called "the 200 families," determined both personnel and policy. The bank favored budget balances above all, without which it would not cooperate.

Along with a tight monetary policy came a tight fiscal policy. It was austerity all the way round. From 1932 to 1936 government spending was cut by one-fifth, industrial production fell nearly a quarter, the real exchange rate rose, and the money supply collapsed. Meanwhile, the Bank of France encouraged capital flight. The Bank insisted on budget cuts as the only way forward, and generally vetoed any policies that the democratically elected government promoted that did not meet with its approval. For example, the Bank of France vetoed the reflation policies of 1934–1935. This led to the government's resignation.

The situation deteriorated until the public began to riot. In January 1936, a left-wing cross-party alliance called the Popular Front took over. The Popular Front wanted to follow countries that were breaking with the orthodoxy of austerity. The main obstacle was the Bank of France. Nonetheless, the Popular Front increased wages, reduced working time, and reformed the structure of the Bank of France so that the Regents did not control the government council. This simply led to another round of capital flight, interest-rate increases, and more deflation. Reflationary policy, in the absence of effective capital controls means that capital flight wins, especially when it is aided and abetted by the central bank. When the leader of the Popular Front suggested capital controls, he was forced out.

Even when France abandoned gold in September 1936, there was little improvement. With devaluation, spending had to pick up the slack. However, the central bank gave a *de facto veto* on all policies except austerity. Thus, devaluation simply increased the import bill and deepened the slump. The countries that left gold behind rebounded through devaluation combined with increased public spending, even if it was through rearmament. The Bank of France routinely vetoed budget increases that would have allowed the French military to modernize, and even mobilize, to meet the German threat. As a consequence, French defense spending between 1934 and 1938 was one-tenth that of Germany. Laughably, the Bank of France chafed at the ruinous level of military spending and called for defense cuts as late as 1940. Meanwhile, Hitler knew that the franc would be defended at all costs, even if it meant the loss of France. The franc was the symbol of France. Meanwhile, romance moved from Paris to Casablanca, along with Humphrey Bogart and Ingrid Bergman. The French were hopelessly compromised.

A Hamlet-like Tragedy in the Kingdom of Denmark

A paper by Giavazzi and Pagano in 1990 highlights Denmark's expansionary contraction during 1982–1986, claiming that a political regime shift to the right, plus devaluation, plus a peg to the deutsche mark promoted growth.[9] They were tempted to say that the same thing applied to Ireland. Later, Alesina and Ardagna found that "regardless of the initial level of debt, a large fiscal adjustment that is expenditure-based and accompanied by wage moderation and devaluation is expansionary."[10] The 2009 update of this paper found nine examples of expansionary fiscal adjustments, and in every case "successful fiscal adjustments are completely based upon spending cuts accompanied by modest tax cuts."[11] The key channel for expansionary austerity to work, across all the cases, is the rational

---

[9]Francesco Giavazzi and Marco Pagano, "Can Severe Fiscal Contractions be Expansionary? Tales of Two Small European Countries," NBER Working Paper 3372, May 1990.

[10]Alberto Alesina and Silvia Ardanga, "Tales of Fiscal Adjustment," *Economic Policy* 13, 27 (1998), p. 516.

[11]Alberto Alesina and Silvia Ardanga, "Large Changes in Fiscal Policy: Taxes Versus Spending," NBER Working Paper 15438, 2009, p. 12.

expectations of consumers. Do they prove the case for austerity? The answer in short is "no."

Alesina and Ardanga note that the size of the adjustment in Denmark was large, around 10% of GDP, and was "divided about equally between spending cuts and tax increases."[12] They contend that centralized wage-bargaining institutions held the line on wage growth while the currency was pegged rather than devalued. This led to disinflation rather than a devaluation, which nonetheless led to falling unit labor costs. Still, after the initial successful consolidation, growth fell dramatically in 1988–1989 while unemployment rose, the main cause of which was the end of centralized wage bargaining — thus for them the case is "mixed." Perotti also notes that growth ground to a halt and consumption declined for three years.

To explain the slump and keep the expectations channel as the main avenue for adjustment would mean that the regime shift was not credible after all, which could make it hard to explain the original expansion via expectations. The whole notion of a confidence fairy appears to be an ill-woven tale. Later work by the IMF does not see Denmark as an example of "fiscal consolidation motivated by a desire to reduce the budget deficit"[13] because the economy was overheating when the consolidation was undertaken. That is, the cuts were taken in a boom, not a slump! Expansionary policies during a boom are naturally expansionary. The austerity tragedy in Denmark could well have been written by William Shakespeare.

The Luck of the Irish

Routinely appearing on the list of positive cases of expansionary austerity is Ireland in the late 1980s. Alesina and Ardanga relate the Irish experience from 1987–1989. When Irish debt-to-GDP reached 16% in 1986, a right-wing government came to power that slashed transfers,

---

[12]Alberto Alesina and Silvia Ardagna, "Tales of Fiscal Adjustment," *op. cit.*, p. 528.

[13]Jamie Guajardo, Daniel Leigh, and Andrea Pescatori, "Expansionary Austerity: New International Evidence," IMF Working Paper 11/158, July 2011, p. 33.

the government wage bill, and taxes. Devaluation and negotiated wage moderation reduced unit labor costs by 12% to 15%. Growth rates and foreign investment both soared. Key to this was the large expenditure-based cut plus wage moderation and devaluation. The devaluation of Sterling made foreign goods cheaper and expanded the international market. Stephen Kinsella offers a different story. He writes of the late 1980s and of the aftermath of the banking crisis of 2008. Ireland did have an expansion following a consolidation, but the correlation is not causation. Rather, this consolidation "coincided with a period of growth in the international economy, with the presence of fiscal transfers from the European Union, the opening up of the single market and a well-timed devaluation in August 1986."[14] Roberto Perotti also argues that in the Irish case the depreciation of Sterling and the expansion in the U.K. boosted Irish exports and the Irish economy.[15] Traditional expansionary policies led to the expansion. The timing was as lucky as a four-leaf clover.

The expansion was further bolstered by a simultaneous income tax amnesty that raised the GDP by about 2%. Better still, "the average industrial wage rose by over 14% in the period 1986–1989 [which] boosted government revenue and increased ... private consumption."[16] The Irish expansion was not a case of expansionary austerity but rather a classic instance of Keynesian demand pull. Pay increases and global upswings provided the pull. As would be predicted, government revenue rose with payrolls. Expansionary policies worked to Ireland's benefit, but they were of the traditional Keynesian variety.

The REBLL Alliance and the Debt Star

The question remains: Can smaller nations take it on the chin and expand? Attention in 2008 shifted to Estonia, Latvia, and Lithuania.

---

[14] Stephen Kinsella, "Is Ireland Really the Role Model for Austerity?" *Cambridge Journal of Economics* 36, I (2012), p. 233.

[15] Roberto Perotti, "The 'Austerity Myth': Pain without Gain," Bank of International Settlements Working Paper 362, December 2011, p. 5.

[16] Kinsella, *op. cit.*

The trio embraced an extraordinarily deep fiscal adjustment, while keeping their currencies pegged to the euro while internal prices and wages collapsed. In 2009, Romania and Bulgaria joined them in this self-flagellation. By 2011, they had all returned to higher growth levels than the rest of Europe, especially Southern Europe.

Praise came from prominent sources. IMF director general Christine Lagarde said that Latvia was an inspiration for Southern Europe. Olivier Blanchard, IMF chief economist and austerity skeptic, noted how the Latvians can take the pain. Moreover, the Romanians and the Bulgarians received praise from the austerity camp later that summer, thus joining the Baltic States' austerity alliance.

To understand why the praise was misplaced, we need to visit the REBLL's growth model. It is based on massive foreign investment, even more massive foreign borrowing, and economic institutions that could only be described as open to money coming in and people going out. That is, the reliance was on capital inflows and worker outflows. The problem with the model was its vulnerability to transnational capital flows.

The REBLLs deindustrialized. This prompted the migration of between 10% and 30% of the most active part of their labor force in Eastern Europe. These losses compounded an already weak capacity to develop infrastructure, which in turn led to the concentration of investment in real estate and finance rather than manufacturing. Exports were never a strong foreign currency earner, which meant a shortage of foreign exchange to cover imports. In turn, this led to an increased dependence on foreign capital inflows and remittances from all the expatriate labor to provide for the financing of large payments deficits.

The REBLLs were encouraged by the prospect of European Union membership. With membership, their assets would appreciate simply by adopting the euro. Eastern European banks were bought wholesale by Austrian, French, German, Swedish and Greek banks. These banks made little contribution to industrial investment. Rather, they provided credit to consumer and to real estate speculators. This transnational credit pump created a phenomenal consumption bubble. This led to a banking crisis in 2008.

Exports slumped as financing for imports dried up and deficits, already large, exploded. The real estate bubbles burst once the foreign banks that held as assets securitized mortgages tried to cover their losses in the credit crunch. The banks looked to liquidate assets elsewhere in the portfolio to cover the real estate losses. Because of capital flight, the Western banks did not own their banks, they owned their money supplies as well. Money flowed out, demand abroad contracted, construction bubbles popped, and the REBLL economies collapsed. Table 2.1 shows the extent of the debacle.

Fortunately, the European Union and the IMF intervened and orchestrated a massive bailout of Central and Eastern European financial systems — in other words, of the Western banks' wholly owned foreign subsidiaries — just when current accounts in these states were exploding. An agreement in Vienna prevented the liquidity crunch from spreading to the rest of the REBLLs, so long as the same balance-sheet guarantee (austerity) was applied elsewhere — and it was. Once again, it was all about saving the banks, and the bill for doing so in the form of austerity, high interest rates, unemployment and the rest, was dumped once again on the public-sector balance sheet of the state concerned. In 2009, while the U.S. and Western Europe were rediscovering Keynes, the REBLLs were enforcing local austerity packages to save core European Union banks.

The size of consolidation following the collapse was massive — 17% of GDP in Latvia, 13% in Lithuania, and 9% in Estonia, with half of it enforced in the first year, and most of it, on the expenditure side.

Table 2.1: REBLL GDP and consumption contraction in 2009.

Country	Change in GDP	Change in consumption
Romania	−6	−10.1
Estonia	−14	−15.6
Bulgaria	−5.5	−7.6
Latvia	−7	−12.6
Lithuania	−14	−17.5

Source: Eurostat.

Double-digit public-sector wage cuts became the norm across the REBLLs. The expenditure cuts wreaked havoc in health, education, and social protection. Regressive value-added taxes (VAT) and labor taxes were increased. Massive tax evasion worsened the overall fiscal situation.

The REBLL cases prove that expansionary austerity fails. Only after huge welfare losses does an upward growth trajectory appear. Close to 4% of Latvians left the country between 2008 and 2011. In 2009, 79% classified the economic situation in their country as "bad." IMF projections have Latvian unemployment remaining in double-digit territory until 2017, and that is with rosy GDP forecasts.

Austerity is supposed to reduce debt. In fact, that is its ultimate objective. While the REBLLs had low levels of debt going into the crisis, Latvia's debt rocketed from 10.2% of GDP in 2007 to 42% in 2012. The REBLLs will be saddled with much higher debt levies for a long time because of their austerity. Far from blowing up the Debt Star, they have built themselves a bigger one. In sum, the REBLL alliance does not prove the case for expansionary austerity.

Conclusion

The case for austerity has been made as economics and as economic policy, and is found lacking in both respects. Austerity simply has not worked. While it looks like "expansionary fiscal consolidations," it is found that these cases are either driven by factors other than what austerity proponents maintain, or those proponents simply got the case wrong. Expectations leading to consumer confidence fairies really are tall tales. The few positive cases are easily explained by currency devaluations and accommodating pacts with trade unions. Instead of progress, austerity has instead brought class politics, riots, political instability, more rather than less debt, assassinations, and war. It has proven to be a dangerous idea.

3

The Housing Bubble Collapse

The seeds of the global Great Recession were sown before the downturn. The massive shift in the income and wealth distributions beginning with Reaganomics set the stage. When so many financial assets are in the hands of so few, Wall Street becomes anxious to find new financial instruments. Out of these Austrian-styled financial innovations, bubbles can be made. At their inception, we could usually find Alan Greenspan.

Alan Greenspan: Maestro of Monetary Policy, 1987–2006

It helps immensely to know that Greenspan had not only connections to the Austrians but also to Ayn Rand. Alan Greenspan was the single most powerful figure affecting the global economy between 1987 and 2006, when he served as head of the Federal Reserve. He had substantial influence before then as an economic adviser to Presidents Richard M. Nixon and Gerald Ford. Even after retirement, he remained an important political force. He has been called apolitical, someone so detached from politics that he can always be trusted. Above all, he is the detached observer subservient to no political motive or operative. He is *pure*. He wants also to maintain the purity of the Federal Reserve System so as to insulate the Fed from the influence of politicians, who surely cannot be trusted.[1]

---

[1] The following is based on E. Ray Canterbery, *Alan Greenspan: The Oracle Behind the Curtain* (Singapore, New Jersey, London: World Scientific Publishing, 2006), pp. 1–21. The book provides a biography of Greenspan while giving a history of his monetary policymaking.

Greenspan's purity — as with most self-consciously persistent claims — is a myth. Moreover, the purity of the Federal Reserve System is a sham. In the instance of Mr. Greenspan, "purity" generally has meant selfless dedication to an objective view of economic conditions untarnished by decisions benefiting special interests. To the contrary, we best understand this wizard behind the veil of money through a realistic understanding of his aims.

Greenspan's policies were always directed at the protection of the greatest financial wealth holders. Whether it is dealing with stock market bubbles, currency crises or the bailout of giant financial institutions, his actions and those of the Federal Reserve generally have been forces shifting the income and wealth of Americans toward the top and away from the bottom and middle classes. Only through this prism can his policy positions be understood. These effects go beyond the U.S.; it is a global strategy carried out not only though the Fed, but through multinational financial institutions, including

Illus. 3.1: Alan Greenspan.

Source: Wikipedia at http://en.wikipedia.org/wiki/Alan_Greenspan.

the International Monetary Fund, the World Bank and private hedge funds. The Federal Reserve and the wizard have a unified defense for such policies: A central bank cannot influence the configurations of family incomes and wealth. This is simply and categorically wrong. It is the view of an Austrian orthodoxy.

Maestro Greenspan's background ideally prepared him for his historic conducting of monetary policy. From his early days in New York City he quietly groomed himself for the uncompromising ideological stance he would take. In this respect, he is not quite as dull as he appears. His first career was as a musician, once even playing professionally with a 1940s swing band. Alan entered famed Juilliard as a clarinet major in the winter of 1943, but left the first week of the next year to play in Henry Jerome's swing band. Jerome's band was several notches below those of Benny Goodman, Glenn Miller, or Artie Shaw. Jerome played the "businessman's bounce," more Guy Lombardo than Artie Shaw, at unhip places. It did not matter; the swing era was coming to an end by the mid-1940s.

Jerome switched to bebop late in 1944 — a new craze pioneered by Dizzy Gillespie, Charlie Parker and others. With its new hip style Jerome's band attracted several very talented young musicians, but the band never made it in the record business mostly because of wartime shellac shortage required for the old-fashioned 78 rpm records. Henry Jerome's band disbanded in 1945, with Greenspan quitting a few months ahead of Jerome. While Greenspan was a pretty good amateur musician, he was only average as a professional. It was like the difference between playing golf under the USGA and the PGA.

Greenspan, the "Keynesian," is even more difficult to conjure up than Greenspan, the jazz musician. Always a bookish sort, Greenspan next enrolled in New York University's School of Commerce, and was among the few pursuing a degree in economics. One of the first economics books that Greenspan read on his own was Dudley Dillard's *The Economics of J. M. Keynes*, perhaps the best popular exposition of Keynes' work. In Keynes' *General Theory* [1936], a government could end a business recession or depression by spending more than its tax revenue — willingly running federal budget deficits, a very radical idea at the time. It not only became Franklin Roosevelt's fiscal program during the Great Depression, but was the policy choice to fight business downturns of most economists until Reaganomics hit the fan.

Greenspan, seemingly impressionable, soon would be persuaded that Dillard, Keynes and Roosevelt were wrong. Geoffrey Moore, one of Greenspan's teachers, assigned *Measuring Business Cycles* by Arthur Burns and Wesley Mitchell [1946]. Moore, an incurable collector of economic data, developed a leading indicator of economic activity that Greenspan would later use in his work. Then, when young Alan went to graduate school at Columbia University, Arthur Burns was one of his professors and ultimately, his mentor. Burns, initially noted for hair parted down the middle, large round wire-rimmed glasses and a ubiquitous pipe, was one the few critics of John Maynard Keynes at the time. Burns was asking Greenspan's class: "What causes inflation?" While his students remained silent, Burns' answered with a slap in Keynes' face, "Excess government spending causes inflation".

Arthur Burns' powerful personality was sufficient to turn young Greenspan into the staunch supporter of *laissez-faire* and limited government that neoconservatives around the globe have grown to love. As we will come to know, this is unfortunate. Eventually, Burns' free market credentials would guarantee him the chairmanship of the Federal Reserve System where he would instill the fear of inflation from government deficit in American minds.

The switch from jazz musician to economist, from liberal Keynesianism to conservative *laissez-faire* political economy, would not be Greenspan's final reversals. Ten months after a blind date with Joan Mitchell — an extraordinary blond in her early 20s, elegant and highly cultured — they were married. Alan had dropped out of Columbia because he was having trouble coming up with the tuition. Besides, Arthur Burns had gone to Washington to serve as chairman of the Council of Economic Advisers (CEA) in the Eisenhower administration. Greenspan went to work at what was then the National Industrial Conference Board, later shortened to the Conference Board, a not-for-profit business research organization.

Meanwhile, Joan was spending a lot of time with a group of New York "intellectuals" interested in a philosophy called objectivism. Alan and Joan drifted apart and their marriage was annulled in 1953. Joan became a good friend post-annulment.

Greenspan and Ayn Rand

With the end of his marriage, Greenspan did a turnabout on objectivism; he had hated it when married to Joan but grew to admire Ayn Rand, the feisty woman behind the philosophy. From Greenspan's late 20s to his early 40s, objectivism was a major part of his life, as he spent many hours in the company of Rand and her narrow circle, sufficiently wide nonetheless to make his head spin. She was to have as much influence on Alan as Arthur Burns. And, she did not even part her hair in the middle — rather, she wore bangs. Ayn Rand was formidable; she was brilliant, charismatic, iconoclastic, logical to the point of insanity, and capable of dramatic displays of incendiary temper. Some claim that she was mentally ill.

By now, Alan Greenspan was well to the political right of the Eisenhower Republicans. He still is. As for Dwight D. Eisenhower, Ayn Rand considered him a closet communist. As for Greenspan, he became one the first students at the Nathaniel Branden Institute, the "think tank" founded by Rand's lover to further her ideas. Rand called Greenspan "the undertaker" because — among other things — he always dressed in a black suit matching his demeanor, much like the one he wore to her funeral. He also was a bit of a pessimist who was not sure that he could prove he existed. Greenspan, as Fed chair, took to wearing only blue, perhaps so he would seem less the villain to blue-collar workers.

Greenspan was a member of a radical right group known to themselves as the Collective and, to Rand, as the Class of '43, modestly named for the year of her novel, *The Fountainhead*. Summing theologically the Collective's philosophy, Rand evokes radical individualism as the theme of *The Fountainhead*, which she called "individualism versus collectivism, not in politics, but in man's soul". Its hero, Architect Howard Roark (Gary Cooper in the film), embodies a philosophy of pure self-interest. He designs a gigantic government housing project for the poor only under the condition that he designs it *his way*. In the end, Roark cannot save the project from the many evil doers opposing him in the name of some greater good, such as the Robin Hoodesque — taking from the rich and giving to the poor. Thus, Roark is justified in destroying his butchered creation with a charge of dynamite! The poorly housed are left with rubble, but Roark has saved Rand's philosophical theme: the evil "do-gooders" put the heroic entrepreneur in the awkward but defensible position of having to blow up their project.

The Collective converted Greenspan into a lover of free markets, a man not only suspicious of do-gooders but having a righteous hatred of government. No doubt Alan came under the spell of objectivism's narrow focus on rationality and individualism. Under this new philosophy, Greenspan was able to convince himself that he did, indeed, exist. Once converted, Rand came to admire Alan; now they both were fellow radicals for capitalism. In 1974 Greenspan tells *Newsweek*: "When I met Ayn Rand, I was a free enterpriser in the Adam Smith sense, impressed with the theoretical structure and efficiency of markets. What she did was to make me see that capitalism is not only efficient and practical, but also moral". He had become a moralist.

Rand thought the neo-Austrians such as Hayek to be too theoretical and not sufficiently radical. Clearly, nonetheless, Greenspan had a close affinity to the Austrians. They shared an interest in the mandates of the free market and the morality of capitalism.

Greenspan helped Rand with some of her research for her next novel, *Atlas Shrugged*. While *The Fountainhead* had been about architecture, her new novel would be about the world of heavy, really heavy industry. Not only did Greenspan know much about railroads, oil derricks, and steel mills, he now occupied a heavy role in the Collective. On top, of course, was Rand, followed by Nathaniel Branden, then Barbara Branden, then Greenspan. Bennett Cerf, an editor faced with a novel of 645,000 words, suggested that perhaps a few words could be cut. "Would you cut the Bible?" was Ayn Rand's cutting reply. The reviews, such as "The worst piece of fiction since *The Fountainhead*," were savage.

In response to a scathing review by Granville Hicks in the *New York Times*, Alan Greenspan was moved to write an angry letter (published November 3, 1957) in which he wondered "about a person who finds unrelenting justice personally disturbing."

Still, passionate devotees were found for *The Fountainhead* and *Atlas Shrugged*. Enough that in 1958 Nathaniel Branden was able to fund his modestly named Nathaniel Branden Institute. It opened with a series of 20 lectures called "Basic Principles of Objectivism." Greenspan developed a 90-minute lecture entitled "The Economics of a Free Society" that would make Ronald Reagan's General Electric speech on free enterprise appear to be a communist manifesto. Eventually there would be a magazine called the *Objectivist*; Greenspan was a frequent contributor.

Greenspan certainly never wandered far from his Randian roots or from Wall Street, a short walk away. In 1954, he and an older bond trader, William Townsend, established the New York-based consulting firm Townsend–Greenspan & Company. The company not only made Greenspan a millionaire (when it meant something), but also introduced him to the biggest banks in New York. At Ayn Rand's aggressive prodding, Greenspan entered the political arena as the director of domestic policy research for Richard Nixon's 1968 presidential campaign. Staying on as an informal Nixon adviser, the future central banker easily bridged the ideological gap between Wall Street and Washington. From Townsend, Greenspan learned how inflationary expectations could depress bond prices and increase long-term interest rates, something he never forgot.

The volatile mixture of Randian philosophy, Wall Street values, and Washington reality, nonetheless sometimes exploded. For instance, Greenspan created a problem for Nixon by setting in motion a proposal to free Wall Street from regulations. Since persons on Main Street did not trust Wall Street and still do not, the idea of deregulating Wall Street was very unpopular. Nixon had to reverse Greenspan. Still, the president asked a seemingly reluctant

Greenspan to head the president's Council of Economic Advisers. What happened next was fortuitous, for Greenspan had little admiration for Nixon's dark side. About the time of Greenspan's appointment, Nixon was forced to resign under a cloud of impeachment and the future maestro was named President Gerald Ford's chief economic adviser.

Ayn Rand came down from New York, along with her hard-drinking, long-suffering husband, Frank O'Connor, for Greenspan's inaugural ceremony on September 4, 1974. For Rand, Greenspan's appointment comprised some vindication for her beliefs: someone from her small circle was in a position of power, which she called "a heroic undertaking" — much like Howard Roark in a black suit. Alan Greenspan's invitation of Rand to the ceremony was itself heroic, testimony to his fervent belief in her doctrines. Greenspan, a born again opponent of government and now the chief economic adviser to the president, moved into the Old Executive Office Building wonderfully situated next to the White House. From there, he moved to the Federal Reserve.

Ironically, Greenspan as Fed chair was greeted by one of the greatest market failures in world history. On August 3, 1987, the U.S. Senate had confirmed Greenspan as chairman of the Reserve. On Monday, October 19, 1987, the Dow plunged 508 points, losing more than a fifth of its value and nearly $1 trillion in wealth in one day. It was the largest percentage loss ever in one day, eclipsing the worst days of the 1929 crash. It was a bubble that burst. Alan Greenspan never thought that his days of dealing with bubbles had ended with the 1987 stock market crash and the total unraveling of the Nasdaq in 2000–2001. After that, he was claiming "risk management" to be the main role of the Federal Reserve. Greenspan and his neoconservative cousins had created enough risks to make risk management a growth industry. Again, Mr. Greenspan and company were busily creating conditions so volatile that only a whirling dervish could dodge them all.

Thanks to the stock market bubble and especially the bursting of the Nasdaq, wealthy people and institutions needed to shift their funds into different assets. Those 35% to 55% returns in securities had essentially disappeared except in hedge funds which were again under pressure, some even collapsing. The housing market, especially second homes, vacation homes, and investment condos became the new playground for the rich. Ultimately, as ever, families that could not afford to play did get in on the action and would be the most vulnerable, just as they are in stock market. They have little to lose, but it is all they have.[2]

The conventional wisdom among real estate, finance, and economics professors is that a bubble cannot form in housing — in part, because housing is not simply straw, brick, or timber, but Home Sweet Home. Reminding ourselves that current conventional wisdom is the equivalent of conservative ideology and Greenspan is an ideologue, we naturally expect him to take the same position. We need to recall, however, in the interest of full Fed disclosure, Greenspan's pattern of taking opposing stances on everything, sometimes on the same day, seldom in the same speech. Though usually never mentioned explicitly, the housing and construction industries are central to Fed policy. As a basic industry housing construction is also central to economic growth.

The Fed's Open Market Operations

Now we will briefly review the Fed's open market operations in order to understand the Fed's influence in housing. To stimulate business activity, the Fed provides more reserves to banks for overnight lending (as Fed funds). In turn, this act of increasing the reserves in the banking system lowers short-term interest rates. Since private banks mark-up all other loan rates such as the prime rate from the Fed funds rate, the interest rates of longer maturities are lowered. The first effects are to reduce interest rates on credit cards issued

---

[2]During the era of bubbles in the stock markets a rash of articles appeared claiming that speculation in such markets was rational. For a critique of "rational bubbles," see E. Ray Canterbery, "Irrational Exuberance and Rational Speculative Bubbles," Presidential Address to the International Trade and Finance Association, *The International Trade Journal*, Spring, 1999, pp. 1–22.

by these private banks. Next, housing and construction are especially stimulated by lower interest rates. Employment and incomes in those industries increase, thus stimulating other parts of the economy through the Keynesian multiplier effect. Conversely, to slow down business activity, the Fed provides fewer funds to banks for overnight lending so as to hopefully raise interest rates across the spectrum. In turn, credit is reduced and the construction industry slows down, eventually taking most of the balance of the economy with it. In these two processes, overall credit is expanded and contracted.

The foregoing explains why during 2001–2003 Alan Greenspan embraced housing as a new miracle economic driver. The economy had been faltering at the turn of the century and Greenspan needed some source of stimulus for the economy. He saw it in real estate as he lowered the Fed funds rate in stair-step fashion through mid-2003. Mortgage rates and credit card rates are tied to the prime loan rate and 5- or 10-year bonds, all of which are tied to the Fed funds rate. Lower interest rates were combined with financial innovation in the way of adjustable-rate mortgages that set off a boom in housing. Before Greenspan, the USA had been bubble free for half a century.

Illus. 3.2:   Bursting bubble photo by Bigi-/Photobucket.
Source: http://media.photobucket.com/user/Bigi.

The Nasdaq Bubble and Bust

Meanwhile, the stock market had been under tremendous pressure since it peaked in March 2000. In 2002 the Nasdaq declined another 32%, while the S&P 500 sank 24%. From its peak in 2000, the Nasdaq would tumble a shocking 74%, and the S&P 500 a substantial 43%. Throughout the sharp run-up on the stock markets Greenspan denied that there was a bubble, while at the same time saying that if a bubble were to exist, the central bank and others would not know about it until after it burst. But since a bubble could not exist (in his mind), he could easily ignore the unmistakable sound of air going out of the stock market as it deflated.

With the stock market no longer available for pulling along the economy (nor the associated profits on Wall Street), real estate seemed to be the only motor left to start. New financial products that included derivatives, asset-backed securities, collateralized loan obligations, and collateralized mortgage obligations (CMOs) had made firms and individuals independent of specific institutions for funds. All this contributed to a more flexible and efficient financial system. At the time this meant that regulated banks were being superseded by unregulated markets. It was to make the financial system ultimately more vulnerable. These "innovations" led to the financial market turmoil of late 2007 in which many large financial firms approached bankruptcy. They were innovations of the neo-Austrian variety rather than the more substantial Schumpeter species.

Attractive mortgage rates bolstered the sales of existing homes and made possible the use of the home equity loan. Low mortgage rates encouraged homeowners to take on larger mortgages when refinancing their homes. This provided still larger home lines of equity. At the time this seemed to be a safe thing to do since the housing market had not been a source of speculation during most of the 1990s. Still, the growth rate of mortgage debt outstanding accelerated, until by 1998 it was galloping at an annual rate of 9.5%. Wall Street stood ready to securitize this rising mortgage debt. Government-sponsored enterprises such as Fannie Mae and Freddie Mac were also rapidly expanding their activities. Sharply falling interest rates added fuel to the smoldering fire.

Greenspan suggested that the usual analogy between the stock market and real estate market was imperfect. This was convenient because the stock market had already crashed. Unlike the stock market, sales in the real estate market incur substantial transactions costs and, when most homes are sold, the seller must physically move out. The turnover in the stock market is something like 100% yearly whereas the turnover of home ownership is less than 10% yearly. Besides, the market for homes is local; a home in Portland, Maine, is not a good substitute for a home in Portland, Oregon; the national housing market is a collection of local segmented markets. Nonetheless, his arguments did not prevent a housing bubble.

The Bubble in Housing

A multitude of forces led to the housing bubble. The increased availability of mortgage loans combined with lower initial monthly payments increased home buyers' ability to pay and pushed prices upward. Since borrowers could always refinance when their mortgages became unaffordable, making mortgage-backed securities and collateralized debt obligations (CDOs) more attractive to investors and to the investment banks that created them, prices could continue to climb. The higher price also induced existing homeowners to take out home equity loans, which provided more raw material for asset-backed securities. The home became an ATM machine. At the same time, lower risk reduced the price of credit default swaps on mortgage-backed debt, making CDOs and synthetic CDOs easier to create. The enhanced Wall Street demand for mortgages to feed the securitization pipeline funneled cheap money to mortgage lenders. By the early 2000s subprime lending became a larger and larger share of the market, not only in the USA but in much of the rest of the world.[3]

---

[3]What follows is based on E. Ray Canterbery, *The Global Great Recession* (Singapore, New Jersey, London: World Scientific Publishing, 2011), pp. 123–137. Much more detail on the roles of financial innovations such as the CDO, the subprime mortgage, and credit default swaps is found in Canterbery, *ibid.*, Chapter 7.

Despite the ability to pass risk along, some banks kept some of the risk anyway. They used financial innovation in the form of structured investment vehicles (SIVs), which were used to raise money by issuing commercial paper and investing it in longer-term, higher yielding assets. Citigroup, for example, used SIVs to buy over $80 billion in assets by July 2007. These SIVs allowed banks to invest in structured securities without having to hold capital against them. Thus, the SIVs-enabled banks to take out more leveraged risks with the same amount of financial capital — that is, as long as housing prices soared. When things did go bad in 2007 and 2008, many banks, including Citigroup, bailed out of their SIVs, incurring billions of dollars of losses.

How big was the bubble? Historical housing data from Robert Shiller, a 2013 Nobel Prize winner in economics, are displayed in Figure 3.1. There, we can see how real U.S. housing prices fell off a cliff, beginning around 2006. The picture is worth a thousand words. Before that, as noted, mortgages were already in trouble by 2005, as the housing boom approached its peak, a peak not reached, according to U.S. census purchase prices, until the second quarter

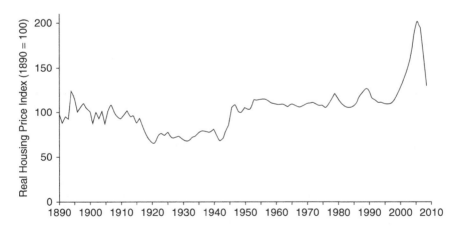

Figure 3.1:   Real U.S. housing prices, 1890–2009.

Source: Robert Shiller, *Irrational Exuberance* (Princeton: Princeton University Press, 2000), updated by Simon Johnson and James Kwak, *13 Bankers* (New York: Pantheon Books, 2010), p. 130.

of 2007. The picture is made more dramatic by the inclusion of data from 1890 through the estimated value in 2010. Those who report that U.S. housing prices "doubled" are using the Schiller Index with 1890 as the base year. The Shiller and (later) Standard & Poor's Case–Shiller index is based on a sample of 20 cities and metropolitan areas. The index may be a more accurate view of the real estate bubble in the U.S. After all, the bubbles were in particular cities. Still, one thing is clear: speculators in housing were reluctant to leave the market, irrespective of their locale.

Unlike Greenspan, Robert Shiller has a good track record in calling bubbles. Just before the stock market crashed in 2000, he warned about the prospects for Nasdaq stocks. Just before housing prices dropped in 2006, he again called the turn. There are many housing indexes that bear Shiller's name, but we will consider one more in Figure 3.2. The bubble actually peaks in the second quarter, but there is very little difference between each of the four quarters of 2006. According to our version, we have an 89% bubble, if the year 2000 is used as the base. This is only slightly different from the annual data results and not wildly different from the broader U.S. Census index.

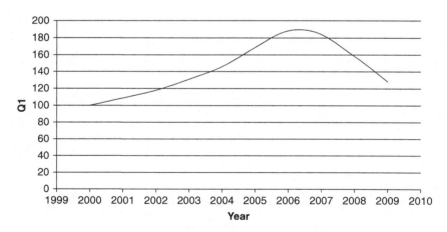

Figure 3.2:   First quarter Standard & Poor's Case–Shiller Index values (rounded to the nearest whole number).

Source: *Wikipedia* at htp://en.wikipedia.org/wiki/Case-Shiller_index, November 2, 2010, p. 4.

The expansion of the bubble had begun much earlier. By October 2002 the real estate market was experiencing multi-year gains. Between the autumns of 1997 and 2002, the average home price in the USA rose 42%. In particular cities the increases were much greater — 75% in Boston, 88% in San Francisco, and 67% in New York City. People were moving out of the stock market and were seeking wealth in real estate. Many households had turned themselves into quasi-ATM machines. As interest rates continued to fall, homeowners refinanced their houses with mortgages in excess of the value of their homes, and then borrowed on the equity. Whereas homeowner's average equity equaled 70% of the house's market value in 1997, in 2003 it was down to 55%.

This nascent housing bubble sustained the demand for new construction. Housing construction is a form of investment. In short, mortgage markets were a powerful stabilizing force during the first couple years of the economic growth slowdown. In still other words, the home ATM machine was doing well. In turn, the ATM machine had a powerful effect on consumer spending. All this happened during a time when other asset values were being eroded. Housing had saved the day.

Just to be sure, Greenspan cut rates for the 13th time on June 25, 2003. This brought the Fed funds rate down to 1%, where it would remain for nearly a year. By July 2003, home prices had gone up 20% during a bear market in stocks. Many analysts began to fear that when home prices did start to go down, they would fall remarkably far. In Japan, home prices were down to less than half what they were during the Japanese bubble.

The first signs that the beneficial side of rising home values were vanishing, emerged as early as near the end of 2003. Prior to the death of irrational exuberance, the foundation of rapidly growing wealth was in securities. The equity ascent — off to a flying start after 1994, peaking in early 2000 — was a source of great accumulations of wealth at the very top. Wealthy bond holders also did remarkably well. Those ordinary people with financial assets in their pension plans went along for the ride, but also for the fall. Overall, $5 trillion in market value of corporations was lost from March 2000 to

October 2002. This period defined the end of the dot-com bubble. The value of real estate, somewhat more democratically held, began to accelerate well before the bottoming out of Nasdaq equity prices in 2004.

For an interminable time, Alan Greenspan denied that the U.S. was in the early stages or any stage of a housing bubble. He noted the great demand among hardworking immigrants for houses (on Greg Norman's exclusive golf course resorts?). Housing, he said too, is a local market, making it virtually impossible to experience a national housing bubble. Moreover, he added, it is hard to speculate in a house a family lives in because, when they sell, they have to buy another and pay all those closing costs.

Despite Greenspan's romantic window on poor immigrants, a realist should not be surprised to find that rich people own more mansions and estates than do the poor or the middle class. Although it may be embarrassing to the neoconservative wealthy family to see typical families benefit from asset inflation, the transfer of wealth out of securities and into large homes, as well as into palatial second homes on beaches and golf courses, did not leave upper-middle class households behind. Aided by exotic financing innovations so praised by Greenspan, many were buying homes and condos that they could not afford.

At a time when an article in the *Wall Street Journal* by James R. Hagerty in 2003 was raising a few red flags, Greenspan continued to say that there was no bubble in housing. However, the oracle's past record in bubble spotting ranks right up there with the captain of the Titanic in spotting serious icebergs. Greenspan once said that there is no way to identify a bubble until it bursts; he also told fellow economists on January 3, 2004, "… our strategy of addressing the bubble's [the Nasdaq bubble] consequences rather than the bubble itself has been successful." Although the economists at the American Economic Association (AEA) gave him a standing ovation and muttered about his greatness, others were reminded of the inadequacy of the life boats on the Titanic. If the captain of money policy chose not to address a "bubble" that he could not identify but nonetheless dealt with "its" consequences, does that not mean that he knew of a bubble before and after?

As with the Nasdaq, and contrary to Greenspan, it is possible to know a bubble when it pops up. A bubble in housing prices is different from that in securities but has some shared characteristics. Buying is based only on anticipation of rising prices rather than on fundamentals. Expectations of returns are based on recent gains rather than on historic norms. Some historical norms can change, but not over a fortnight. Buyers lose all respect for risk and refuse to believe that higher returns are closely linked to higher risks. In housing, as in other assets, at some price the focus on perceived risk is "not being on board" rather than "possibly losing money." Minds lose the battle of rationality against irrationality and greed.

Greed and agreed, housing is different in an important respect. We cannot inhabit the shares of Microsoft stock, no matter how many shares we have. Normally, buying and selling properties requires paying commissions and other "transactions costs." Normally, it takes months or even a year to sell a house above the current market price. As finance people put it, the market for houses is not as liquid as that for securities; it takes considerable time to "cash out" of a house or other property. This much we grant Alan Greenspan for normal times.

Nonetheless, a house is a home only in normal times. It is precisely when a house is not a home that a housing bubble exists. During the bubble, price appreciation overwhelms 6% commissions and closing costs; besides there are ways to buy at pre-construction costs that require no costs before the deal is closed and the property cannot be resold (flipped) before closing time. During a bubble, a house can be sold the day it goes on the market. What normally is an illiquid market becomes liquid. Besides, through a process called securitization a bundle of real estate properties can be packaged and resold as a piece of paper; houses are converted not to homes, but to derivatives.

Still, Greenspan has a point about real estate markets being local. Real estate agents live and die on that premise. Of course, this idea is modified by securitization or even by real estate management trusts (REITS). All of which brings us back to the *Wall Street Journal.*

James Hagerty cites a study by house price gurus Karl E. Case of Wellesley College and Robert J. Shiller of Yale; they find that national measures of housing trends can be misleading. While house prices rise gradually along with a slow growth in personal incomes of most families, states with cities short of land for residential construction such as California (Bakersfield, Riverside–San Bernardino, Los Angeles–Long Beach, Redding, Fresno, San Diego, Orange County) and coastal Florida (West Palm Beach, Boca Raton, Miami, Fort Myers, Cape Coral, Fort Lauderdale) are more likely to swing from boom to bust in a hurry. The Case–Shiller view would seem, at first *rougissent*, to support the view of Coe Lewis, an agent at Century 21 Award who says that people worry too much about prices. "They get paralyzed," Ms. Lewis says. "They almost over think the process. They think there's got to be a dip. There's not going to be a dip. I'm not afraid at all of a bubble in Southern California". We wonder how well that worked out for Ms. Lewis.

With the *Wall Street Journal* ahead of the pack, by early spring 2005 business analysts in the U.S. seemingly could not write or speak of anything other than a herd instinct in the housing market itself. Even Case and Shiller began to refer to a national bubble. Alan Greenspan, so early to cry wolf about Dow stock prices, joined this hunt very late in the season. At last, in response to questions following a luncheon speech on May 20, 2005, he told the Economic club of New York: "At a minimum, there's a little froth in the market. We don't perceive that there is a national bubble, but it's hard not to see that there are a lot of local bubbles". In frothing about "local" bubbles, Greenspan appears to endorse the earlier Case–Schiller view. Besides "lather" and "fizz," however, a synonym for froth is "bubbles". The man who once claimed that bubbles cannot be found until they burst now finds bubbles all over the place, including locally. "Local" can mean "narrow" so he may have been speaking of only tiny bubbles, perhaps reminiscing about the era of Lawrence Welk and those big bands.

While Greenspan is notorious for saying one thing and meaning another or claiming one thing but denying he meant what they say he said, he generally has recognized a financial disaster after it has happened. Greenspan got smarter as the bubble got larger. We have to worry then when we see the maestro going so quickly from "it can't happen" to "froth" which means bubbles. As to what is local, in the Case–Shiller study, there were so many local bubble cities in California to make it a bubble state. California's economy is about the size of the U.K.'s. If California and Florida were merged into the "Sunshine Boys," their economy would about equal Germany's. In a country where Treasury officials worry about how the U.K. or a Germany business recession likely adversely affects American interests, California and Florida are essentially countries within the U.S. As to Century 21 Award, it is a national franchise, so frothy local speeches by its agents are suspect.

As to a housing bubble, "Greenspan" was now likely to be correct, but which Greenspan? His inability to recognize (or at least admit to) the greatest financial bubble in world history is not encouraging. The Federal Reserve, the organization he happened to be heading at the time, issued some new guidelines to mortgage lenders during the same week as Greenspan's "frothy" speech. Among regulators' the top concern was the surge in popularity of interest-only loans, which allows people to pay only interest in the initial years but face the entire principal later. If there really is a bubble, however, toothlessly mouthed warnings will not stop most lenders from lending as usual. Was, in fact, Greenspan again saying one thing and doing another? He and other Fed officials denied that they were continuing to raise interest rates to slow housing asset inflation.

Once enough people believe that a bubble will continue to expand, it probably will. Once four-fifths of *Wall Street Journal* readers believe (as reported May 2005) that there is a housing bubble, it is a short step from believing that a bubble will continue and believing that not participating in it will be a lost opportunity. *Wall Street Journal* subscribers have the wealth to keep it going in California and Florida. The August 12, 2005 *Journal's* "House of the Week" was a 106 room, 11 bedroom, 13 bathroom little fix-me-up mansion for $21.5 million, and it was in the Berkshires of Massachusetts, not even in California. When sky high prices are accepted as "normal," much as Greenspan ultimately decided that Internet and tech stock prices were just what the market ordered during the early 2000s, look out below! This particular housing bubble reached a peak in September 2005, but this was not the end of the fallout, only the beginning.

Whither the Fundamentals?

The existence of the bubble could have been verified. From 1895 to 1995, a 100 years epoch, nationwide house prices in the U.S. tracked the overall rate of inflation. On average, house prices rose at the same rate as the price of food, cars, clothes, and so on. While house prices in places like San Francisco and New York did rise far more rapidly than overall inflation, these price increases were offset by prices that trailed inflation in places like Gary, Indiana and St. Louis, and Missouri.

In 1995, house prices began to outstrip the overall rate of inflation. By the summer of 2002 house prices had already outpaced inflation by 30%, creating more than $3 trillion of housing bubble wealth. The question arises: Was there anything in market fundamentals — either on the demand or supply side of the market — that would explain the $3 trillion? The two main elements on the demand side are income and population. If income grows rapidly, people may want bigger and better homes, or even second homes. By the same token, a more rapidly increasing population will lead to more rapid growth in the demand, especially if the growth rate is high among people in their 20s, who are forming their own households for the first time.

Neither of these factors provides an explanation for the fast run-up in house prices during this period. Income growth had been healthy during the late 1990s, but was not extraordinary. The rate of growth of median family income over the four years from 1996 to 2000 was no more rapid than the growth rate over the long boom from 1947 to 1973. Further, the country had fallen into a recession in 2001, and family income had begun to decrease. Income growth was weak through the rest of the bubble years, even though some modest gains happened in 2005 and 2006. In any case, income growth alone cannot explain the bubble in house prices during this time.

Population growth is an even less likely explanation. Though Greenspan had cited immigration as a factor pushing up prices, the reality is that the inflow of immigrants in the 1990s and the following decade was a relativity minor element compared with the demographic bulge created by the baby-boom cohort. In truth, the rate of household formation was far more rapid in the 1970s and early 1980s. When baby boomers were first forming their own households, but there was no bubble then. By the mid-1990s, the majority of the baby boomers who would ever be homeowners already owned a home. By the end of the housing bubble, the oldest baby boomers were already in their 60s.

What about supply-side fundamentals? Alan Greenspan once suggested that environmental constraints on building was one cause of the house price rises. Despite some environmental restrictions on building during the era of the housing bubble, that era was not the high point of the environmental movement. There essentially was little difference between the earlier decades and the bubble years.

Greenspan was the source of still other "reasons" for above-trend house prices. There was a limited supply of building land in desirable urban areas. True, land in urban areas is limited, but this condition was not new to the mid-1990s. This constraint had not been the source of a run-up in house prices over the prior 100 years. Why would it have made these prices suddenly rise nationwide in 1996?

There is a simple way to assess whether supply constraints were causing increases in house prices; look at the rate of housing construction during this period. We were building houses at a rapid pace in the 1990s and at an even more rapid pace in the first decade of the 21st century. The USA was building new housing units at a record rate from 2002 to 2006, when starts averaged

1,880,000 annually. This rate was about at the five-year peak from 1969 to 1973. There was no supply constraint on housing during the bubble era.

Another place to look would be rental prices during the bubble years. While rental prices outpaced inflation by a small amount in the late 1990s, in the following decade they kept even with the over-all rate of inflation or even trailed it slightly. This trend is still further evidence that the fundamentals, the supply and demand elements, were not driving the rapid increase in house prices.

Herein we have the definition of a housing bubble. Soaring prices of houses cannot be explained by the fundamentals of demand and supply; the excess markup must constitute a bubble. The evidence was there for everyone to observe.

Collapses Around the World

While some countries only experienced a steady rise in housing prices, others saw bubbles even more extensive than the ones that happened in some regions of the USA. The run-up in housing prices happened in many countries beginning later than in the USA, but with declines starting sometime in 2008. Some countries, especially former communist countries, saw an unprecedented rise in housing prices followed by an even steeper bust. In Estonia, price changes between the lowest and highest levels in the decade of the 2000s reached some 600%. In Singapore, Dubai, Latvia, Iceland, and the U.K. price declines following dramatic price bubbles range between 19% and 50% as of the first quarter of 2009. Australia, although see-ing a slight dip in prices at the end of 2008, was beginning to worry about a potential housing bubble in 2009. At about the same time Singapore was experiencing the beginning of a drop.[4]

The data trends show that local home prices, affected by the performance of the local economy and even varying considerably within a country, are increasingly influenced by international varia-bles. Foreign buyers, especially rich ones, consider the benefits of

---

[4]This section is based on Canterbery, *The Global Great Recession, op. cit.*, pp. 156–160.

purchasing homes abroad. Those markets more susceptible to global economic conditions and fluctuations find maintaining affordable property prices of local residents to be challenging. Where bubbles exist, demographic trends, incomes, and urbanization do not fully explain the outcomes. However, increases in credit and liquidity and the demand for assets adds fuel to the expanding bubbles. Even though their timing may be different, the causes of the bubbles remain universal.

The Research Division of the National Association of Realtors (NAR) conducted an extensive study of recent historical housing prices in 17 countries.[5] Each bubble is measured from the first quarter of 2000 as the base year (Year 2000 = 100). Moreover, the ending date for the bubbles are selected as either the fourth quarter of 2008 or the first quarter of 2009. What is notable are the sizes of the bubbles in the other 16 countries compared with the U.S., the exception being Singapore, where its bubble was just getting underway. Estonia has the biggest bubble in the sample with 322%, followed by Iceland, 135%, and Australia, with 114%. After that is France with 104.5%, and Sweden with 87.1%. The bubbles ending in the first quarter of 2009 are uniformly large, with New Zealand leading, followed by Iceland. We should note that price peaks for the bubbles did not necessarily coincide with the somewhat arbitrary ending dates. But, as in the U.S., price increases did not turn negative right away. The bubbles were often enduring.[6]

The NAR percentage increase of 21.8% greatly understates the U.S. bubble compared with U.S. Census data. This results partly because the Census peak comes much earlier than that for the National Association of Realtors (which is based on their own data collection). Moreover, median prices and a base year of 2000 = 100 was used in the NAR survey compared with the Census with purchase prices and a base point of 1991, first quarter = 100.

---

[5] The study is available at www.REALTOR.org/research. My analysis of the data differs in some cases from theirs.

[6] The results of the NAR study are summarized in Table 7.2 in Canterbery, *The Global Great Recession, op. cit.*, p. 158.

Do the lags and leads of the peaks versus the selected ending dates for the bubbles tell us anything about cause and effect? That is, did the U.S. bubble leak over into the global economy or was the countries' bubbles independently generated? The peak came for the U.S. bubble first, which provides only one criterion for cause to effect. The peaks for the other 16 countries came during the money and banking panic in the U.S. (to be considered next). This too was the time of the unraveling of the subprime mortgages and CDOs, which made the effects of the bubble much worse. The banks in the U.S. had counter-parties in the sweet 16, the exception possibly being Estonia. Subprime mortgages were common in the U.K. and its 90.4% bubble may have been generated independently of the U.S.

Alan Greenspan had not only been the cheerleader for subprime lending, he had facilitated the bubble early on with aggressively easy monetary policy. Thus far we have seen what this process did for financial markets and the housing market. The American bubble in mortgages and house prices preceded most of the bubbles abroad. Later, we will consider other causes and effects. Next, we consider the implications for Main Street USA where its homeowners reside.

4

Housing's Trickle-Down Effects

When the music stops, in terms of liquidity, things will be complicated. But as long as the music is playing you've got to get up and
dance. We're still dancing.

— Charles Prince, Chair and CEO, Citigroup, July 2007

Alan Greenspan understood the tight connection of housing to
construction and to the balance of the economy. He had
counted on these connections to restore economic growth. As luck
would have it, these connections remain intact when housing goes
south. Ben Bernanke by now was in charge of the central bank. On
February 14, 2009, Bernanke told the Senate Banking Committee
that the serious housing slump and a credit crisis triggered by rising
defaults in subprime mortgages had greatly strained the economy.
"The outlook for the economy has worsened in recent months and
the downside risks of growth have increased," Bernanke told the
committee. "To date, the largest economic effects of the financial
turmoil appear to have been on the housing market, which, as you
know, had deteriorated significantly over the past two years or so."
He still did not predict a full-blown recession, only sluggish growth.
Some economists said that he had underestimated the coming
calamity. The Dow Jones Industrials fell 175 points the next day, as
if to highlight Bernanke's remarks.

The Tipping Point

Weighing heavily on the stock market that day in February was Bear
Stearns, the venerable investment bank, which lost nearly half its

market value in a matter of minutes. On the verge of a collapse that could have shaken the very foundations of the U.S. Financial system, Bear Stearns was bailed out by a rival and the Federal Reserve. It was too-big-to-fail. J. P. Morgan and the Federal Reserve rushed to pump new money into the Wall Street firm. J. P. Morgan and the central bank agreed to extend loans for 28 days to Bear Stearns, then the nation's fifth-largest investment bank and the one hit hardest by the subprime mortgage mess.

Two hedge funds managed by Bear Stearns had failed during the prior summer, setting off a credit crisis that swept up banks and brokerages around the globe. We were at a global tipping point. Now Bear Stearns itself was endangered. In backing up J. P. Morgan, the Fed had dusted off a rarely used Depression-era provision to provide loans to investment banks. This represented a major shift in Federal Reserve policy. The Fed is required only to provide loans to commercial banks. Bernanke also said that he was ready to step in to fight an erosion of confidence in the nation's largest financial institutions.

The J. P. Morgan deal was valued at $236.2 million or initially $2 a share for Bear Stearns. At their peak the shares had traded at $159.36. While the Fed had agreed to fund up to $30 billion of Bear Stearns' less liquid assets, the deal did not go through. A combination of risky bets on securities tied to subprime mortgages and loan's given to customers with poor credit histories had crippled Bear Stearns. J. P. Morgan's attempted acquisition of Bear Stearns represented roughly 1% of what the investment bank had been worth just 16 days prior. As it turned out, the $2 a share offering did not stick.

There were problems everywhere. Conditions in early spring 2008 foreshadowed dark prospects for the American and global economies. In March, nervous employers in the U.S. slashed 80,000 jobs, enough to vacate a small city. With the most jobs lost in five years, the national unemployment rate climbed to 5.1%, modest only in retrospect. Job losses were nearing a quarter million for the year in just three months. It had been the third month in a row that total U.S. employment had shrunk; the sharp sustained increase was a sign of tremendous economic stress. Even Ben Bernanke used the word "recession," acknowledging the possibility.

Illus. 4.1:   A global tipping point.
Source: Photograph by Christopher Gould, from the web.

Illus. 4.2:   Creative destruction in housing — incredible building explosion.
Source: Picture #3 izismile.com.

Bernanke began to realize what he was facing. In a rare weekend move, The Federal Reserve took bold action on a Sunday evening (March 16) to provide funds to the financially squeezed Wall Street investment houses. Moreover, the central bank cut its lending rate to financial institutions to 3.25% from 3.50%, effective immediately, and created another lending facility for big investment banks to secure short-term loans. The new lending facility was available to the big Wall Street firms on St. Patrick's Day. The investment houses needing immediate help included Goldman Sachs, Lehman Brothers, and Morgan Stanley. The CEO at Goldman Sachs was Lloyd C. Blankfein; at Lehman Brothers, Jasjit S. ("Jesse") Bhattal; and John J. Mack at Morgan Stanley. They were some of the biggest names in the business.

The Fed slashed its Federal funds rate a remarkable three-quarters of a point on March 18, capping its most aggressive two months of action in a quarter-century. The Fed had now cut the Federal funds rate by three-fourths of a percentage point twice in 2008, the first coming at an emergency meeting on January 22, only to be followed by a half-point cut at a regularly scheduled meeting on January 30. These rapid-fire rate cuts comprised the most aggressive credit easing since mid-1982, when Paul Volcker was trying to move the nation out of the deepest recession since the Great Depression. Now, with the Federal funds rate at a mere 2.25%, the real interest rate (adjusted for consumer price index (CPI) inflation) was below zero and heading even lower. Soon, at a regularly scheduled meeting on March 30, 2008, the Fed funds rate was trimmed to 2.00%. Bernanke knew that the Federal Reserve was running out of bullets.

Were these aggressive moves enough? The housing crisis could not have come a worse time in terms of national politics. Not only was George W. Bush a lame duck president, his popularity was at an all-time low. Still, President Bush proposed an ambitious plan for the Federal Reserve to take on the unwieldy role of the cop in charge of financial market stability. Other regulatory agencies would see their influence diminished.

The CPI, which had gone up only 2.8% in 2007, was now headed for an annual rate of 4%. The real Federal funds rate was headed for –1.75. While this complicated matters for monetary policy, the inflation proved to be temporary.

The U.S. housing industry was in worse shape and with foreclosures, there was further dampening in consumer demand for durable goods. In March 2008, sales of new homes plunged to the slowest pace in more than 16 years. Worse still, the median price of new homes in March compared with the previous year fell at the fastest clip in 38 years. Sales of new homes dropped by 8.5% to a seasonally-adjusted annual rate of 526,000 units, the slowest sales pace since October 1981, according to Commerce Department figures. According to a Realty-Trac Inc. Report, the number of U.S. homes heading toward foreclosure more than doubled in the first quarter-year from the year before. The median price of homes sold in March dropped by 13.3%, compared with March 2007, this the largest year-over-year price drop since a 14.6% plunge in July 1970.

Foreclosures comprised the size of small city during the first three-quarters of 2006, but escalated thereafter. The rise in foreclosures was especially steep during 2007, then showing an increase in the first quarter of 2008 of 23% over the previous quarter. Thus, by spring 2008 the foreclosures would equal a *major* city. Moody's Economy.com estimated that one in four USA families with mortgages had zero or negative equity in the first quarter of 2008; they already owed more than the current value of their homes and were "underwater." This translated into 2.3 million foreclosures in 2008. By early 2009 some 12.2 million homeowners would be underwater. According to the U.S. Census, there were about 75 million homeowners in America. The latest estimates suggested that some 6.4 million homes are at risk of sinking into foreclosure by the end of 2012. This was a number without precedent. There was a plague on most houses.

Congress passed Bush's tax rebate bill that would have temporarily beneficial results. Some $50 billion of the economic stimulus payments were sent out by the end of May 2009, slightly less than half of the $106.7 billion scheduled for 2008. The immediate effect was to increase retail sales by about 1% in May. Without the tax rebate package, the U.S. would have had relatively flat growth over the middle of the year. The results were nonetheless temporary and all eyes turned to monetary policy as the source of continuing stimulus. A surge in oil prices past US$140 a barrel and warning of trouble in financial, automotive and high-tech industries sent the Dow down 358 points on June 26. In particular General Motors was being hurt by the fallout of the prolonged housing slump and the nearly year old credit crisis. Citigroup, headed by Vikram S. Pandit as Chief Executive, fell sharply after an analyst placed a "sell" rating on the stock and warned investors to expect less from the brokerage sector in the uneasy economic climate.

Housing had boomed for five years, but now was in a prolonged slump. Prices were being depressed by the continued huge inventory of unsold homes, a backlog from rising mortgage defaults that were dumping more homes on an already overbuilt market. Meanwhile, AutoNation Inc., the nation's largest auto retailer, said that decelerating vehicle sales in Florida, California, and other key states were the result of these sagging home prices. AutoNation saw no light at the end of the tunnel until 2009. Even Wendy's hamburgers were in trouble, not unrelated to the housing crisis. Triare companies, the owner of Arby's and its roast beef sandwiches, bought Wendy's, after Wendy's stock had fallen from a high of over $40 a share in summer 2007 to a buyout price of around $26 a share. Homeowners were dining in to save money. With minority stock financing from Warren Buffet, candy maker Mars Inc. on April 28, 2008 offered to buy confectioner Wm. Wrigley Jr. Co. for an estimated $223 billion in cash, making it the largest confectioner in the world. Even candy was getting concentrated.

Concerns come full circle to those commercial banks holding mortgages on homes that homeowners cannot afford. The Babbits of real estate had done all too well. Moreover, all those derivatives were off the twin balance sheets of banks and hedge funds. Then, there were the brokerage firms that had sold puts and calls to the hedge funds. The round-robin continues as the commercial banks lent to troubled brokerage firms to keep them afloat. They were all in a life raft that had sprung more than one leak.

There was the fast-moving decline of IndyMac Bank, a mortgage lender that was one of the nation's largest savings and loans. It illustrated how wide and deep the problems of the U.S. banking system had become. IndyMac did a lot of business in Alt-A mortgages, which are described as just below qualifications for a prime mortgage, but better than for a normal subprime mortgage. The

U.S. government seized IndyMac Bank around mid-July 2008. More likely that the kind of exodus of depositors that quickly sank IndyMac is what some bankers were describing as a slow motion "walk on the bank," which could cripple financial institutions already weakened by credit problems. IndyMac had Depression-like lines of people waiting to withdraw their money from the bank, the largest regulated thrift to fail.

Treasury Secretary Henry Paulson sought to reassure an anxious public that the banking system was sound, while also bracing people for more troubled times ahead. He testified before the House Financial Services Committee on July 10. "The three big issues we're facing right now are, first, the housing correction which is at the heart of the slowdown; secondly, turmoil of the capital markets; and thirdly, the high oil prices, which are going to prolong the slowdown," he said. "But remember, our economy has got very strong long-term fundamentals, solid fundamentals." The latter echoed comments coming from President Herbert Hoover and his secretaries during the Great Depression. Democratic leaders, including presidential candidate Barack Obama, were pushing for a second, smaller economic stimulus. Paulson said he did not want to speculate about the idea.

Austrian-Styled Innovation in Housing

Scary stories began to circulate among mortgage brokers. One in particular should have raised the eyebrows of regulatory authorities. There was bad underwriting, fraudulent income documentation, and even equity lines equaling 125% of the equity that persons had in their homes. The ATM machine had gotten larger. These practices were becoming standard operating procedures.

One of the industry's innovations was the aforementioned Alt-A Mortgage. These are the nonprime mortgages without standard documentation such as income and credit references, often referred to as "liar's loans." Alt-A mortgages soared more or less in tandem with equity lines of credit. While Alt-A mortgage debt was about 3% of total mortgage debt in 2003, it averaged about 15% during

2005–2007. Meantime, home equity loans soared from an average of about 5% of total mortgage debt in 2001–2003 to about 15 in 2006–2007. The housing bubble approached a peak in 2005, leaving all those subprime mortgages, liar's loans, and equity lines of credit hanging out to dry. The housing ATM alone was responsible for a large share of GDP growth during 2000–2005. Other innovations in the form of derivatives would follow.

Unlike the stock market bubble, the real estate bubble of 2000–2005 was fueled by debt. Then from 2004 to 2007, banks and mortgage companies were making trillions of dollars of ultra-liberal adjustable rate mortgage loans to millions of unwitting Americans who had little or no chance of servicing these loans to maturity. By counting on rising real estate prices to tide them over, this lending spasm turned the U.S. housing market into a system of Ponzi finance, as defined by Post Keynesian Hyman Minsky. Ever rising house prices would shore up the mortgages before the truth was revealed, or so it was thought.

Derivatives Complicate the Mix

Wall Street configured residential mortgage portfolios into structured bonds through collateralized mortgage obligations (CMOs). An entire portfolio of mortgages could be dedicated to support the issuance of a family of bonds. The bonds were tiered in horizontal slices, or tranches, and portfolio cash flows were preferentially directed to the top tranches. Wall Street pushed the tranching technology to an extreme and triggered a serious mortgage market crash in 1994. As the market slowly recovered, more conservatively structured residential mortgage-backed securities (RMBS) replaced many of the CMOs in most big investor portfolios.

Following the RMBSs, the commercial mortgage-backed securities (CMBS) entered stage right. Unlike the residential mortgages, commercial mortgagers do not lend themselves to pooling. To solve this problem, rating agencies were used to construct the pool. The financials, management, tenant history, maintenance records, and mortgage details were collected by banks. Then, rating agencies used proprietary models to estimate default risk and negotiate the pool structure. For example, a CMBS might have five or six tranches, and might include 140 buildings with face value mortgages in the $10 million range and upward. These served to broaden the investor base for such mortgages and tightened interest spreads. Several other financial innovations were to follow.

The rating agencies played a big role. As long as the documentation of credit was done with the rating agencies, anything could be securitized. Businesses began to sell asset-backed securities (ABS) to finance equipment, fleets of vehicles, and other things of value. General Electric, for example, became an early ABS issuer. Furthermore, investment banks created collateralized bond obligations (CBOs), and commercial banks issued collateralized loan obligations (CLOs). As noted earlier, collateralized debt obligations (CDOs) became the generic name for all types of security assets, including the old-fashioned mortgages. In most cases a trust, technically independent of the parent, would be created to purchase the assets, a purchase financed by selling securitized paper, usually with a tranched structure. Banks continued to conduct these transactions off their balance sheets.

It got still more complicated. New credit derivatives such as the credit default swap (CDS) were invented. Suppose a U.S. bank is underexposed to credits in Brazil. It used to be that this could be fixed by buying some Brazilian bank branches or partnering with a local bank. A credit default swap cuts through this process. For a fee, the U.S. bank can guarantee against any losses on a loan portfolio held by the Brazilian bank and can receive interest and fees on those loans. The Brazilian bank will continue to service the loans, so its local customers will see no change, but the Brazilian bank will have purchased insurances for its risk portfolio, freeing up regulatory capital for business expansion. The notional value of credit default swaps grew from $1 trillion in 2001 to $454 trillion by mid-2007.

Meanwhile, the credit agencies were doing quite well, thank you. Between 2002 and 2006, Moody's doubled its revenue and more than tripled its stock price. Their main customers were the big commercial banks and investment banks, and the agencies slanted their ratings to please these clients. Despite the high ratings for bonds, their default rates were rising.

Leverage was compounded. There were even CDOs of CDOs. Risky tranches of a number of CDOs were collected and used to support a new CDO, with a range of high-to-low risk-rated tranches. Among all this mess was the highly inflated ratings for bonds. Often, the AAA rating for a senior tranche was extrapolated to the entire CDO.

This was a house of cards destined to collapse. Events in the fall of 2007 led to an evolving slow-motion crisis in the banking industry. The top banks had committed to some $300 billion to $400 billion in bridges for private equity deals that were still being completed when the subprime debacle hit. CDO financing stopped, and the banks were in trouble; the CDOs had played a critical role in maintaining bank liquidity. Moreover, the rates on commercial paper, issued by the banks for short-term liquidity, suddenly spiked up nearly 20% in early September. Among the banks in trouble were the giants Citibank and J. P. Morgan (later JPMorgan Chase). In October the big banks and investment banks reported some $20 billion in losses, with $11 billion of that at Citibank and Merrill Lynch, mostly in subprime-based CMOs. Within a few weeks the banks revised their losses to more than $45 billion. Again, some $20 billion was at Citibank and Merrill Lynch.

We can begin to see how home mortgages led to a banking crisis. Investment bankers created mortgage bonds by pooling thousands of home loans or home equity lines of credit. You might think that mortgage bonds made up of thousands of home loans would provide safety through diversity. It did not happen that way. These bonds became so toxic that they poisoned banks and threatened the entire economy.

Look under the hood of one of these diversified bonds and you can understand why banks were in trouble. The mortgage bond holds other mortgage bonds made up of the riskiest portions of other bonds, some of which are themselves a collection of other poorly rated mortgage bonds. In a rising real estate market, such risks are deemed acceptable. When first issued, the mortgage bond might have been rated AAA. But when things unwind, it is a different story as any default gets compounded by the chain of linked bonds. While say 4.4% of typical loans tied to the mortgage bond are in default, nearly 59% of the investments are now worthless. The mortgage bond has become a toxic asset.

The banks come back into the picture. Banks hold tens of billions of dollars in mortgage bonds, and as the bonds fall in value or are wiped out completed, they erase precious capital the banks need to survive. Then Secretary of Treasury Timothy Geithner said that he wanted to start a public–private partnership to buy up such toxic assets.[1] Geithner and others believe that rescue banks for these bonds will save the commercial banks. To pull that off, the bond has to be priced to sell. Once again, the Black–Scholes formula comes back into play. The price has to be right. A look at Jupiter High Grade V, one of these mortgage bonds, illustrates just how difficult setting the price would be. Jupiter owns 223 other mortgage bonds. One of those bonds is Mantoloking, which in turn owns 126 other bonds. Those mortgage bonds are then all made up of thousands of actual loans, some of which may be current, while others may have expired.

A Goldman Sachs report estimates that most investment banks believe bonds like Jupiter are worth 40% less than what was paid for them, or 50 cents for every dollar invested. But because so many of Jupiter's bonds have gone bad, you could just as easily guess that it is worth 41 cents on the dollar. Given where loan defaults are headed, the best part of the bond could be worth as

---

[1] Geithner stayed on until February 28, 2013 when Jack Lew was sworn in as the new Secretary of Treasury. By November of 2013, Timothy Geithner had gone through a revolving door to become managing director of Warburg Pincus, a private equity fund. We will find him in a different role in Chapter 5.

little as 5 cents. If some entity, be it the Treasury or the Federal Reserve, buys these assets, there will be very little new capital on either balance sheet. And, all of this traces back to the foreclosure crisis.

The various mortgage transactions involved commercial banks. The overall effect was found in bank failures. By May 22, 2008 some 36 banks had been taken over by the Federal Deposit Insurance Corporation (FDIC), which arranged for a merger of the failing bank with a "healthier" bank where possible. All FDIC checking accounts are insured up to $250,000. Since the inception of FDIC during the Great Depression, no depositor has lost money unless their account exceeded the insurance limit. Although there were only three failures in all of 2007, many more banks were distressed throughout 2008. The largest bank failure by far was that of the aforementioned saving and loan IndyMac Bank, which was seized by regulators on July 11 with about $32 billion in assets and deposits of $19 billion. On August 22, 2008, Federal regulators shut down Columbian Bank and Trust Company in Topeka, Kansas. The FDIC was appointed receiver of Columbian Bank, which had $752 million in assets and $622 million in deposits as of June 30. It was the ninth failure in 2008 of an FDIC-insured bank. Later banks seized were Strategic Capital Bank and Citizens National Bank, both in Illinois. The closure of Strategic Capital Bank is expected to cost the FDIC $173 million, while Citizen National Banks' closure will cost about $106 million. The banking crisis worsened in 2009, but did not end then.

The most recent cases contrast with the about $46 million in uninsured deposits at Columbian bank that exceeded the insurance limit. Concern continues to grow over the solvency of some banks amid the housing slump and the steep slide in the mortgage markets. Banks are being subjected to tumbling home prices, rising foreclosures, and tighter credit conditions, afflicting both large and small banks across the USA. The FDIC had been adding to the staff of examiners to handle the expected failures and planned to raise insurance premiums paid by banks and thrifts to replenish its reserve funds after the huge payout to IndyMac.

Late in July 2008, Merrill Lynch announced plans to write down another $5.7 billion tied to bad mortgage debt, raising fears that other banks and financial firms will follow. Merrill Lynch said it would sell repackaged mortgage-backed securities for just $7 billion only a few weeks after they had been valued at $31 billion.

Illus. 4.3:   Ben Bernanke official portrait.
Source: *Wikipedia*, the free encyclopedia.

In response, the Federal Reserve gave emergency loans to Wall Street firms, a practice continued in 2009, and held in reserve thereafter. As financial companies racked up multi-billion dollar losses on sour mortgage investments and credit problems spread to other areas, firms have hoarded cash and clamped down on lending. That had crimped spending by consumers and businesses, which in turn has weighed on the national economy, a vicious cycle the Fed desperately wants to break.

The Global Dimension

The world's central bankers admired the ingenuity and even the elegance with which Bernanke and Geithner engineered the rescue of Bear Stearns. They presumed that the next time a major financial institution teetered on the brink, the two would be up to the task of saving it. As it turns out, the same forces that brought down Bear Stearns were endangering Lehman Brothers. And, now they found that there were little that they could do. Like Bear Stearns and many other Wall Street firms, Lehman was heavily involved in the creation of mortgage-backed securities. It also relied to a great extent on borrowed money, with $700 billion in total assets against only $25 billion in capital. In July, Lehman came to the New York Fed with a proposal that it convert itself into a bank holding company, the sort of institution that would come under explicit oversight by the Fed, and in exchange gain access to the full range of central-bank programs that insure steady funding. But why should the Fed pretend it was a bank?[2]

Meanwhile, New York Fed markets desk chief Bill Dudley laid out a proposal for how the central bank might deal with a Lehman failure. His idea was to divide Lehman in two: a "bad or ugly bank," consisting of $60 billion of complex mortgage and other securities, of which $55 billion would be funded by the Fed, and a "clean Lehman" consisting of everything else, which would be a more liquid, less leveraged investment bank stripped of ugly assets, a pretty bank. In exchange for providing billions for the ugly bank, the Fed would be given stock in the pretty bank, the lady in red.

While the concept had theoretical elegance, the Fed lawyers in Washington were appalled. The prior emergency lending authority they had used with Bear allowed them to lend against safe collateral, not to invest in the stock of an investment bank. That is, they did not go into the business of banking. But there were no good options. As Lehman's finances became ever more fragile in the

---

[2]Parts of what follows is based on Neil Irwin, *The Alchemists* (New York: The Penguin Press, 2013), especially Chapters 10 and 11.

summer of 2008, the consensus was that they needed a buyer. After months of a low murmur of worry, the actual collapse in confidence happened over just a few days, on the heels of the U.S. government's putting Fannie Mae and Freddie Mae into conservatorship, a form of bankruptcy. The crisis was back, and the markets were zeroing in on Lehman.

On the morning of Thursday, September 11, New York Fed officials sent colleagues in Washington a plan titled "Liquidation Consortium," a plan to bring together the heads of the financial firms that had the most to lose if Lehman went down. The idea was to let Wall Street bail out its own. This would prevent Lehman's insolvency and prevent widespread financial devastation. The basic problem was the dependence of many other financial institutions on Lehman. Many more could follow Lehman on the bankruptcy path.

The next two days were the most consequential for global capitalism in modern times. Wall Street had to bail out Lehman Brothers. Geithner and Hank Paulson scurried between rooms, looking desperately for a buyer, or at least for a consortium of stronger firms that might, as Geithner phrased it, put "foam on the runway" for Lehman's crash.

Meanwhile, abroad, the central bankers and finance ministers of Europe gathered at one of the grandest villas in the south of France, nestled between Nice and Monaco in the village of Beaulieu-sur-Mer. They clinked champagne glasses in a house that was built at the start of the 20th century for appropriately enough, a banking heiress, Beatrice Ephrussi de Rothechild. Apart from the absence of ball gowns on the women and white ties and tails on the men, the scene looked as if it were taking place before World War I. But, then, central bankers always seem to meet in exotic places.

The opulent setting was not the only thing that called to mind the Great War. Charles Bean, Deputy Governor for monetary policy of the Bank of England, said, "We thought a year ago, when this crisis first emerged, that it 'might be over by Christmas,' a bit like World War I, but as it has gone on we have realized that there are far deeper and more well-seated problems that will take longer to unfold."[3] In fact, the global crises would go on for years more and profoundly endanger European unity, much like the events after World War I.

On that moonlit evening on the French Riviera, and the next day in Nice, the mood was one of confidence that the Americans would take care of their mess, as they had before. For one thing, the Bank of America seemed poised to buy up Lehman. However, as the Europeans left Nice on the evening of Saturday, September 13, the Americans were watching everything fall apart. Bank of America had elected to acquire Merrill Lynch, *not* Lehman Brothers. And British bank regulators were uncomfortable with Barclays buying Lehman, which could turn the American government's problem into the British government's problem. On Sunday, the Americans had no buyer for Lehman.

The idea of a consortium had collapsed, in part due to the fragile finances of the very banks that it would have comprised. They were all in bad shape. Moreover, the Fed is allowed to lend money only against sound collateral. A loan would not solve the problem of Lehman, which was insolvent. There was no legal way for Bernanke or Paulson to hand money over to a private firm. Lehman Brothers would have no choice but to file for bankruptcy protection first thing Monday morning. The French, in particular, were terrified.

There was little time for remorse. On Monday, September 15, 2008, Geithner and his colleagues at the New York Fed faced a new crisis. American International Group (AIG), an insurance company with a $1 trillion balance sheet and 116,000 employees, was on the brink of collapse. Worse, AIG had operations in almost every corner of the world economy: writing insurance policies against fire for homeowners, guaranteeing pension plans for municipalities, and leasing 747s to airlines. As luck would have it, the worst part of its balance sheet was financial. AIG had developed a wildly lucrative business of guaranteeing those seemingly high-quality mortgage bonds created by Wall Street. With AIG's assurance,

---

[3]Treasury Committee Hearing on Bank of England, August 2008 Inflation Report (Sept. 11, 2008).

investors considered these securities virtually riskless. AIG, in turn, viewed the odds of losing money on insuring these super-safe bonds as so low that it did not reserve any money for payouts.

As the mortgage securities AIG guaranteed lost value, its clients — global banks including the French Socie'te' Generale, Germany's Deutsche Bank, and the United States' Goldman Sachs — demanded that AIG put up billions of dollars to ensure it would make good on the potential losses. The firm's insurance arms were heavily regulated, however, and could not simply shift cash over to its troubled financial products division.

One might suppose that AIG could easily borrow money to buy itself time to sell off some of its profitable businesses. But commercial banks were not in the mood to extend $75 billion in loans to a troubled company. They had their own problems — becoming the next Lehman chief among them. Raising the money on the stock market was not an option either. After Lehman Brothers had filed for bankruptcy protection that Monday morning, the Dow Jones industrial Average fell 504 points, one of the largest single-day drops in its history, and many of the overseas investors who had made large-scale investments in big U.S. financial companies earlier in the crisis had seen their money all but wiped out. The appetite of investors for new shares of AIG was non-existent.

Geithner was convinced that the collapse of AIG would be catastrophic for the financial system, even though, as late as Lehman Brothers weekend, essentially no one within the Federal Reserve understood the risks the company had been taking or what might happen if it were to go under. "The failure of AIG, in our estimation, would have been basically the end," Bernanke said in a lecture years later. "It was interacting with so many different firms … . We were quite concerned that if AIG went bankrupt, we would not be able to control the crisis any further."[4] Unlike with Lehman, there was a plausible option. Under the same "unusual and exigent" emergency lending authority it had used with Bear

---

[4]Ben Bernanke, lecture, George Washington University, Washington, DC, March 27, 2012.

Stearns, the central bank could make the multibillion-dollar loan to AIG that private banks were unable or unwilling to make. The loan would be secured by AIG's insurance businesses, which the firm would have to sell in order to raise repayment funds. This prevented a domino effect.

By the time that AIG had been put to bed, another nightmare happened. On September 16, Bernanke and Geithner focused on what to do about Reserve Management Co. It was one of the earliest innovators of a product that had transformed the way many people around the world save, as well as how many companies fund themselves. The Reserve Primary Fund, like all money market mutual funds, performed many of the functions of a bank, both for savers and for borrowers, but without all the costly regulation and overhead of a bank. The managers of the fund invest money in safe, short-term investments — commercial paper issued by General Electric to manage its cash flow, for example, or Treasury bills issued by the U.S. government, or the repurchase agreements that investment banks use to fund themselves.

Unlike a bank, a money market fund does not have to maintain a large cushion of capital; rather, it invests nearly all of its investors' money in securities. It can generally pay a higher rate of interest to savers and demand lower interest rates from borrowers. But it lacks the range of government guarantees that the banking system has — Federal deposit insurances, as well as access to emergency Fed lending. These funds exploded in popularity in the 1970s and 1980s in no small part to get around regulations, specifically caps on banks' interest rates.

Of Reserve Primary Funds' $62 billion in assets, some $785 million was invested in securities from (yes) Lehman Brothers. When Lehman went under, the entire fund came close to collapse. When people demanded their money back, it meant that the fund's managers needed to sell other assets to get the necessary cash. As it turns out, the week of September 14, 2008, was one of the worst weeks in the history of finance to try to sell commercial paper and other short-term investments. While the Reserve Primary Fund was not a bank, it was experiencing a run nonetheless. On Tuesday evening it announced that it would have to "break the buck," meaning that shares in the fund normally worth $1 would in fact be worth only 97 cents. In response, investors started pulling their money out of other money market funds, making $159 billion in withdrawals the very next day. A vicious cycle had set in. With money flowing out of the funds, the funds were forced to dump still more commercial paper into the market to free-up cash, causing their value to fall further, creating more losses. At the same time, the withdrawals threw into doubt the funding that many U.S. corporations use to pay for everyday operations. These corporations too, rely on the commercial paper market.

The dangers were great and widespread. If the money market funds collapse, so would the solvency of banks that had otherwise weathered the collapse of Lehman and the near collapse of AIG, along with the ability of much of corporate America to make its payroll. "We came very, very close to a depression," Bernanke told *Time* magazine in 2009. "The markets were in anaphylactic shock."[5]

It was not over. Just three days after the Reserve Fund broke the buck, came the Asset Backed Commercial Paper Money market Mutual Fund Liquidity Reserve Facility, or AMLF. This fund, located in the Federal Reserve Bank of Boston, lent money to banks, which could then buy the securities the money market funds were selling off and pledge them to the Fed, with the banks themselves taking no financial risk for their role as intermediary. The program lent out $24 billion on its first day of operation, and $217 billion before the panic wound down, routing money through banks like State Street and JPMorgan Chase to mutual funds run by household-name companies such as Janus and Oppenheimer.

The Commercial Paper Funding Facility (CPFF), announced on October 7, focused on the other side of the problem, the difficultly companies were having selling their commercial paper, due in large part to the money market funds not being available as a buyer. With the CPFF, the Fed used its 13(3) authority to lend money in "unusual and exigent circumstances" to fund a "special purpose

---

[5] Michael Grunwald, "Person of the Year 2009," *Time*, December 16, 2009.

vehicle" (SPV) that purchased commercial paper from eligible issuers. Participants in the program could sell to the SPV only after paying a fee of 0.1% of their total commercial paper balance — a requirement designed to provide the Fed some measure of protection. If borrowers defaulted, the losses would be covered by these fees. Before it was over, in early 2010, some $738 billion in commercial paper had been purchased from affiliates of 82 different companies. Big banks, both domestic and foreign, were on the list. So were some of the mainstays of the U.S. corporate sector. For example, Ford Credit, GMAC, Chrysler Financial Services took part in the program. So did General Electric and Golden Funding Corp.

The results were summed up when *Time* magazine named Bernanke "Person of the Year." It said Bernanke "conjured up trillions of new dollars and blasted them into the economy; . . . lent to mutual funds, hedge funds, foreign banks, investment banks, manufacturers, insurers and other borrowers who had never dreamed of receiving Fed cash; jump-started stalled credit markets in everything from car loans to corporate paper; . . . and generally transformed the staid area of central banking into a stage for desperate improvisation."[6]

Then, too, there was lending to foreign central banks. By December 10, foreign central banks had borrowed $580 billion of Fed money or a quarter of the U.S. central bank's total assets. The Fed also pumped dollars into individual foreign banks that had U.S. subsidiaries; at peak levels, $85 billion for the Royal Bank of Scotland, $77 billion for Switzerland's UBS, $66 billion for Deutsche Bank, $65 billion for the U.K.'s Barclays, $59 billion for Belgium's Dexia, and $22 billion for Japan's Norinchukin. In effect, Europe had become the 13th Federal Reserve district.

Bernanke made clear to Paulson that the central bank would no longer bail out ordinary business firms. It was time for the Treasury to step in. He, along with Paulson, advocated the $700 billion Troubled Asset Relief Program (TARP). Congress passed TARP on October 3. The major banks were told that they would have to take money from the program or else face regulators. Citigroup and

---

[6] *Ibid.*

Morgan Stanley were told how much capital they would receive. TARP turned out to be one of the most unpopular government programs ever legislated. It did not prevent the necessity of a globally coordinated monetary easing that followed on October 8, 2008. The Bank of Canada, the Bank of England, the European Central Bank, the Federal Reserve, Sveriges Riksbank, and the Swiss National Bank all announced reductions in policy interest rates. The Bank of Japan expressed its strong support of these policy actions.

These monetary and fiscal policies did not prevent a steep decline in the world economy. But the worse had been avoided. There was no global economic depression. But there was far more work to do. There was the Great Recession and a glacial recovery.

5

The Great Recession

If the financial crisis of 2008–2009 produced a king of Wall Street, it would most likely be Jamie Dimon, CEO of JPMorgan Chase. (Lloyd Blankfein of Goldman Sachs would the other likely contender, as the prince in waiting.) JPMorgan Chase had over $2 trillion in assets, not counting positions recorded off its balance sheet, such as derivatives; it had $155 billion in balance sheet equity; and it earned $4.1 billion in operating profits in the second quarter of 2009. In comparison, the 1985 Salomon Brothers, after converting to 2009 dollars, only had $122 billion in assets, $5 billion in equity, and $2 billion in operating profits for an entire year. Goldman Sachs had $890 billion in assets.

The Financialization of the American Economy

A lot had changed in the quarter century prior to the great money and banking panic. For one thing, there was a wave of mergers that created fewer and fewer but larger and larger financial institutions. And bigger did not necessarily mean better. JPMorgan Chase emerged out of the mergers of Chemical Bank, Manufacturers Hanover, Chase Manhattan, J. P. Morgan, Bank One, and First Chicago, to be followed by the acquisition of Bear Stearns and Washington Mutual in 2008. Salomon was acquired by Travelers, which then merged with Citicorp into Citigroup.

Along with this growth, the financial sector got bigger and bigger. In 1978, all commercial banks together held $1.2 trillion of assets. By the end of 2007, the commercial banks had grown to

$1.8 trillion in assets. But there was more. Investment banks, including Salomon, grew from $33 billion in assets, or 1.4% of GDP, to $3.1 trillion in assets, or 2.2% of GDP. Asset-backed securities such as collateralized debt obligations (CDOs), which barely existed in 1978, accounted for $4.5 trillion in assets in 2007, or 3.2% of GDP. The debt held by the financial sector grew from $2.9 trillion or 125% of GDP in 1998 to over $36 trillion in 2007, or 259% of GDP. The financial sector had grown in importance; every dollar of GDP required $2.59 in financial debt. The USA was leveraged.

Most of the growth in the sector was due to the increasing financialization of the economy, the conversion of one dollar of lending to the real economy into many dollars of financial transactions. Again, in 1978 the financial sector borrowed $13 in credit markets for every $100 borrowed by the real economy; by 2007, that had grown to $51. These figures exclude the off-balance sheet derivatives. Globally, over-the-counter derivatives, which essentially did not exist in 1978, grew to over $33 trillion in market value — over twice the U.S. GDP — by the end of 2008. A great portion of these derivatives was held by U.S. financial institutions, the world leaders in the business.

From 1978 to 2007 the financial sector grew from 3.5% to 5.9% of the economy, while its share of corporate profits climbed much faster. While from the 1930s until around 1980, financial sector profits grew at roughly the same rate as profits in the non-financial sector, from 1980 until 2005, financial sector profits grew by 800%, adjusted for inflation, while non-financial sector profits grew by only 250%. Although the sector's profits plummeted at the peak of the financial crisis, they quickly rebounded; by the third quarter of 2009, financial sector profits were over six times their 1980 level, while non-financial sector profits were little more than double that of 1980. These patterns are highlighted in Figure 5.1.

Bankers' salaries and bonuses grew alongside these gigantic profits. In 1978, average per-person compensation in the banking sector was $13,153 (in 1978 dollars), essentially the same as in the private sector overall. After 1982, banking pay took off, until by 2007, the average banker was making over two times as much as the

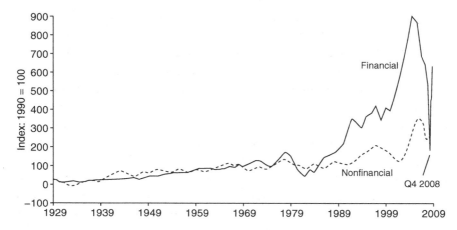

Figure 5.1:   Real corporate profits, financial versus non-financial sectors.

Source: Simon Johnson and James Kwak, *13 Bankers* (New York: Pantheon Books, 2010), p. 61.
Notes: Bureau of Economic Analysis, *National Income and Product Accounts*, Tables 11.4 and 6.16.
Financial sector excludes the 12 Federal Reserve banks. Annual through 2007, quarterly Q1
2008–Q3 2009.

average private sector employee. Early on, the comic poet Ogden
Nash put it in the title of a poem — "Bankers Are Just Like Anybody
Else, Except Richer." In comparison though, the money in hedge
funds was obscene. In 2007, five fund managers earned at least
$1 billion eclipsed by John Paulson, who made $3.7 billion from
betting against the housing market and mortgage-backed securities
built on top of it. Needless to say, Paulson won the bet.

Deregulation of Banking and Finance

Along with all this growth came greatly diminished regulation. The
deregulation trend begun in the administration of Jimmy Carter
was transformed into a crusade by Ronald Reagan. The financial
services industry had broken free from the constraints placed on it
by the Great Depression. The result was an out-of-balance financial
system that still enjoyed the full backing of the Federal government.
This free-market ideology extended to the derivatives markets

where the Black–Scholes formula was being used to calculate the prices of financial derivatives.[1]

In 1982, the Garn–St. Germain Depository Institutions Act lifted many regulations on the savings and loan (S&L) industry, allowing them to expand into new businesses, engage in commercial lending, and invest in junk bonds. The bill also authorized state-chartered banks to offer mortgages with adjustable rates. At the same time Lewis Ranieri, one of the legendary traders at Salomon Brothers, worked directly with Reagan officials to create a new market for mortgage-backed securities. A new bill, the Secondary Mortgage Market Enhancement Act of 1984, which Ranieri helped create and defend, cleared away state regulations that had hampered Salomon's earlier efforts to create its own mortgage-backed securities out of Bank of America mortgages. The new market for private mortgage-backed securities also helped commercial banks and S&Ls to pass on the risk of their fixed rate mortgages to investors in these new securities. These new laws were good for investment banks and their fees. Still, 23,000 banks failed between 1985 and 1992. Only 79 banks had failed during all of the 1970s.

Salomon Brothers also pioneered arbitrage trading. Traders could make certain money by finding two securities that should but did not have the same value; buying one, selling the other, and waiting for their prices to converge. Or, the same goal could be achieved by buying the interest payment on the final principal payment on a 30-year bond separately while selling the whole 30-year bond (including interest and principal) for a higher price. Arbitrage trading soon spread to other investment banks. The popularity of arbitrage fueled the rapid growth of hedge funds which grew from less than $30 billion in assets in 1990 to over $1.2 trillion in 2005, and then on to $2 trillion by 2008.

On the coattails of high-yield debt, securitization, and arbitrage trading came the modern derivatives market. This revolution began with the invention of the interest rate swap by Salomon Brothers

---

[1]Much of what follows is based on E. Ray Canterbery, *The Global Great Recession* (Singapore, New Jersey, London: World Scientific, 2011), pp. 177–197.

in 1981. Interest rate swaps allow companies to exchange fixed rate payments or floating rate payments, or vice-versa, "swapping" interest rate risks between the two parties. It was like wife-swapping except at a price. In a similar way, currency swaps allow companies to swap currency risks by exchanging different currencies for combinations of currencies. The two kinds of swaps can be combined into one. By mid-2008, the market for over-the-counter interest rate swaps had grown to over US$350 trillion in face value (the amount on which interest is calculated) and over US$8 trillion in gross market value.

The credit default swap played an important role in the financial crisis, as we have noted. It is a form of insurance on debt; the buyer of the swap pays a fixed premium to the seller, who agrees to pay off the debt if the debtor fails to do so. Typically, the debt is a bond or a similar fixed income security, and the debtor is the issuer of the bond. These credit default swaps were popularized by J. P. Morgan in the late 1990s. This explosion of new products provided vast new profit-making possibilities for financial institutions.

The Rise and Fall of Mega-banks: "Banks too-Big-to-Fail"

Banks not only got bigger, they got broader with the help of derivatives and commercial paper; they began to look matronly. We should not lose sight of the fact that the traditional role of commercial banks is to raise money for corporations. At least, that was once their role. In 1978, Bankers Trust began placing commercial paper (short-term debt) issued by corporation with investors. The Federal Reserve opened up another loophole in 1985, allowing commercial banks to set up affiliated companies (through a bank holding company) to deal in specific securities that were otherwise off-limits to commercial banks. Over the next decade, Alan Greenspan expanded the loophole, which began with government bonds, mortgage-backed securities, and commercial paper, to include corporate bonds and equities. Soon the loophole was a chasm. Commercial banks were taking on the functions of investment banks, which had been prohibited by the Glass–Steagall Act. At the same time, investment banks encroached on the business of commercial banks. For example, Merrill Lynch introduced the cash management account (CMA), a money market account with check-writing privileges. The major commercial banks used acquisitions not only to become larger, but also to move into investment banking. What was once a divide between commercial banks and investment banks became a divide among mega-banks. These mega-banks became the new Wall Street.

The mega-banks and their operations were aided and abetted by further deregulation, as the dismantling of the regulatory system constructed in the 1930s was completed in the 1990s. Derivatives now enter the picture. The Riegle–Neal Act of 1994 mostly eliminated restrictions on interstate banking, allowing bank holding companies to acquire banks in any state and allowing banks to open branches in new states. The Gramm–Leach–Bliley Act of 1999 demolished the remaining barriers separating commercial and investment banking by allowing holding companies to own subsidiaries engaged in both businesses as well as insurance. At the same time the government refused to regulate derivatives. It was thought that market forces would be sufficient to prevent fraud and excessive risk-taking. The rapid growth of the derivatives market was proof that they were socially beneficial; this was the view of Alan Greenspan.

Greenspan was not the only one to celebrate financial innovation. In 2006, even as he warned about potential risk management challenges form derivatives, Timothy Geithner (then New York Fed President) said of the wave of financial innovations:

> These developments provide substantial benefits to the financial system. Financial institutions are able to measure and manage risk much more effectively. Risks are spread more widely, across a more diverse group of financial intermediaries, within and across countries. These changes have contributed to a substantial improvement in the financial strength of the core financial intermediaries and in the overall flexibility and resilience of the financial system in the United States.[2]

---

[2]Timothy F. Geithner, "Risk management Challenges in the U.S. Financial System" (lecture, Global Association of Risk Professionals, 7th Annual Risk Management Convention and Exhibition, New York, February 26, 2008).

These remarks, delivered on Wall Street's front steps, were silent on the benefits for the real economy, which were nil. In April 2009, *during* the financial crisis, Ben Bernanke, Greenspan's successor, said, "Financial innovation has improved access to credit, reduced costs, and increased choice. We should not attempt to impose restrictions on credit providers so onerous that they prevent the development of new products and services in the future."[3] Derivatives would do everything except prevent war as we know it. They faced little danger from regulators who extolled their virtues.

It did not take long to find out how deregulation worked out. In 2006, borrowers unable to refinance their mortgages, began defaulting in sharply rising numbers. In 2007, the mountain of assets based on housing values began to crumble as increasing defaults torpedoed the prices of mortgage-backed securities and CDOs. The avalanche almost brought down the global financial system in 2008. Yet, big, risk-loving banks had become crucial to the USA economy and to our way of life.

In truth, the nine banks sitting on this mountain of crumbling assets were too-big-to-fail. On October 13, 2008, with their stock prices in decline and the short-term viability of their firms in doubt, the heads of nine major banks — Bank of America, Bank of New York Mellon, Citigroup, Goldman Sachs, JPMorgan Chase, Merrill Lynch, Morgan Stanley, State Street, and Wells Fargo — arrived on the door steps of the Treasury for a meeting with then Treasury Secretary Henry Paulson. The government was stepping in to protect the massive USA financial system and, by extension, the global economy.

The October 13th deal was structured as a purchase of preferred shares, which meant that the Treasury loaned the banks money, at an initial 5% annual interest rate, that never had to be paid. The purchases meant that the government now owned part of the banks. The banks in turn received virtually free money. At the meeting, the government began guaranteeing debt issued by the banks, allowing

---

[3] Ben S. Bernanke, "Financial Innovation and Consumer Protection" (lecture, Federal Reserve System's Sixth Biennial Community Affairs Research Conference, Washington, DC, April 17, 2009).

them to raise money by selling bonds to private investors who knew that the government would guarantee their investments. Meanwhile, Lehman Brothers went bankrupt, Bear Stearns and Merrill Lynch were sold, and Goldman Sachs and Morgan Stanley fled into the safety of bank holding company status, which gave then enhanced access to emergency lending from the Federal Reserve.

The banks were facing a liquidity crisis and needed more capital. In March 2008, Bear Stearns, the weakest of the big five investment banks, collapsed. The cause? Bear Stearns was brought down by a modern-day bank run. It was more exposed to structured mortgage-backed securities than its rivals. The Fed first attempted to lend Bear Stearns money by using Morgan Chase as an intermediary; as an investment bank, Bear was not eligible for direct loans from the Fed. As noted earlier, this failed to bolster confidence and Paulson, Bernanke, and Geithner attempted to broker the sale of Bear to J. P. Morgan for a miserly $2 per share. J. P. Morgan refused to go along even with this bargain price without government help. The New York Fed agreed to assume all the losses on $30 billion of Bear's illiquid securities. The deal was renegotiated to a purchase price of $10 per share. It was a coup for J. P. Morgan, which was paying for Bear Stearns approximately what its building was worth. To prevent the other investment banks from the same fate as Bear Stearns, the Federal Reserve immediately created the Primary Dealer Credit Facility, which would allow investment banks for the first time to borrow money directly from the Fed. It was a dramatic expansion of the safety net for the investment banks.

No one knew the value of toxic assets setting on major banks' balance sheets, or how much they would lose if they were forced to sell. The banks were taking major write-downs. In 2007, Citigroup took $29 billion in write-downs, Merrill Lynch $25 billion, Lehman $13 billion, Bank of America $1 billion, and Morgan Stanley $10 billion. In 2008, Citigroup took another $53 billion in write-downs, Merrill $39 billion, Bank of America $29 billion, Lehman $14 billion, JPMorgan Chase $10 billion, and Morgan Stanley $10 billion. It was like a fire sale. If some of the major banks were to acknowledge the true decline in the value of their assets, they might be insolvent.

Next, Lehman Brothers was short of cash. Over that famous weekend of September 12–14, Paulson and Geithner cast about for a buyer.[4] No taxpayer money was to be used this time. When a plan for Barclays to acquire Lehman fell though on Sunday, the backup plan was bankruptcy early on Monday morning. The demise of Lehman triggered a chain reaction that ripped the financial markets. The aforementioned American International Group (AIG), struggling with its derivatives, faced downgrades by all three major credit rating agencies. These downgrades, in turn, could force it into bankruptcy. On Tuesday, the Fed stepped in with $85 billion credit line to keep AIG afloat. If the insurer defaulted on its hundreds of billions of dollars in credit default swaps, its counter-parties

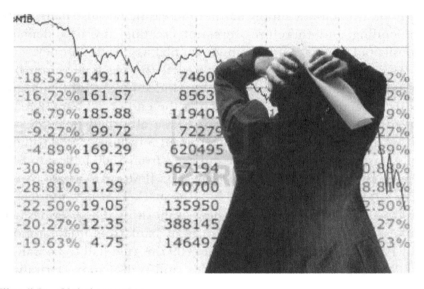

Illus. 5.1:   Global recession.

---

[4]A book by a Wall Street TV reporter is devoted to this hectic weekend. For a detailed account of the personalities, the many phone calls, the conflicts of the Wall Street CEOs with each other and with Fed and government officials, see Maria Bartiromo (with Catherine Whitney) *The Weekend That Changed Wall Street* (New York: Penguin, 2010).

would suffer devastating losses or at the least, fear of such losses would end liquidity in world financial markets.

Banks, Big and Small, Fail

The mighty continued to fall. As noted, the Reserve Primary Fund announced that it would "break the buck," because of losses on Lehman debt. Washington Mutual collapsed as depositors pulled out their money, thus far the largest bank failure in U.S. history. Wachovia, on the brink of failure, was acquired by Wells Fargo. Running out of cash, banks stopped lending. Money moved toward the safety of U.S. Treasury bills and stayed there. There was a liquidity trap. Overnight lending rates were near zero and could go no lower, no matter how fast the money supply was increased. In any event, the money supply was not increasing because banks were not lending and therefore were not creating any new demand deposits (a large part of the money supply) as "inside" money.

The financial crisis of 2008–2009 left the big banks even bigger. Bank of America absorbed Countrywide and Merrill Lynch and saw its assets grow from $1.7 trillion at the end of 2007 to $2.3 trillion in September 2009. JPMorgan Chase absorbed Bear Stearns and Washington Mutual and grew from $1.5 trillion to $2.0 trillion. Wells Fargo absorbed Wachovia and grew from $500 billion to $1.2 trillion. By mid-2009, Bank of America, JPMorgan Chase, Wells Fargo, and Citigroup controlled half the market for new mortgages and two-thirds of the market for new credit cards. The U.S. has had a rule since 1994 that prohibits any single bank from holding more than 10% of total retail deposits. In 2009 this rule had to be waived for JPMorgan Chase, Bank of America, and Wells Fargo. Derivatives became more concentrated; at the end of June 2009, five banks had over 95% of the market for derivatives traded by U.S. banks, led by JPMorgan Chase.

By 2010, there were at least six banks too-big-to-fail — Bank of America, Citigroup, Goldman Sachs, JPMorgan Chase, Morgan Stanley, and Wells Fargo. "Too-big-to-fail" creates three major problems for society. First, these institutions have been bailed out by the government when they did come to the brink of failure. Second, giant financial institutions have a strong incentive to take excessive risk, since the government will bail them out in an emergency (moral hazard). Third, giant financial institutions are bad for competition, and this is bad for the economy. Even during the financial crisis, the large banks could pay 0.78% points less for money than small banks.

Not surprisingly, small banks are continuing to fail. In 2009, 115 U.S. banks failed, the most since deposit insurance was introduced in the 1930s. In 2010, 157 banks (mostly small ones) had failed, a pace faster than that of 2009. The closings in 2010 included 29 in Georgia, 23 in Illinois, 20 in California and 18 in Florida. Week after week, banks were failing — in Norcross, Georgia; Springfield Illinois; San Clemente, California; and Fort Myers, Florida. The failures in the bubble states of Arizona, Nevada, California, and Florida were modest in 2008, but massive in 2009–2010 and could be large again. There were mounting losses on loans in the toughest economic climate since the 1930s. The failures — especially of small banks — have continued with 92 in 2011, 53 in 2012, slowing to 24 in 2013. These failures have sapped billions of dollars out of the Federal Deposit Insurance Corporation (FDIC) fund, which fell into the red during 2009. Its deficit stood at $20.7 billion as of March 31, 2010.[5]

Small banks are important to the overall economy. Giant corporations such as IBM and Microsoft depend on the large banks, those already bailed out. Some 64% of the loans of small banks are to USA small businesses, which in turn create about 65% of all new jobs and employ about half of the private sector workforce. Worse, the FDIC had 829 banks at risk of failure (as of October 29, 2010), most of them small ones. These are likely to fail unless the climate in business changes very soon.

Time magazine has provided the story of one community bank that destroyed a Georgia town's faith in government, the economy, and itself. It is a microcosm of what we might expect soon across small

---

[5] The FDIC now enjoys a small surplus and had finagled a guarantee of a $500 billion loan from the Treasury.

town America.[6] The Community Bank & Trust (CBT) headquarters is in Cornelia, Georgia. Behind Daniel Bell of the FDIC on January 29, 2010, a team of 25 experts swooped down on CBT, taking control of the coded Federal Reserve tokens that allow access to payment systems and seized the terminal on which interbank transfers are made. The FDIC knew that the balance sheet of CBT was a mess. Though Community Bank had thrived in flush times, its practices led to hundreds of residential and commercial foreclosures in the local economy (and may produce thousands more). Both homes and businesses underwritten by CBT have been foreclosed in 2010, 1500 loans are in serious trouble, and at least 2700 were so poorly documented that no one is sure whether they should be foreclosed or not. In other words, CBT is part of the mortgage mess which is driven by subprime mortgages, including liar's loans. All this despite the bank having been well-managed for many years.

Although the FDIC had the option of taking over the bank and running it, it decided to find a buyer. The buyer is South Carolina Bank and Trust (SCBT) based in Columbia. SCBT itself had been stabilized with the help of Troubled Asset Relief Program (TARP) funds in 2009, and made the best of five competing bids for CBT. For taking on nearly all of CBT's assets and liabilities, SCBT was given $158 million with the agreement to cover 2% of losses on outstanding residential and commercial loans up to $233 million and to cover 5% on loans above that amount. The new owners proceeded to close 10 branch offices, declined to rehire 120 employees and began an investigation of the old bank's 10,822 loans. While they moved 1500 to a special asset group, they foreclosed on 224 loans originally worth $49 million, 35 residential, the rest commercial.

Not everyone was happy with what the FDIC did. "Cornelians believe SCBT is foreclosing on the bad loans so rapidly that it is taking the local economy down the tubes."[7] CBT had foreclosed on just 2.14% of its business loans and 1.75% of its residential mortgages,

---

[6]Massimo Calabresi, "Death of a Small-Town bank," *Time*, September 1, 2010, pp. 57–60.

[7]*Ibid.*, p. 60.

all of which were more than 100 days delinquent. The problem is the shift of faith from CBT to SCBT. It is a problem facing small bank after small bank. This lack of confidence overlooks some basic facts. SCBT can get reimbursement on losses from the FDIC whether or not it forecloses on delinquent loans. Moreover, if SCBT keeps its losses on CBT's loans under $233 million, the FDIC will wire a check to SCBT for 50% of the difference. This gives SCBT a reason to keep loans that can produce interest income. CBT is a small bank but the process is still complicated. Attempting to reassure Cornelians, SCBT kept the CBT name. If other small banks fall in the same way, and the FDIC assures us they will, the USA faces the crisis of failing banks along with failing confidence in those that survive.

U.S. Bank Credit and the Stock Market

Most Americans live in a small circle as either debtors or creditors, but some are stock holders. We can summarize the effect on two financial indicators that the Federal Reserve watches closely. One is bank credit, the other is stock market price indexes. This is not to say that these are the only financial indicators of the Fed, but they comprise parts of the financial outcomes. The relevant bank credit can be divided between commercial/industrial loans and real estate loans (mostly mortgages). The percent change (year over year) in the level of bank credit is shown in Figure 5.2. Both measures began to slump slightly in 2005, with real estate credit falling in 2007 and taking a steeper descent in 2008 and 2009. Late in 2009 the percentage changes turn negative and remain so through the latest reported data. The decline for real estate loans in September 2010 is −3.3%.

The credit crunch measured by commercial and industrial loan activity did not hit until early 2008, that pivotal year. The divergence of the two types of credit reveals much about the institutions of banking compared with overall mortgage credit. The banking system proved to be more vulnerable than the mortgage lenders. Commercial banks are purely private, especially during this time of virtually no regulation. Despite the Federal Reserve's best efforts,

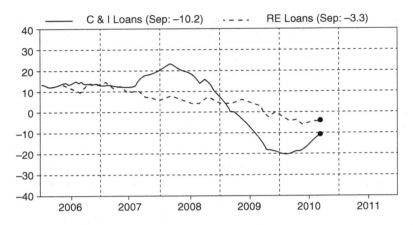

Figure 5.2:   Bank credit: Percent change over year-ago level.

Source: Haver Analytics, Federal Reserve Board of Governors website.

Notes: C & I Loans equals Commerical and Industrial Loans. RE loans equals Real Estate Loans.

commercial and industrial credit fell sharply after early 2008 and accelerated in 2009. By September 2010, despite having leveled off early in the year, commercial and industrial (C & I) loans declined 10.2% from their level a year earlier. In contrast, the mortgage industry experienced slower downward changes. The mortgage market was cushioned by the presence of Fannie Mae and Freddie Mac, despite all their problems. This is not to deny the severe repercussions of the subprime debacle.

The stock market price index favored by the general public is the Dow industrial, which is a blue chip indicator. A broader index and the one apparently favored by the Fed is Standard & Poor's 500 Composite index. Its behavior during the Great Recession is displayed in Figure 5.3. After peaking in late 2007 near 1600, the S & P 500 stair-steps its way downward and then falls off a cliff around mid-2008. It reached its near-term bottom in early 2009, only to begin a recovery punctuated by three dips. It had recovered to 1183.8 by October 28, 2010. By May 2, 2014, it had soared to 1881 on the way to 2000. This market is driven by the presence of very low rates of interest. Uniquely, losses of wealth occurred in both the housing and the stock markets during the money and banking panic.

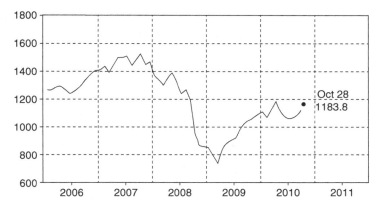

Figure 5.3:   Stock Market Index: Standard & Poor's 500 composite.
Source: Haver Analytics, Federal Reserve Board of Governors website.

The Decline in the Real Economy

The turmoil in housing and banking, not to mention the stock market, had to affect the real economy. Economic problems spread from the housing and banking sectors to industry even as the credit crisis deepened. The Institute for Supply Management announced that its reading for the nation's manufacturing fell to 49.9 in August from 50 in July. A reading below 50 signals contraction. This was only the beginning of a long slide. General Motors reported a $15.5 billion second-quarter loss, the third-worst quarterly performance in its nearly 100-year history. Through the first half of the year, it used up more than $7 billion in cash, including $3.5 billion from April through June. Thus began a long sales slump in the auto industry. Because of a lack of financing auto sales continued to slump in September. Ford sales were down 34% from the year before, followed by Chrysler down 33% and GM down 16%. GM sales were buoyed temporarily by its pricing vehicles at employee rates. Auto sales were to drop by three million for the year 2008.

Meanwhile, troubles in the financial sector worsened. Earlier, we related the story of Lehman Brothers, Merrill Lynch, and the

Bank of America. They were battling the nation's worst financial crisis since the Great Depression. This spilled over into the real economy.

The erosion of confidence had invaded Main Street. Consumer spending which is 70% of GDP, dropped a sharp 0.3% in September. A survey by the University of Michigan showed consumer confidence in October fell to 57.6%, the biggest one-month drop in the survey's history (dating to 1978). The cuts in spending for durable goods such as automobiles were especially sharp. Soon the nation's personal saving rate would reach historic highs as consumers further retrenched. The damage to consumer confidence would prove to be long-lasting. This condition is heightened by unemployment. The number of out-of-work Americans continuing to draw unemployment benefits surged to a 25-year high in late October. An extension of unemployment benefits was included in the Congressional stimulus package. Fortuitously, unemployment benefits had been established during the Great Depression.

It was increasingly clear that the American automobile industry was being trampled by the economic downturn and the crisis in the financial markets. It is an industry critical to the real economy. Despite a request by the automakers for an additional $50 billion in

Illus. 5.2:   Global belt-tightening during economic recessions.
Source: The web.

loans from Congress to help them survive tough economic conditions and pay for health care obligations for retirees, the Bush administration refused to broaden the $700 billion financial bailout to include producers of products other than financial instruments, including derivatives. Bush was favoring the non-basic financial sector at a risk to the basic manufacturing sector. Any money would be in addition to the $25 billion in loans that Congress passed in September to help retool auto plants to build more fuel-efficient vehicles. The heart of the USA manufacturing sector and the jobs of tens of thousands of American workers were at risk. President-elect Barack Obama said his transition team would explore policy options to help the auto industry. In a sign of the times, General Motors ended an endorsement deal with Tiger Woods, who had attracted younger buyers to the Buick brand.

A $14 billion rescue package for the nation's imperiled auto industry sped to approval in the Democrat-dominated U.S. House on December 10. The legislation would provide money within days to cash starved General Motors and Chrysler. Ford said it had enough money to stay afloat, but would also be eligible for Federal aid. On January 2, 2009, the U.S. Treasury supplied Chrysler with a $5 billion loan that was necessary to keep it operating. This was an initial loan for a company that generally pays its suppliers $7 billion every 45 days. This followed a similar transfer of $4 billion from Treasury to General Motors, the tranche of a $9.4 billion loan.

The National Bureau of Economic Research, the caller of such things, had concluded on December 1, 2008 that the country had been suffering through a recession since December 2007. Everyone knew this except perhaps Wall Street where the news sent the Dow industrials down 680 points the next day. The Institute for Supply Management reported that its index of manufacturing sank to 36.2 in November, a 26-year low. The unemployment rate in October zoomed to 6.5%, a 14-year high. The news was worse in Japan. Output at that nation's manufacturers tumbled 8.1% in November, the largest drop since Tokyo began measuring such data in 1953. Japan's automakers and others slashed production to cope with slowing global demand (including falling imports from the U.S. and Europe).

The jobless rate jumped and household spending fell. The contraction in China's steel production, a global bellwether for heavy industry, deepened in November, driving the nation's factory output to its worst performance on record.

Meanwhile, in the USA, median household income, adjusted for inflation, fell 3.6% during 2008 to $50,303, the steepest year-over-year drop in 40 years. The poverty rate, at 13.2%, was the highest since 1997. About 700,000 more people did not have health insurance in 2008 compared to the year before. Half of all income went to the top fifth of American households. About 54 million people were living under 125% of the poverty line, about three million more than in 2007. The number of "deep poor" — people whose earning put them at less than half the poverty line — increased by 1.5 million to 17 million people.

On December 16, 2008, the Federal Reserve used its last measure of conventional monetary policy. It was entering a new era lowering its benchmark interest rate virtually to zero and declaring that it will now fight the recession by pumping out vast amounts of money to businesses and consumers through an expanding array of new lending programs.

On the fiscal front, there was only the TARP, the $700 billion bailout, which originally had three purposes. First, it was to refinance mortgages; this Secretary John Paulson refused to do. Second came the mortgage related securities. There were several rationales for buying troubled mortgage-backed securities. For one thing, panic had virtually shut down the markets for securities that must be restarted to restore the system of mortgage finance. For another, one source of that panic was that nobody knew what the securities were worth, the Black–Scholes formula notwithstanding. Finally, many mortgages are buried in complex securities. Buying the securities would allow the government to refinance the underlying mortgages. Buying mortgage-backed securities helps the government acquire mortgages to refinance; refinancing mortgages to avert foreclosures enhances the values of these securities, bolstering the finances of banks.

Third came the recapitalizing of banks. The Congress gave the Secretary catch-all authority to buy "any other financial instrument," which offered the flexibility to respond to unforeseen circumstances, such as an auto bailout, for example. But the TARP funds were used exclusively for recapitalizing banks and other financial institutions. Treasury bought preferred stock with no control rights. And there were no public purpose *quid pro quo*, such as a minimal lending requirement. So banks just sat on the capital, or used it to make acquisitions (which does not create any new capital). Paulson bent over backward to make the terms attractive to banks. He contended that wide participation was essential and even forced money on several bankers who did not want it. This was the way that the first $350 billion was spent. The remainder was left to the discretion of the Obama administration.

So, TARP was used to save the banks and other financial institutions. Fiscal austerity was for Main Street. Under Ben Bernanke, the Federal Reserve Bank of New York began to do what TARP had failed to do. On January 5, 2009, the New York Fed began buying mortgage-backed securities in an effort to bolster the battered housing market. The program allows the Fed to spend $500 billion on mortgage-backed securities guaranteed by mortgage giants Fannie Mae and Freddie Mac and an additional $10 billion to directly purchase mortgages held by Fannie, Freddie and the Federal Home Banks.

It is useful to summarize in a few snapshots the effects of the Great Recession in employment and output. Table 5.1 shows the unemployment rate in the U.S. for March 2008 through December 2010. Although the unemployment rate peaked in October 2009, it remained stuck in the 9.5 to 9.8 range thereafter. By November 2010 the number officially unemployed had grown to about 5 million, enough to fill a state almost three-quarters way between the populations of Pennsylvania and New York state. The "official" recession began with an unemployment rate of only 4.9% and "ended" with an unemployment rate of 9.5%. The unemployment rate did not peak until 2009, four months after the "official" recession was over. Moreover, the rate was 9.9% in April 2010 and got stuck at 9.5% by August 2010. What do we call the dreadful 18 months since the official recession ended?

Now we go behind the unemployment figures to industrial production in the basics industry and to the broader measure of GDP,

Table 5.1:   Unemployment rates in the U.S.

December 2007	4.9%	June	9.5%
Janaury 2008	4.9	July	9.4
February	4.8	August	9.7
March	5.1	September	9.8
April	5	October	10.2
May	5.5	November	10
June	5.6	December	10
July	5.8	Janaury 2010	9.7
August	6.2	February	9.7
September	6.2	March	9.7
October	6.6	April	9.9
November	6.8	May	9.7
December	7.2	June	9.5
Janaury 2009	7.6	July	9.5
February	8.1	August	9.6
March	8.5	September	9.6
April	8.9	October	9.6
May	9.4	November	9.8
		December	9.4

Source: Bureau of Labor Statistics.

which includes financial services. Let us look first at industrial production because this must be the measure used by the NBER to set the start of the recession in December 2007. The NBER still considered manufacturing to be the core of the economy. Figure 5.4 shows the pattern of percentage changes in industrial production for the U.S. from the first quarter of 2006 through the second quarter of 2010. Manufacturing declined in the fourth quarter of 2005, as a forewarning of unfolding events. There was a rebound during the next two quarters, to be followed by a weak 1.1% gain in the third quarter of 2007, only to be upended by the decisive drop of −0.5% in the fourth quarter. This was an early warning of what was to come. Thereafter, we see the configuration of a deep recession in industrial

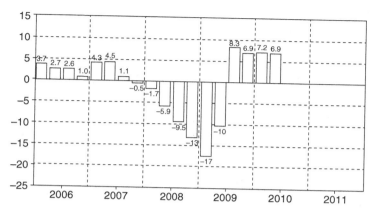

Figure 5.4: U.S. industrial production: Annualized percentage change.
Source: Haver Analytics, Federal Reserve Board of Governors website.

output for seven quarters, with the jolting fall of 17% in the first quarter of 2009.

Alarms were set off at the Federal Reserve by the sharp deterioration in what I have called the basics industry. A –10% reading in the second quarter of 2009 was followed by rebounds during the last two quarters and the first two quarters of 2010. Most of this rebound — with a healthy 8.3% gain in the third quarter, followed by 6.9% in the fourth quarter — came from personal consumption expenditures unrelated to the automotive industry. Automotive sales, including that for parts and engines, nosedived after the cash for clunkers program ended. The rebound in consumption for other durables such as appliances stemmed from improvements in employment and personal incomes, much of which were companions of the stimulus package. The extraordinary near-deflation may have abetted this improvement even as it wreaked havoc on monetary policy. Still, industrial production slowed to a 5.4% gain in September 2010 (monthly figures are not shown) compared with a 6.9% gain the previous quarter.

The broader measure of GDP growth rates are shown in Figure 5.5. As noted, this is the measure commonly used for economic growth. The first decline of the Great Recession came in the first quarter of

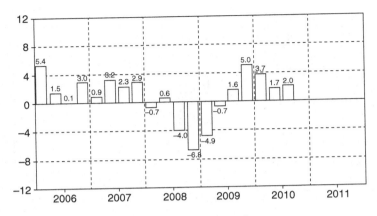

Figure 5.5:   GDP growth: Annualized percentage change.

Source: Haver Analytics, Federal Reserve Board of Governors website.

2008, a quarter after the NBER designated date for the start of the official recession. After a modest uptick for one-quarter, the GNP growth rate falls off a cliff with the low point being a growth rate of −6.8% in the fourth quarter of 2008. While the worst was behind us, modest growth resumed in the third quarter of 2009. Thereafter, the recovery was tepid despite a 5% gain in the fourth quarter of 2009. The gain then and the gains in 2010 were part of a "jobless recovery."

Unemployment in Other Countries

In February 2009, just prior to the "official" ending to the Great Recession, economists Mike Elsby, Bart Hobijn, and Aysegul Sahin made some interesting projections, which proved to be more accurate than those of the European Commission. Their rule of thumb is the percentage increase in unemployment is well-approximated by the percentage increase in inflows plus the percentage increase in duration of unemployment.[8] In this view, rises in unemployment are preceded by an increase in unemployment inflows as jobs are

---

[8]Michael W. Elsby, Ryan Michaels, and Gary Solon, "The Ins and Outs of Cyclical Unemployment," *Macroeconomics*, **1**(1), 84–110 (2009). For the annual estimates on the VOX website as well, see Michael W. L. Elsby, Ryan Michaels, and Gary Solon, "Unemployment Dynamics in the OECD," *NBER Working Paper 14617* (2008).

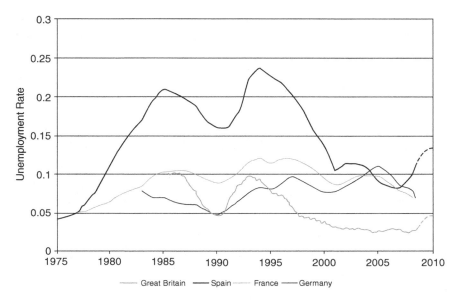

Figure 5.6: Unemployment rates in Britain, Spain, France and Germany.

Source: Mike Elsby, Bart Hobijn, and Aysegul Sahin, "Unemployment in the Current Crisis," VOX website, February 14, 2009, p. 3.

Notes: Dashed lines are future unemployment rates under the assumption that in flow rates and duration increase so further.

destroyed, followed by a rise in the duration of unemployment as workers fail to quickly find new jobs. Elsby, Hobijn, and Sahin find that the rapid inflow of workers into unemployment during what I have called the Great Recession confirms that this is one of the most severe recessions in U.S. History. They forecast a further weakening of the labor market, an outcome that proved to be true.

Their forecasts for the unemployment rates in Great Britain, Spain, France, and Germany appear in Figure 5.6. They include the most recent unemployment rate available at the time. Germany and France both continue to enjoy declining unemployment rates, whereas Spain experiences a substantial rise in unemployment, and Britain experiences a moderate rise. Upon closer inspection, since 2007 inflows rose by 50% in Britain and 23% in Spain, while outflow rates fell (and hence unemployment duration increased) by 23% in Britain and 14% in Spain. The role of job losses was more important in Europe. Inflow rates reached levels last seen in the mid-1990s, when Spanish unemployment soared about 20% and Britain was still recovering from the early 1990s recession.

Like in the U.S., both inflows and duration began to rise in Great Britain and Spain in 2007, suggesting that the origins of the 2009 slowdown also was apparent some time before the financial crisis of 2008–2009. This naturally raises the question of why the increase in British unemployment was more modest, at least through 2010. According to Elsby, Hobijn, and Sahin, the European labor markets are much less dynamic than their American counterparts. European workers take far longer to leave unemployment, whereas Americans workers exit unemployment on average six times faster than European workers. In Europe, it takes time for unemployment to respond to changes in the rate at which workers flow in and out of the unemployment pool. My answer is somewhat different, at least for Britain. The quick implementation of Keynesianism is a part of the answer; Keynes has never been far from the minds of the British, the exception being during the Thatcher government. Moreover, much of Europe, Spain excepted, have a very strong unemployment compensation programs which ease the income effects of unemployment. In Britain, at least, the social programs were being dismantled in October 2010, which is likely to change the unemployment rate increase from "modest." At about the same time France was raising its social security age retirement age from 50 to 52 in the face of violent protests.

Although Elsby, Hobijn, and Sahi show that changes in unemployment flows provide advance warning of unemployment increases, their admittedly "conservative" estimates of 5% unemployment in Britain, and 3.5% in Spain proved to be just that, conservative. According to Eurostat, the unemployment rate in Britain was 5.4% in 2005 and 5.3% in 2007. Elsby, Hobijn, and Sahin were assuming that labor market conditions would get no worse in either country. Notably, the actual unemployment rate in Britain stayed well below that of the U.S. in the 2008–2010 period.

According to the International Monetary Fund (IMF), the Spanish unemployment rate was 11.3% in 2008 and 18.2% in 2009.

The official rate for February 2010 was 22%. In France, the IMF has an unemployment rate of 7.9% for 2008 and 9.5% for 2009. The International Labor Organization also reported an unemployment rate of 9% in 2008, 7.8% in 2009, and 8.2% in 2010. However, Germany's Federal Employment Office estimated a seasonally adjusted rate of 10.8% for 2008. The unemployment rates in Europe depend very much on who is doing the estimating. The sharp downward trend depicted by Elsby, Hobijn, and Sahin did not prevail through 2008–2010 for France and Germany. However, the earlier unemployment rates (Official or IMF rates) were right on track. In contrast, China's unemployment rate in the 4% range remained lower than U.S. and European rates during 2007–2010, but the sheer number of unemployed Chinese was huge. Still, China remained isolated from the effects of the U.S. Great Recession, but much of the rest of the world did not.

We should not neglect Russia. The CIA has estimated Russian unemployment rates as 6.6% for 2007, 6.2% for 2008, 6.4% for 2009, and 8.9% for 2010. These too are conservative estimates. Until the fall of 2008, that pivotal year of the Great Panic, Russia appeared to be a safe haven with its steady, high growth rate of 7% a year. It also had massive international currency reserves, which peaked at US$598 billion in August 2008. By October 2008, this all changed. The Russian stock market tanked, falling 80% from May to October 2008. In 2009 Russia's GDP fell by 8%, more than any other country of the G-20 largest economies in the world. Among its high technology industries only computer software has emerged as a growth industry. It also has problems with its exports such as liquefied natural gas. Russia has chosen to remain mostly isolated from the U.S. and still remains aloof, despite overtures by the Obama administration. Thus far, Russia has refused to join the World Trade Organization (WTO), which could improve its trade position.

Roubini: A Cassandra Who Became a Prophet

Could much of the disaster been avoided? Alan Greenspan, by his own admission, did not see speculative bubbles emerging much less bursting. Ben Bernanke did not recognize the housing bubble until after the collapse. Both were busy creating the bubble environment. This raises the question of whether anyone could foresee what was to come.

Among those who did see the future, Nouriel Roubini (1959–) stands out. Roubini is a professor of economics at the Stern School of Business, New York University and chairman of RE Monitor, an economic consultancy firm. In September 2005, he warned a skeptical IMF that: "The United States was likely to face a once-in-a-lifetime housing bust, an oil shock, sharply declining consumer confidence, and, ultimately, a deep recession." He also foresaw "homeowners defaulting on mortgages, a trillion dollars of mortgage-backed securities unraveling worldwide and the global financial system shuddering to a halt."[9]

In September 2005, Roubini outlined the end of the real estate bubble. He suggested that the trend for 110 years was for supply increases to lead to a fall in prices. But since 1997, real home prices have increased by about 90%. There was no economic fundamental — real income, migration, interest rates, demographics — that could explain this. It means there was a speculative bubble. He went on to suggest that the bubble was now bursting. Furthermore, he argued, contrary to the conventional wisdom, that central banks should take action against asset bubbles.[10]

In Roubini's view, the U.S. has been growing through a period of repeated big bubbles. He suggests that too much human capital has gone into financing the most unproductive form of capital, namely housing, and would like to see the U.S. invest in more productive activities. Moreover, he saw housing bubbles in the U.K., Spain, Ireland, Iceland, and in a large part of emerging Europe, like the Baltics all the way to Hungary and the Balkans. As of February 2009, he remained pessimistic about the U.S. and global economy.

---

[9]Roubini quoted by anonymous columnist in "Eight Who Saw it Coming," *Fortune*, August 2008.

[10]Nouriel Roubini, "Why Central Banks Should Burst Bubbles," *International Finance*, Spring, 2006.

In *Foreign Policy* he writes: "Last year's worst-case scenario came true. The global financial pandemic that I and others had warned about is now upon us. But we are still only in the early stages of this crisis. My predictions for the coming years unfortunately, are even more dire. The bubbles, and there were many, have only begun to burst."[11]

What has happened *was* predictable. To understand why Nouriel Roubini got it right when others failed, we only need to revisit the original John Maynard Keynes and his stress on uncertainty as well as the Post Keynesians such as Hyman Minsky. Roubini is a follower of Minsky. The believers in austerity had nothing to say on the subject.

---

[11] Nouriel Roubini, "Warning: More Doom Ahead," *Foreign Policy*, January/February 2009. See also Nouriel Roubini and Stephen Mihm, *Crisis Economics* (New York: The Penguin Press, 2010).

6

Public Debt and Global Austerity

During economic recessions government expenditures rise, Federal tax revenues fall, and budget deficits rise. As these deficits are cumulative, the national debt rises as a share of the GDP. These problems became especially severe during the Great Recession. The financial crisis was a protracted affair; the asset market collapses were deep and prolonged. Declines in real housing prices averaged 35% stretched out over six years and equity price collapses averaged 56% over about three and a half years. This was associated with profound declines in output and employment. The unemployment rate rose an average of 7 percentage points during the down phase of the cycle, which lasted on average more than four years. Output declines were more than 9% on average, although the duration of the downturn, averaging roughly two years, was considerably shorter than that of unemployment. The decline in employment was protracted.

During such episodes, the value of government debt tends to explode. It rose an average of 86% (in real terms, relative to pre-crisis debt) in the major post-World War II episode. Ironically, the main cause of the debt explosion was not the costs of bailing out and recapitalizing the banking system. Rather, the biggest driver of debt increases was the collapse in tax revenues as incomes fell and unemployment rose. Many countries also suffered from spikes in the interest burden of the debt, for interest rates soared, and in a few cases (most notably that of Japan in the 1990s), countercyclical fiscal policy effects contributed to the debt buildup.

Historical Housing Crises

In Figure 6.1, we look again at the housing bust phase of housing price cycles surrounding banking crises in an expanded data set. Included are a number of countries that experienced crises from 2007 on. The latest crises are represented by bars in dark shading, past crises by bars in light shading. From peak to trough, the cumulative decline in real

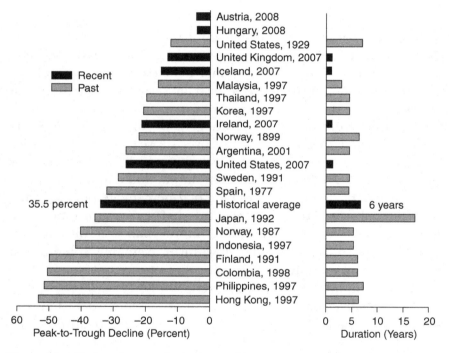

Figure 6.1:   Cycles of past and ongoing real house prices and banking crises.

Source: Carmen M. Reinhart and Kenneth S. Rogoff, *This Time is Different* (Princeton, NJ: Princeton University Press, 2009), p. 227.

Notes: Each banking crisis episode is identified by country and the beginning year of the crisis. Only major (systemic) banking crisis episodes are included, subject to data limitations. The historical average reported does not include ongoing crisis episodes. For the recent episodes, the calculations are based on data through the following periods: October 2008, monthly, for Iceland and Ireland, 2007, annual, for Hungary; and Q3, 2008, quarterly, for all others. Consumer price indexes are used to deflate nominal house prices.

housing pries average 35.5%. The most severe real housing price declines were experienced in Finland, Colombia, the Philippines, and Hong Kong. Their crashes were 50% to 60%, from peak to trough. The crash in the U.S. during the latest episode was almost 28% through late 2008, or more than twice that registered in the U.S. during the Great Depression.[1]

The decline in housing prices averaged six years, with Japan lasting 17 years. The equity price declines that accompanied banking crises were far steeper than the housing price declines, but shorter lived (see Figure 6.2). The average historical decline in equity prices was 55.9%, with downturn lasting 3.4 years. Indonesia, Korea, Austria, Thailand, and Iceland experienced peak-to-trough equity price declines far exceeding the average. The duration was short in Iceland and long in Thailand. The U.S. was below the average.

A combination of bailout costs and higher transfer payments and debt servicing costs lead to a rapid and marked worsening in the fiscal balance. Finland and Sweden stand out in this regard, with the latter going from a pre-crisis surplus of nearly 4% of GDP to a whopping 15% deficit-to-GDP ratio, the former going from a surplus of 1% to almost 11% deficit-to-GDP ratio. Table 6.1 shows these as well as other results. Argentina experienced a 9.5% increase in its deficit. Notably, eight of the countries were enjoying fiscal surpluses prior to the crisis.

Real Debt Crises Across Nations

Figure 6.3 shows the cumulative increase in real government debt in the three years following a banking crisis. The deterioration in government finances is startling, with an average debt increase of 86%. The debt increases are mostly tied to tax revenue losses rather than bank bailout costs (which are minor contributors to the post-crisis increase in debt burdens). Spain, Indonesia, Chile, Finland, and

---

[1]Most of the figures in this chapter are taken from Carmen M. Reinhart and Kenneth S. Rogoff, *This Time is Different* (Princeton, NJ: Princeton University Press, 2009), Chapters 14 and 15.

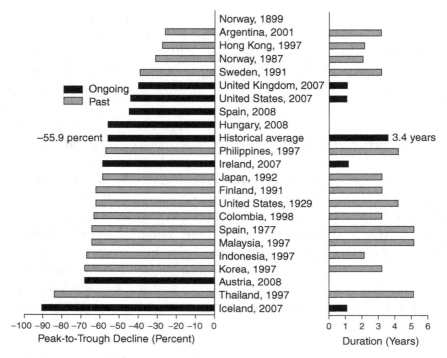

Figure 6.2:   Cycles of past and ongoing real equity prices and banking crises.

Source: Carmen M. Reinhart and Kenneth S. Rogoff, *This Time is Different* (Princeton, NJ: Princeton University Press, 2009), p. 228.

Notes: Each banking crisis episode is identified by country and the beginning year of the crisis. Only major (systemic) banking crisis episodes are included, subject to data limitations. The historical average reported does not include ongoing crisis episodes. For the recent episodes, the calculations are based on data through December 2, 2008. Consumer price indexes are used to deflate nominal equity prices.

Colombia are among those above the average of 86%. Thailand, Sweden, Korea, the Philippines, Norway, and Japan are below the average.

Sovereign risk, though uneven, was incurred. Figure 6.4 highlights the sovereign default, debt restructuring and/or near default (avoided by international bailout packages) that were characteristic of financial crises. Countrywide credit rating during the crisis declined. Advanced economies do not go unscathed. Finland's

Table 6.1: Fiscal deficits (central government balance) as a percentage of GDP.

Country, crisis year	Year before the crisis	Peak deficit (year)	Increase or decrease (−) in the fiscal deficit
Argentina, 2001	−2.4	−11.9 (2002)	9.5
Chile, 1980	4.8	−3.2 (1985)	8.0
Colombia, 1998	−3.6	−7.4 (1999)	3.8
Poland, 1991	1.0	−10.8 (1994)	11.8
Indonesia, 1997	2.1	−3.7 (2001)	5.8
Japan, 1992	−0.7	−8.7 (1999)	9.4
Korea, 1997	0.0	−4.8 (1998)	4.8
Malaysia, 1997	0.7	−5.8 (2000)	6.5
Mexico, 1994	0.3	−2.3 (1998)	2.6
Norway, 1987	5.7	−2.5 (1992)	7.9
Spain, 1977	−3.9	−3.1 (1977)	−0.8
Sweden, 1991	3.8	−11.6 (1993)	15.4
Thailand, 1997	2.3	−3.5 (1999)	5.8

Source: International Monetary Fund.

sovereign risk rating score went from 79 to 69 in three years, leaving it with a score close to those of some emerging markets, but still below the historical average decline of −15.1%. Japan suffered several downgrades from the more famous rating agencies as well. The emerging countries of Chile, Argentina, Indonesia, Malaysia, Korea, and Thailand suffered the greatest ratings declines, all being above the average.

The Great Depression and the Global Great Recession: A Comparison

The magnitude of the global great recession and its scope invites comparison with the Great Depression. Figure 6.5 contrasts the crises of the 1930s with the deep post-World War II crises in terms of the number of years over which output fell from peak to trough.

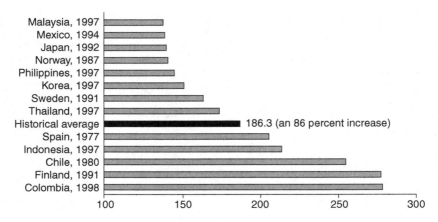

Figure 6.3: The cumulative increase in Real Public Debt in the three years following past banking crises.

Source: Carmen M. Reinhart and Kenneth S. Rogoff, *This Time is Different* (Princeton, NJ: Princeton University Press, 2009), p. 232.

Notes: Each banking crisis episode is identified by country and the beginning year of the crisis. Only major (systemic) banking crisis episodes are included, subject to data limitations. The historical average reported does not include ongoing crisis episodes, which are omitted altogether, because these crisis began 2007 or later and the debt stock comparison here is with three years after the beginning of the banking crisis. Public debt is indexed to equal 100 in the year of the crisis.

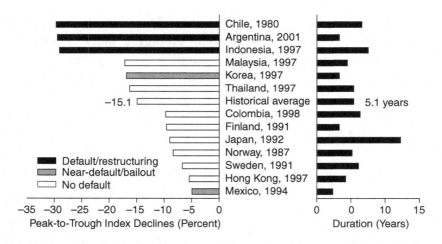

Figure 6.4: Cycles of *Institutional Investor* sovereign ratings and past banking crises.

Sources: *Institutional Investor* and Carmen M. Reinhart and Kenneth S. Rogoff, *This Time is Different* (Princeton, NJ: Princeton University Press, 2009), p. 233.

Notes: *Institutional Investor's* ratings range from 0 to 100, rising with increasing creditworthiness.

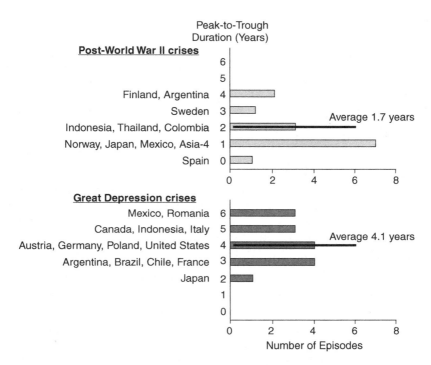

Figure 6.5: The duration of major financial crises: Fourteen great depression episodes versus fourteen post-World War II episodes (duration of the fall in output per capita).

Source: Carmen M. Reinhart and Kenneth S. Rogoff, *This Time is Different* (Princeton, NJ: Princeton University Press, 2009), p. 324.

Notes: The 14 post-war episodes were those in Spain, 1977; Norway, 1987; Finland, 1991; Sweden, 1991; Japan, 1992; Mexico, 1994; Indonesia, Thailand, and (grouped as Asia-4 in the figure) Hong Kong, Korea, Malaysia, and the Philippines, all 1997; Colombia, 1998; and Argentina, 2001. The 14 Great Depression episodes were comprised of 11 banking crisis episodes and three less systemic but equally devastating economic contractions in Canada, Chile, and Indonesia during the 1930s. The banking crisis were those in Japan, 1927; Brazil, Mexico, and the United States, all 1929; France and Italy, 1930; and Austria, Germany, Poland, and Romania, 1931.

The upper panel shows post-war crises including those in Colombia, Argentina, Thailand, Indonesia, Sweden, Norway, Mexico, the Philippines, Malaysia, Japan, Finland, Spain, Hong Kong, and Korea — 14 in all. The lower panel shows 14 post-Depression crises, including those in Argentina, Chile, Mexico, Canada, Austria,

France, the U.S., Indonesia, Poland, Brazil, Germany, Romania, Italy, and Japan.

Each half of the diagram forms a vertical histogram. The years each country or several countries were in crisis is measured on the vertical axis. The number of countries experiencing a crisis of any given length is measured on the horizontal axis. The recessions accompanying the Great Depression were of a much longer duration than the post-war crises. Output typically fell from peak to trough for an average of only 1.7 years after the war, with the longest downturn of four years experienced by Argentina and Finland. In contrast, during the Great Depression, many countries experienced a downturn of four years or longer, with Mexico and Romania experiencing a decrease in output for six years. During the Great Depression the average duration of output declines was 4.1 years.

Apart from the duration and steepness of the declines, is the behavior of output after the downturns. A different perspective is presented in Figure 6.6. Here we measure the number of years it took for a country's output to reach its pre-crisis level. The results are stunning. It took an average of 4.4 years for output of the post-war episodes to claw its way back to pre-crisis levels. Japan and Korea were able to do this relativity quickly, in only two years, whereas Colombia and Argentina took eight years. This is bad enough, but things were much worse during the Great Depression. Countries took an average of 10 years to bring their output back to pre-crisis levels, in part because no country was in a position to export its way to recovery since world aggregate demand had imploded. The U.S., France, and Austria took 10 years to rebuild their output to pre-depression levels, while Canada, Mexico, Chile, and Argentina took 12. If we take the Great Depression as the benchmark, the potential trajectory of the financial crisis of the late 2000s looks more daunting.

We need to look at one more picture. In Figure 6.7, we depict the evolution of real public debt during the Great Depression era. Public debt grew more slowly in the aftermath of these crisis than it did in the post-war crises. After the Depression, it took six years for real public debt to grow by 84% (versus half that time in the post-war crisis). Some of this difference reflects the very slow policy response

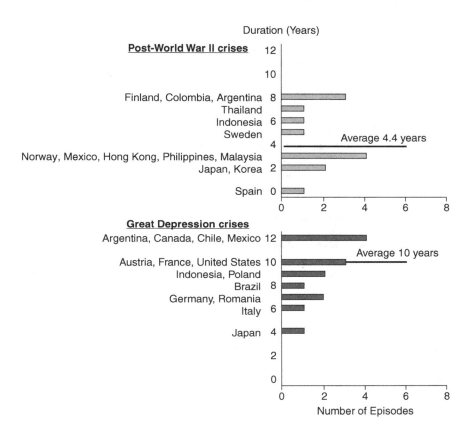

Figure 6.6: The duration of major financial crises: Fourteen Great Depression episodes versus 14 post-World War II episodes (number of years for output per capita to return to its pre-crisis level).

Source: Carmen M. Reinhart and Kenneth S. Rogoff, *This Time is Different* (Princeton, NJ: Princeton University Press, 2009), p. 236.

Notes: The 14 post-war episodes were those in Spain, 1977; Norway, 1987; Finland, 1991; Sweden, 1991, Japan, 1992; Mexico, 1994; Hong Kong, Indonesia, Korea, Malaysia, the Philippines, and Thailand, all 1997; Colombia, 1998; and Argentina, 2001. The 14 Great Depression episodes were comprised of 11 banking crisis episodes and three less systemic but equally devastating economic contractions in Canada, Chile, and Indonesia. The banking crises were those in Japan, 1927; Brazil, Mexico, and the United States, all 1929; France and Italy, 1930; and Austria, Germany, Poland, and Romania, 1931. The pre-crisis level for the Great Depression was that of 1929.

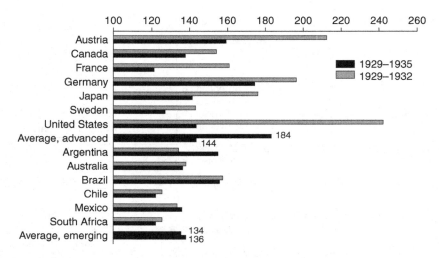

Figure 6.7:   The cumulative increase in Real Public Debt three and six years following the onset of the Great Depression in 1929: Selected countries.

Source: Carmen M. Reinhart and Kenneth S. Rogoff, *This Time is Different* (Princeton, NJ: Princeton University Press, 2009), p. 237.

Notes: The beginning years of the banking crisis range from 1929 to 1931. Australia and Canada did not have a systemic banking crises but are included for comparison purposes, because both also suffered protracted economic contractions. The year 1929 marks the peak in world output and hence is used as the marker for the beginning of the Depression episode.

that occurred in the Great Depression. That began with Herbert Hoover expecting an automatic recovery. Noteworthy also is that public debt in emerging markets did not increase in the later stages following the crisis. Some of these emerging markets had already drifted into default (on both domestic and external debt); others may have faced external constraints such as debt intolerance and therefore had little capacity to finance budget deficits.

These pictures of the aftermath of severe post-war financial crises show that these crises have had a deep and lasting effect on asset prices, output, and employment. Unemployment increases and housing prices declines have extended for five and six years, respectively. Real government debt has increased by an average of 86% after three years. The lesson is unmistakable. It takes a long time to recover from severe financial crisis and each has a legacy of deep and long-lasting national debt.

The global nature of the recent crisis makes it more difficult for individual countries to grow their way out through higher exports or to smooth the consumption effects through foreign borrowing. The planned quadrupling of IMF resources may ease the pain. The next round of defaults could play out in slow motion. Otherwise, defaults in emerging market economies tend to rise sharply when many countries are at the same time experiencing domestic banking crises. There is another policy that helps which the Great Depression years lacked, namely an extremely easy monetary policy with interest rates near zero in many countries. All this did not prevent asset prices and other standard crisis indicator variables to tumble in the U.S. and elsewhere along the tracks laid down by historical precedent. True, equity markets recovered some ground, but this too is in line with historical experience. The more sobering benchmark is laid down by the behavior of output and employment.

The Austerian Tea Party

We now turn to a uniquely American experiment with debt reduction, with attributes that will spill over to other nations. The Tea Party is an American political movement that is primarily known for advocating a reduction in the U.S. national debt and Federal budget deficits by reducing U.S. government spending and taxes. The name is derived from the Boston Tea Party of 1773, an iconic event in American history. Anti-tax protestors in the U.S. have often referred to the original Boston Tea Party for inspiration. There were references to the Boston Tea Party at Tax Day protests held throughout the 1990s and earlier. By 2001, a custom had developed among some conservative activists of mailing tea bags to legislators and other officials as a symbolic act. Some Tea Party affiliated Republicans, such as Michele Bachmann, Jeff Duncan, Connie Mack IV, and Tim Scott, voted for progressive Dennis Kucinich's resolution to withdraw from Libya. However, other members such as Sarah Palin, Dick Armey, Marco Rubio, and Ted Cruz favored domestic tax reform. Koch

Illus. 6.1:   Tea Party in DC.
Source: *Wikipedia*, the free encyclopedia.

Industries has been providing financial and organizational support to the Tea Party movement.

The Tea Party has become a powerful wing of the Republican Party. They say they have no choice for their positions: deficits are out of control; something must be done and soon. They triggered a shutdown of the Federal government in October 2013, then refused to raise the debt ceiling without concessions. They feel that politicians have addicted Americans to a government that is not sustainable. For them, the debt-ceiling deal reached by the Senate on October 16 is merely a cease-fire.

They have had some success stories to tell. Events have gone the movement's way ever since Republicans wrested control of the House of Representatives in the 2010 midterm elections. Discretionary spending has been falling, Federal-employee head count is down. And since 2010, deficit reduction has been more rapid than in any three-year period since the demobilization following World War II.

And, this has been happening during a period of slow economic growth and high unemployment. It has been a victory over Keynesianism.

Discretionary spending (that is, spending excluding transfer payments and interest) will fall even more in the decades ahead if the laws that the Tea Party helped get on the books stay there. The non-partisan Congressional Budget Office projects that, under current law, by 2038 total spending on everything other than the major healthcare programs, Social Security, and interest will decline to the smallest share of the economy since the 1930s.

Ronald Reagan had nothing on today's Tea Party when it comes to shrinking the ability of a government that requires annual appropriations by Congress. That part of the budget has been cut more significantly than anyone would have expected before the 2010 elections. While Tea Partyers like to see themselves as underdogs in the war against profligate spending, the truth is they have already won.

The victory has come at a high price. Austerity has come at an inopportune time. The Tea Party pushed for heavy spending cuts when the economy was weak, thereby needlessly depressing output and keeping the unemployment rate high. The IMF, which supports long-run deficit reduction, disclosed in June 2013 that the U.S. program was "excessively rapid and ill-designed." It nearly tipped the economy back into recession. The Congressional Budget Office estimated in September that waiving spending caps now would create about 800,000 jobs by the end of 2014.

Worse, the cuts of the Tea Party have come almost entirely on the discretionary side of the budget, choking everything from medical research to anti-poverty programs to food inspection. Discretionary spending is the most vulnerable because it must be appropriated annually. The Tea Party, and Washington in general, have scarcely touched entitlements such as Social Security, Medicare, and Medicaid. That is where the long-run fiscal problem needs to be addressed. It cannot be addressed by cutting discretionary spending.

Politically, the Tea Party's scorched earth strategy has produced some impressive legislative wins but damaged the movement's popularity. Its blunt tactics threaten to make deficit reduction seem like a fringe issue, a concern only to extremists. There is the danger that their victories are Pyrrhic ones. The Greek king Pyrrhus once said, "If we are victorious in one more battle with the Romans, we shall be utterly ruined."

But Tea Party heroes such as Senator Ted Cruz of Texas and Representative Michele Bachmann of Minnesota rail against compromise. Recall that Federal debt jumped by nearly $5 trillion during the eight years of Republican President George W. Bush, of whom most Tea Partyers have little but disdain, even though he is a Republican. Then the Obama administration used deficit spending to fight the worst economic downturn since the Great Depression. The debt has grown an additional $6.1 trillion during President Obama's four and a half years to its current level of $16.7 trillion. Still, it is difficult to argue against the mantra that we need to wait until the economy is healthier before getting deficits under control.

But much of the work has been done. While the economy remains weak, fiscal stimulus is off the table. The Budget Control Act put tight caps on discretionary spending for 10 years starting in 2013. Conservative Republicans insist that these cuts did not go far enough. So the deal also created a 12-member bipartisan super-committee to agree on additional reductions. The fallback in case the super-committee failed (which it did) was sequestration: automatic, across-the-board spending cuts. While these sequestration cuts were never supposed to take effect, they did on March 1, because Congress could not agree on a more rational plan.

Sequestration is indiscriminate and destructive. Meanwhile, the government went into a partial shutdown on October 1, the start of the fiscal year, because Congress failed to pass either a 2014 budget or a continuing resolution to keep spending going at last fiscal year's levels. That has reduced spending below sequestration levels while wreaking havoc on everything from Head Start to collection of delinquent taxes. It has cut the economy's annualized growth rate by 0.1 percentage points for each week it has lasted.

Worse, failure to raise the debt ceiling, either now or in the future, would limit the government spending to only what comes in. The country would have instant budget balance — and, most likely, an instant recession. Business was worried; it was crimping its hiring.

While the downward spending ratchet gets most of the attention, the Tea Party has won on taxes too — insisting successfully that deficit reduction should come from lower spending, not higher revenue. This tight fiscal policy is probably subtracting 1.5 percentage points from the economy's growth rate in 2013, taking into account the year's spending cuts and higher taxes. The Federal Reserve can no longer offset this harm by cutting interest rates because the federal funds rate is already at zero. It has only quantitative easing in its arsenal. So the economy is expected to grow only about 1.5% during 2013, barely above stall speed. Job growth will no longer be sufficient to forestall an increase in unemployment. When unemployment ticks higher, we will be in recession.

Still, Tea Partyers insist on "front-loading" cuts in discretionary spending despite the harm to a still recovering economy — and to the fabric of government — because they do not trust others' commitments to cut entitlement spending at some point in the future. It is hell of a way to run a government.

While the Federal government really does need to tighten its belt eventually, it should not be on the scale and immediacy that the Tea party insists on. However, Tea Partyers are in no mood for nuance. They fear that the Republic is in danger from wily liberals who are skilled in the art of brinkmanship. However, it is the Tea Party that is all too good at brinkmanship. The true believers are winning their battles in Washington, while the rest of the country continues to lose. Only the Tea Party would bring the government to a close and default on the nation's debt. Both policies are not only ruinous but incredibly stupid.

The Politics of the Debt Ceiling

From the start, it was clear that the Tea Party members would make the Federal debt limit the focus of controversy, an ideal ploy for hostage-taking. The Republicans went along. The Republicans either believe, or would have you believe, that the debt ceiling limits the size of the national debt and thus limits government spending. The debt ceiling dates back to America's entry into World War I.

Contrary to a widespread misimpression, it came into existence not as a constraint on congressional spending, but in order to make government fiscal procedures less cumbersome amid the pressures of mobilizing for war. It had — and has — nothing to do with authorizing spending; Congress does that as part of the normal legislative process. Nor does the ceiling have anything to do with annual deficit levels which explains why even today, with the deficit shrinking, Congress still needs to raise the debt ceiling. Rather, the ceiling is an artificial and arbitrary cap, determined by Congress, on the amount that the government can borrow to cover obligations already made.[2]

Through World War II, the limit looked to some like it might actually act as a useful check on government borrowing. But over the decades that followed, as the size of the nation's economy — and with it the national debt — grew exponentially, the debt limit became a vestige of a bygone era. By 1974, it was truly obsolete; that year Congress passed a new law compelling it to approve a budget and thus set borrowing levels annually.

The implication by the Republicans that raising the ceiling will enable the government to spend the nation into bankruptcy all the faster is utterly phony, a pseudo-crisis rooted in no real problem, a fraud manufactured and then stage-managed by the GOP to frighten the public and score political points. It is the Republican radicals, not the Democrats, who are threatening to throw the government into immediate bankruptcy unless they get their way over other issues, above all defunding (which means, basically, repealing) Obamacare.

Since the 1950s, economists have called the debt ceiling an experiment that failed long ago. Addressing Congress in 2003 as chair of the Federal Reserve Board, that Ayn Rand acolyte Alan Greenspan disparaged the debt ceiling as "either redundant or inconsistent with the paths of revenue and outlays you specify when you legislate a budget." Eight years later, as the House Republicans'

---

[2]Much of the following history is based on Sean Wilentz, "A House Divided: Right-wing extremism and the lessons of history," *Rolling Stone*, October 24, 2013, pp. 38–44. Wilentz is George Henry Davis 1886 Professor of History at Princeton.

threatened to shut down the government, Greenspan called the debt-limit problem "unnecessary" and claimed flat-out that the debt ceiling "serves no useful purpose." At last, Greenspan got something correct in real time.

For decades, though, Congress went along with raising the debt limit as a mere formality. Every year from 1941 to 1945, Congress raised the debt ceiling to accommodate the accumulating costs of World War II. Since 1960, Congress has raised the ceiling 78 times, and for good reason. If the debt limit is not raised when necessary, the Federal government will immediately default on some of its obligations that, in turn, would disrupt its ability to pay its creditors, from bondholders and defense contractors to recipients of Social Security and Medicare. A default that lasted for just a single day — and perhaps even the threat of such a default would have dire effects, cause every credit agency to downgrade the nation's credit rating which presents to the rest of the world a bizarre spectacle: the richest and most powerful nation on Earth willfully damaging both its economy and its international credibility. A default that lasted more than a few days would risk triggering a catastrophic financial crisis. Until now, no member of Congress, from either party, has seriously entertained wreaking such havoc.

How has a faction consisting of no more than four dozen House members come to exercise so much destructive power? Wilentz blames the continuing abandonment of professional responsibilities by the nation's mainstream news sources — including most of the metropolitan daily newspapers and the television outlets, network, and cable. At some point over the past 40 years, the bedrock principle of journalistic objectivity became twisted into the craven idea of false equivalency, whereby blatant falsehoods are reported simply as one side of an argument and receive equal weight with the reported argument of the other side. A press devoted to searching for and reporting the truth, wherever it might lead, would have kept the public better informed on the basic details of the government shutdown and debt ceiling showdowns. More importantly, it would have reported seriously the hard truths of the Tea Party "insurgency," including how it was largely created and has since been bankrolled by oil-and-gas moguls such as David and Charles Koch of Koch Industries, and by a panoply of richly endowed right-wing pressure groups like Dick Armey's FreedomWorks and Jim DeMint's Heritage Foundation. It also would have reported on the basic reason for the hard right's growing domination of the Republican Party, which has seen the decay of the party at every level, including what passes for its party leadership. No figure exemplifies the problem better than the GOP's highest-ranking official, Speaker John Boehner, whose background and politics' have largely escaped scrutiny. He is a remainder, the last figure left standing from the Gingrich revolution. It is a matter of history: Boehner is the most pathetic figure ever to serve as speaker of the House. If Boehner is the saddest speaker of the House in American history, the current Congress ranks among lowest of Congresses. While there have been numerous terrible Congresses, the closest parallel in our past had been the relatively obscure 46th Congress in the immediate aftermath of Reconstruction. Then, it was the Democrats who were the Southern conservative party.

According to the usual workings of the American political system, success demands building diverse conditions that contain swings too far to the right or the left. The current Republican Party is the latest angry exception to the rules of normal consensus-building politics, and it is unlikely that the GOP will function as a normal political party once again anytime soon. The GOP's long rightward march — deeply rooted in the revolt against the New Deal headed by Ronald Reagan in the 1980s and accelerated by Newt Gingrich in the 1990s — depends upon the "cannibalism" that Gingrich came to lament; and that cannibalism has devoured, among many things, what had once been the party's strong "moderate" and even "liberal" wings. All that remains as a supposedly tempering force inside the GOP are Republicans so conservative that they cannot really be called "tempering," and so inept and on the defensive that they cannot be called a force. If John Boehner is the last man standing against extremism in the party, there is really nothing to bar the door. And, we cannot expect American austerity to fall anytime soon.

7

Ultra-Austerity in Europe

Unlike Las Vegas, what happens in the U.S. does not stay in the U.S. This much can be said of the 2008–2009 money and banking panic. The economies and markets of the U.S. and Europe are linked in many ways. The connections run both ways. The continuing crisis in the eurozone is a big threat to continued economic recovery in the U.S. Full recovery may await the resolution of the European sovereign debt crisis.

The financial crisis in Europe was partly homegrown, depending on the country. But it was partly shipped across the Atlantic from the U.S. Not surprisingly, then, there are similarities in the two sets of crises.

Both financial crises had their roots in speculative bubbles, obviously in houses, but less obviously in bonds. As noted, the real estate craze was particularly pronounced in Ireland, Spain, Iceland, and the U.K., and less visible elsewhere. The housing crashes in Ireland, Spain, Iceland, and the U.K. were notable. Elsewhere in Europe, naive investors ranging from Belgian widows to German state savings banks deluded by those high AAA ratings, scooped up American mortgage-backed securities with glee, thinking they had struck gold: higher returns without greater risk. This had the ring of America in the bubble years. Moreover, mortgage-backed securities provided one of those links to European banks.

Recessions are Exported to Europe

Recession quickly descended upon Europe when the housing and bond bubbles burst, just as it had in the U.S. Banking infections spread from the U.S. after the Lehman collapse. Virtually every nation experienced a slump, some worse than others. Greece and Iceland were horror stories, with the U.K. and Spain also with scary downturns. Spanish unemployment remains over 25%. Even Germany, a stable and conservative country that lacked a real estate bubble, saw its GDP contract by 6.8% between 2008:1 and 2009:1. The decline was substantially larger than the 4.7% contraction in the U.S.

As in the U.S., the contractions blew holes in government budgets. Tax collections dropped with national incomes. Moreover, the costs of Europe's social safety net — spending on unemployment insurance, health insurance, public pensions, and the like — rose. Most European governments, being Keynesian in downturns, fought the recessions with fiscal stimulus packages of various shapes and sizes, which added to government budget deficits. Then, too, there were the bank bailouts. European parliaments enacted myriad bailouts on a country-by-country basis, some larger relative to GDP than that of the U.S. When the U.S. allowed Lehman to collapse, one European central banker declared, "We don't even let dry cleaners fail."

As in the USA, some countries assumed massive amounts of private (mostly bank) debt. Small in the U.S., massive in Europe. Ireland guaranteed essentially all bank liabilities in September 2008. Subsequently assuming these debts as its own, the Irish government added about 40 points to its debt-to-GDP ratio. In theory, the government could obtain credit on favorable terms. In practice, Ireland's rash actions turned a banking crisis into a sovereign debt crisis. Ireland's annual government budget deficit in 2010 was 32% of GDP, setting a modern-day world record.

So much for similarities. There were numerous differences, most of them stemming from the fact that the 17 countries of the eurozone share a common currency and a common central bank — but not a common government. With the U.S. dollar floating internationally and with one central bank, the U.S. has more direct control over its money supply and interest rates. Greatly divergent European countries share one central bank and one monetary policy.

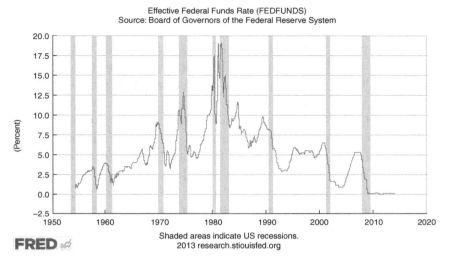

Figure 7.1:   Effective Federal funds rate.

Source: St. Louis Federal Reserve Bank.

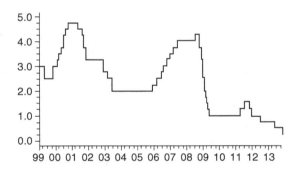

Figure 7.2:   European interest rate ECB.

Source: European Central Bank.

The European Central Bank Practices Austerity

Compared with the Federal Reserve, the European Central Bank (ECB) was a captive of austerity. Figures 7.1 and 7.2 show the two policy rates for the two banks during the Great Recession. The Fed reacted faster to the crisis and much more strongly than did the ECB. By December 2008, the Fed funds rate was already down to virtually zero. As of December 16, 2008, the Federal Open Market Committee (FOMC) had made a change in the funds target rate of a 75 to 100 basis point cut from 1% to a range of zero to 0.25%.[1] The FOMC chose a range rather than a specific rate because a rate of 0% could have had problematic implications for money market funds, whose fees could than outpace yields. This followed the 50 basis point cut on October 29, 2008, and the unusually large 75 basis point cut made during a special January 22, 2008 meeting, as well as a 50 basis point cut on January 30, 2008, a 75 basis point cut on March 18, 2008, and a 50 basis point cut on October 8, 2008. The Federal Reserve was following an anti-austerity policy, in spades.

The stance at the ECB was quite different. The ECB is the central bank of the eurozone. One of its central tasks is the implementation of monetary policy for member nations. Whereas the Fed funds rate is continuously variable, changing with the supply and demand of excess reserves, the ECB rates are fixed for indefinite periods. In December 2008, the ECB's comparable rate was still at 2.5%. Worse, the ECB raised rates twice in 2011 while the Fed was looking for new ways to give the U.S. Economy a boost. Unlike the Fed, the ECB's mandate is to keep inflation low, *period*. Employment be damned. The current ECB rate is 0.25% compared with the near zero rate at the Fed. In recent years, the ECB has been the center of austerity for monetary policy in Europe.

The 17 nations of Europe are not as integrated as the 50 American states. Greece, Portugal, and Ireland were suffering much deeper slumps than, say, Germany, France, and the Netherlands. The weakest countries needed a looser monetary policy than the stronger ones. But, in practice, the ECB cannot run a separate monetary policy for each nation. Its one size has to fit all, no matter how bad the fit.

---

[1] A basis point is 1/100th of 1%. Thus, 100 basis points comprise 1 percentage point. One basis point = 0.01%.

A similar problem exists for the exchange rate. The U.S. has a different exchange rate for each nation, excepting the eurozone. The 17 European countries have only one exchange rate. A currency depreciation is ruled out; this would otherwise spur exports. This is especially a Greek tragedy. If Greece had its own currency in the summer of 2010, the drachma would have plunged in value, making the sunny Mediterranean land an irresistible destination for foreigner vacationers. Greece, probably, would have experienced an export boom, led by tourism, and the Greek recession might have ended right there. Instead, the euro kept Greece expensive and austerity riots scared tourists away.

Another difference between the U.S. and Europe? The U.S. did not have to deal with Greece. Greece has a dismal fiscal history. It has been in default on its public debt roughly 50% of the time since gaining independence in the 1830s. More recently, Greece's budget deficits were large before the crisis and huge thereafter. The Greeks are also poor tax collectors — some say they hardly try. Despite minimum taxes, the government keeps lots of workers on its payroll; they expect to be paid for vacations and to retire young.

Besides, the recession hit Greece especially hard. The economy relies heavily on the export industries of shipping and tourism. In late 2008 and into 2009, world trade suffered a stunning collapse, comparable to that of the Great Depression. There went shipping and the luxury of vacations in Greece. And, there was no exchange rate variation to save exports.

Between the third quarter of 2008 (when Lehman collapsed) and the end of 2010, real GDP in Greece contracted by 10%. Italy continued to fall. By the end of 2011, Greek GDP was about 16% below its 2008:3 peak — and still falling. Greece was on its way to a depression. By comparison, between 1929 and 1933, real GDP in the U.S. fell by almost 27%.

Worse, bad as its budget deficits were, Greece was lying about its budget deficits and national debt. It turns out that some financial engineering by Goldman Sachs had helped the Greek government conceal its mounting debt. By November 2009, the Greek debt-to-GDP ratio was over 120%. Greek interest rates would soon reflect

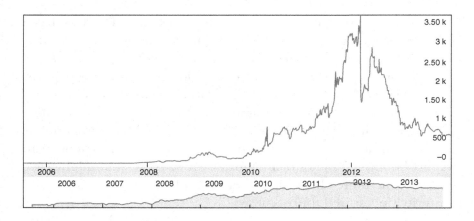

Figure 7.3:   Interest rate spread, Greece versus Germany.

Sources: Greece (http://countryeconomy.com/countries/greece) Country risk (http://countryeconomy.com/tag/country-risk) Spread bonds (http://countryeconomy.com/tag/spread-bonds).

this reality. Starting about this time, Greece's fiscal problems shook faith in many eurozone countries, and even in the euro itself.

A simple way to assess a European government's creditworthiness is to compare its bond rate with that of Germany, the gold standard of rates. Figure 7.3 shows the spread between the interest rate on Greek and German 10-year government bonds. The spread was under 1% as late as October 2008; smaller spreads are found in earlier years. Prior to the crisis, the Greek government apparently was perceived as being almost as good a credit risk as the German government. But, was there a bond market bubble, based on Goldman Sachs accounting? Anyway, the spread on Greek debt widened to nearly 3 percentage points during the height of the worldwide financial crisis in early 2009, as investors shunned risk in every way they could. But then things changed. Starting late in 2009, Greek interest rates began to move up as investor fears escalated and the lies about deficits and debts were revealed. The spreads sharply widened. The Papandreou government reacted by proposing a succession of fiscal austerity programs that were often announced with great fanfare, blessed by the European authorities, and then unraveled.

It was a portent of things to come. The national debt reached 150% of GDP, interest rates went to 6%, and the government must collect 9% of GDP just to pay interest. That was only about 30% of all Greek government revenue. This spelled trouble with a capital T.

All hell broke loose around April 2010. There were more promises of fiscal austerity; more protests and political turmoil; more downgrades from the rating agencies; more discussions of aid packages from eurozone countries, and even from the International Monetary Fund (IMF). Greece's 20-year bond rate breached 12%. The cradle of Western civilization was starting to rock. The first historic bailout deal was reached at the beginning of May 2010, but the relief was short-lived.

Greece was a poor patient with unmanageable politics. A parade of Greek governments had made deals with citizens that the state could no longer afford. Greeks were asked to pay higher taxes, do without some public services, earn lower wages, and live less well. Austerity all the way round. This to satisfy foreign bondholders. Only the bondholding class was doing well.

Papandreou resigned in November 2011, a government replaced by a coalition led by Lucas Papademos, a well-respected economist who had been governor of the Bank of Greece and vice president of the ECB. The Papademos government lasted until May 2012. Then, it took two elections to establish a viable coalition government. Greece has been on the brink ever since. But the debt problems were not unique to Greece.

Trouble of the PIIGS

While the *de jure* lines of authority in Europe are unclear, the German and the French normally take the *de facto* lead. Germany, as Europe's largest economy, is destined to bear the largest share of any bailout. Still, Europe dragged its collective feet. As it did so, more and more countries developed debt problems. Portugal, with its great budget deficits and uncompetitive economy began to look like Greece. Ireland, which had experienced a monumental real estate boom and bust, had to bail out their banks at a colossal public cost. Spain, with its whopping real estate bubble and shaky banks, and Italy, with its great public debt and undisciplined government, were next in line. The long list of troubled European nations became known as the PIIGS (Portugal, Ireland, Italy, Greece, and Spain).

Italy, unlike American banks, was *too big to save.*

In 2010, the PIIGS were in serious trouble, as seen in Table 7.1 that includes Germany for comparison.

The euro became a straitjacket for these countries. They could not fight their slumps with easier money and they could not depreciate their currencies. There was no longer an escudo, a punt, a lira, a drachma, or a peseta — only the dreaded euro. That left only one traditional policy: spending through fiscal policy. But these countries' ability to borrow had disappeared. Eurozone membership became a one-way ticket to a deep, long-lasting recession. It was a ticket to austerity hell.

Notably, the U.K., which experienced a huge financial meltdown, a sharp recession, and a government budget deficit almost the envy of Greece's, fared much better. While suffering a double-dip recession, there was no British sovereign debt crisis; British government bond rates are still low. The British had the advantage of having their own currency and their own monetary policy.

There was also guilt by association. As Greece, Ireland, and Portugal melted down, each requiring a bailout, markets cast a jaundiced eye on Spain and Italy — and interest rates in those

Table 7.1:   The condition of the PIIGS's in 2010.

Country	GDP	Deficit-to-GDP (%)	Debt-to-GDP (%)	Business environment*
Greece	$305 billion	9.6	142	#100
Ireland	$204 billion	32	96	#10
Portugal	$229 billion	7.3	83	#30
Spain	$1.41 trillion	9.2	60	#44
Italy	$2.06 trillion	4.6	119	#87
Germany	$3.32 trillion	3.3	50	#19

*Rank in 2012 World Bank "Doing Business" study of regulatory environment in 183 countries.

countries soared. Even France and Austria lost their AAA credit ratings. Germany, whose credit was the strongest, never worried about rising interest rates — it was the safe haven. However, Germany did worry about the potential breakup of the euro, which would send the deutsche mark soaring, thereby killing German exports.

The tight links between European private banks and their governments opened up new lines of contagion in the crisis. A new line of contagion ran from Greek government debt to Greek bankers (which own a lot of Greek government bonds) and then to banks in other European countries (which have important counterparty relations with Greek banks) and then to the entire world financial system. The contagion is a two-way street. In 2012, a European bailout of Spanish banks cast further doubt on Spanish sovereign debt because it initially took the form of new loans to the Spanish government. Generally, European banks held lots of European government debt, not all of which looked "good as gold."

Illus. 7.1:   Greek protesters clash with police.

Source: http://content.time.com/time/photogallery.

Illus. 7.2:   Italian protesters challenge austerity.

Source: http://content.time.com/time/photogallery/0,29307,2099737_2323025,00.html.

Worse, Europe was not as aggressive as the U.S. in shoring up the capital positions of its banks. Market confidence in American banks soon returned but doubts remained about European Banks. In her first major speech upon becoming head of the IMF, in August 2011, Christine Lagarde, stated bluntly that Europe's banks "need urgent recapitalization." She went on: "This is key to cutting the chains of contagion" and should include "using public funds if necessary."[2] Her stern warning appeared to be directed at France and the ECB.

This raises the question: where was the ECB? After all, one way out of the malaise was for the central bank to buy massive amounts of government bonds of the endangered eurozone countries. Only it had the resources required, since the amount of money needed

---

[2] Christine Lagarde, "Global Risks Are Rising but There Is a Path to Recovery," in *Achieving Maximum Long-Run Growth*: A Symposium Sponsored by the Federal Reserve Bank of Kansas City.

was titanic. The Federal Reserve had pointed the way with Bear Stearns, AIG, QE1, QE2, and more. The Fed's use of asset purchases, financed by creating as much central bank money as necessary, had saved the U.S. financial system. Surely the ECB — and only the ECB — could do the same for Europe.

However, the ECB is quite conservative. It might as well join the Tea Party. It pointed to several reasons for remaining aloof. One was the Maastricht Treaty, which contains a "no bailout" clause:

> The [European] Union shall not be liable for or assume the com-mitments of central governments, regional, local or other public authorities, other bodies governed by public law or public under-takings of any Member State....[3]

The Maastricht Treaty also contains what might be called the "bailout clause":

> Where a Member State is in difficulties ... caused by natural disas-ters or exceptional occurrences beyond its control, the Council, acting on a proposal from the Commission, may provide ... Union financial assistance to the Member State concerned. [4]

The question remains: Do self-inflicted wounds by a member state qualify as "exceptional occurrences" beyond a nation's control?

The ECB reluctance was based, not only on the no-bailout clause, but also on what was considered good central banking prac-tices. The monetary financing of government budget deficits is often characterized as "inflationary finance." This was the main route to hyper-inflation in the Weimar Republic. Still, deflationary conditions prevailed in the eurozone. That the ECB was built in the image of the Bundesbank did not help. The ECB building continues nonetheless to impress.

There was also the moral hazard argument. Purchasing govern-ment bonds would let the national government off the hook and this would ease pressure to get its fiscal house in order. If the ECB bought Greek, Irish, Portuguese, Spanish, and Italian bonds, that

---

[3]Article 125 of the treaty posted on the ECB's web site, European Central Bank.
[4]Article 122 of the treaty posted on the ECB's web site, European Central Bank.

Illus. 7.3:   European Central Bank Building — European Central Bank, Frankfurt Germany.

Source: *Wikipedia*, the free encyclopedia.

would weaken the incentives of the governments to solve their own budget problems. The ECB's attitude helped precipitate changes of government in Greece, Spain, and Italy in 2011. In two of these three cases, technocrats temporarily took over what was supposed to be national unity governments.

These technocrats were economists. One was Mario Monti, sometimes known as "Il Professor" who became prime minister of Italy on November 16, 2011. Just 15 days afterward, another highly regarded Italian economist, Mario Draghi, took over as president of the ECB. Though not related, the pair was dubbed the "Super Mario Brothers." Monti set about reforming Italy; Draghi changed the ECB's course virtually overnight.

It began with interest rates. Under Draghi, the ECB expanded its pre-existing Long-Term Refinancing Operation (LTRO), both in size and maturity. Beginning in December 2011, banks were encouraged to borrow large amounts of money from the ECB for terms as long as three years — a long way from the typical overnight central bank borrowings. The three-year maturities are far longer than any credit extended by the Fed. At this stroke, the ECB made the European banking crisis far less acute. Banks now had some breathing space. From December 2011 through February 2012, the banks borrowed about 1 trillion euros at 1% interest. This new LTRO strategy meant that the ECB would now buy more sovereign debt for its own portfolio.

This was not enough. In early September, Draghi announced a new bond-buying program, called "outright Monetary Transactions" (OMT) that included bonds of maturities of more than three years. The ECB's wallet now is wide open. This made short-term interest rates irrelevant.

Greece remains a basket-case. Its paymasters in Europe and the IMF demand ever more fiscal austerity — higher taxes and less government spending — to shrink the budget deficit. These profoundly anti-Keynesian policies have worsened Greece's depression. This, in turn, makes any budget goal harder to achieve. The same mainly applies to Spain. Greece has already defaulted on some of its debt. Greece teeters on the brink: it may have to leave the eurozone to survive.

Portugal too practiced austerity. It intensified privatization, raised taxes, cut spending, and shaved pensions. But austerity did not work any better as a recovery strategy in Portugal than it did in Greece. Unemployment has risen to 15%. The Portuguese economy shrunk by 3.3% in 2012, one of the worst downward spirals in Europe. Reduced wages and idled workers reduce revenue collections. The debt ratio continues to rise.

The Irish variation on the story was especially perverse, since Ireland had been a model fiscal citizen with low deficit and debt ratios. However, Ireland sank because banks' speculative investments in housing created a massive, debt-financed property bubble that drove its largest banks into insolvency. When the housing bubble popped, and the collateral sank below the value of the debt, the heavily leveraged banks could not roll over their foreign loans and became insolvent. The Irish–American Bank made 72 billion euros worth of loans on property, and lost 34 billion euros of that — almost half of what it had lent.

With the EU's approval, the Irish government gave an unlimited financial guarantee to the six major banks, covering their losses with massive state borrowing. Ireland's debt ratio soared, leaving the Irish government unable to access credit markets and entirely dependent on the tender mercies of others, which required the usual austerity regimen. By 2012, the Irish public debt ratio was 18.2%, right up there with Greece's — but for different reasons. With austerity medicine imposed by the EU, Ireland's unemployment rate eventually reached 15% by late 2012.

Nor did austerity do much good in Britain. In a keynote speech to Conservatives in April 2009, Prime Minister David Cameron called on an "age of austerity." He slashed public spending. By 2012, Britain was back into a double-dip recession. Despite the belt-tightening, Britain's debt ratio has steadily increased — from around 50% when Cameron took office in 2010 to nearly 70% in 2012 — because a deep recession reduced economic activity and government revenues. An unprecedented triple-dip recession seemed likely in 2013. Conservative austerity policy in Britain provided a real-world experiment in the folly of belt-tightening as the cure for the effects of a financial collapse.

We can summarize the European situation with one picture. In the latest IMF forecast for the Eurozone, it is economists who plotted the growth rates of the Euro-countries against a measure of fiscal tightening. It is not a pretty picture. Greece is at the bottom. Overall, this has adverse implications for the U.S. and for the global economy.

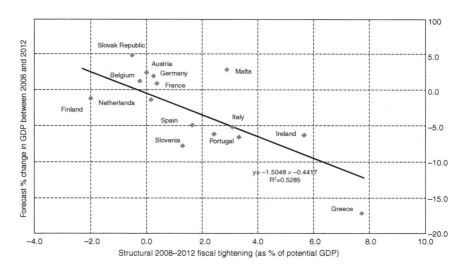

Illus. 7.4:   Fiscal tightening and Eurozone GDP 2008–2012.

Source: IMF, World Economic Outlook Database, April.

8

How Austerity Kills

Politics is nothing but medicine on a grand scale.

— Rudolph Virchow, 1848

Olivia remembers being on fire.

Eight years old, she was scared by the sound of dishes crashing onto the kitchen floor. Her parents were having another fight. She ran up the stairs to her bedroom and hid under a pillow. Exhausted from crying, she fell asleep.

She woke up with a splintering pain on the right side of her face. The room was black with smoke. Her bed sheets had erupted in flames. Screaming, she ran out of her room and straight into the arms of a firefighter who had raced up the stairs. He wrapped her tightly in a blanket. As she would later hear the nurses in the hospital whisper, her father had set the house on fire in a drunken rage.

It was spring of 2009, during the ongoing Great Recession. Olivia's father, a construction worker, had been laid off. Millions of Americans had joined the unemployment rolls, and some turned to drugs or, like Olivia's dad, to alcohol. About 770,000 additional Americans during the Great Recession would binge on alcohol.[1]

Three years later and a half a world away, on the morning of April 4, 2012, Dimitris Christotulas set off to the Greek Parliament building in the center of Athens. At age 77, he saw no other way out.

---

[1] Box *et al.*, "Alcohol Use During the Great Recession of 2008–2009, *Alcohol and Alcoholism*, 2013. Available at http://alcalc.oxfordjournals.org/content/early/2013/01/28/alcalc.agt002.short.

Christoulas had been a pharmacist, retired in 1994, but now he was having trouble paying for his medications. Life had been good, but the new Greek government had slashed his pension, and life was now intolerable.

That morning, Christoulas went to Syntagma Square, the city's central plaza. He walked up the parliament steps, put a gun to his head, and declared, "I am not committing suicide. They are killing me." Then he pulled the trigger.[2]

Olivia and Christoulas may have been 5000 miles apart, but they shared similar fates due to the Great Recession. The Great Recession would take its toll on other people's bodies. They were the victims of the new austerity.

Olivia and Dimitris were not alone. More than 600 Greek citizens killed themselves in 2012. Before the Great Recession, Greece had the lowest suicide rate in Europe. Now that rate has doubled. Greece too is not alone. Suicides in the other European Union countries had dropped consistently for over 20 years until the Great Recession. During the Great Recession, life expectancy in the U.S. fell for the first time in at least four decades. In London, heart attacks rose by 2000 amid the market turmoil. And suicide and alcohol death reports continue to amass.

The Great Depression provides one of our first lessons about the adverse health effects of austerity. Not surprisingly, suicide rates in the U.S. increased significantly, starting in 1929. Suicide rates rose by about 16% from 18.1 per 100,000 population to 21.6 per 100,000 population at the peak in 1932. The trend is shown in Figure 8.1. After the New Deal, nostrums kicked in and the suicide rate dropped. The New Deal included the Federal Emergency Relief Act and Works Progress Administration, which gave 8.5 million jobless Americans work by creating new construction projects; the Home Owner's Loan Corporation, which prevented at least a million foreclosures; the Food Stamp Program which gave vouchers for basic foods to those who could not afford them; the Public Works

---

[2]Niki Kitsantonis, "Pensioner's Suicide Continues to Shake Greece," *New York Times,* April 5, 2012.

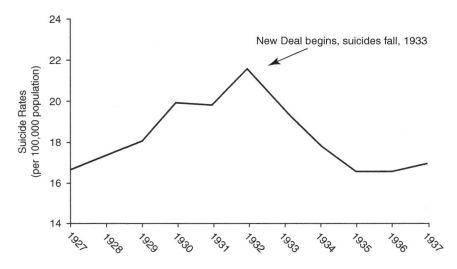

Figure 8.1:   Trends in suicide rates, U.S., 1927 to 1937.

Source: David Stuckler and Sonjay Basu, *The Body Economic* (New York: Basic Books, 2013), p. 11.

Administration which built hospitals and provided immunizations for Americans who could not afford them; and the Social Security Act to combat poverty among senior citizens. During the Great Recession suicide rates accelerated above their previous rates. Before the foreclosure crisis that started in 2007, suicides were already increasing at a rate of one per every 10,000 people per year. When the recession began, the rate jumped to five per every 10,000 per year. Overall, there was a statistically significant increase of about 4750 "excess" suicides during the recession. In the U.K., too, roughly 1000 excess suicides took place (see Figure 8.2).[3]

The Courage of Icelanders

Where anti-austerity measures are invoked in the face of economic adversity, we can expect health to improve. Indeed, this is precisely

---

[3]These estimates were made by David Stuckler and Sanjay Basu, *The Body Economic: Why Austerity Kills* (New York: Basic Books, 2013), p. 112.

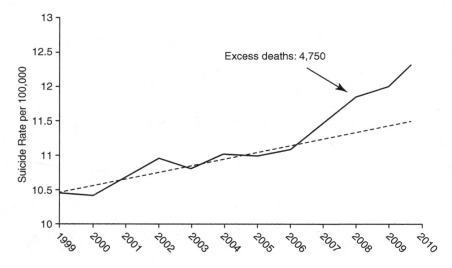

Figure 8.2:   Recession leads to an increase in suicides, United States.
Source: David Stuckler and Sonjay Basu, *The Body Economic* (New York: Basic Books, 2013), p. 112.

what happened in Iceland during the money and banking panic of 2008–2009. Outside the Eurozone, Iceland is a proud and independent nation with its own currency, the Krona. In the mid-1990s, the government decided that the economy needed to expand beyond fish and tourism. Their strategy was to become a private offshore banking center; Iceland reinvented itself as a tax haven for the world's ultra-rich. Commercial and investment banks merged in the early 2000s, paving the way for new methods of loaning money and investing in high-yield commodities. One of the most popular of these new investment innovations would also prove the riskiest. IceSave, an Internet-based banking program run by the private bank Landshanki, offered 6% interest rates to attract foreign capital. IceSave was soon inundated with foreign investments. Following Landshani's success, other Icelandic banks followed suit. The countries' three largest banks moved onto the list of the worlds' top 300 investment trusts. By the beginning of 2007, Iceland had become the fifth richest country in the world. Masses of capital continued to flow into the country.

It was a house of cards. Behind the scenes Iceland's economy balanced on a precipice. In order to maintain the high level of payouts to its bank depositors, the country was running enormous deficits from high levels of imports and vast borrowings of foreign currency, a situation reminiscent of East Asia in the 1990s. Businesses and new building construction were relying on some Icelandic banks. These banks in turn were paying out the loans from dangerous investments overseas, mostly investments that promised high returns that had not yet materialized. Among these, was the notorious mortgage-backed securities of the U.S. When the price bubble in mortgage default swaps bust, everything in Iceland went down the drain. What was not in mortgages was in stocks (which collapsed). Consumers started to withdraw their funds from IceSave, worried that the bank would not be able to pay back their money given the stock market crash in the U.S.

They were right. In October 2008, IceSave began to implode, as a run on the fund began and Iceland's stock market fell by 90%. The country's GDP fell by 13%, and unemployment rates rose from 3% to 7.6% between 2008 and 2010. Nearly 40,000 homeowners were unable to make their mortgage payments as a result of income losses; over a thousand homes were foreclosed. The question arose: With a shrinking tax base, would Iceland be able to pay for public healthcare, unemployment support, pensions, and other social protection programs?

Desperate to find a way to manage its finances, the government turned to the lender of last resort, the International Monetary Fund (IMF). The IMF financial plan for Iceland came with recommendations for austerity. Iceland would get $2.1 billion in loans, but the government would have to slash public spending by 15% of GDP. IceSave's debt was several times the country's entire economy, and the IMF was calling for 50% of Iceland's gross income to be paid to the private investors over a seven-year period. In short, the Icelandic people were being asked to bailout a bunch of rich bankers. This sounds familiar only because this is precisely what was being done in the USA. The public health system faced a 30% cut. In protest, the Prime Minister resigned.

The IMF assumed that the Keynesian multiplier was 0.5 which meant that government spending had a contractionary effect on the economy. A more realistic multiplier of 1.7 has been estimated by Stuckler and Basu.[4] The IMF not only had underestimated austerity's economy harms, it had overlooked the even greater damage that resulted from cutting public health. Health has one of the largest fiscal multipliers, as high as 3. Nor do banker bailouts typically stimulate the economy. In a move partly triggered by riots in early 2009, the government rejected the IMF plan and asked the people what they preferred. 93% of Icelanders voted against paying for the bankers' debts.

Government austerity was thrown out the window. In 2007, Iceland's government spending as a fraction of GDP was 42.3%. This increased to 57.7% in 2008 and has remained about 10 percentage points above pre-crisis levels. In other words, Iceland did not balance its budget through massive cuts in its healthcare system. While currency devaluation meant the National Health Service had less money to import medicines, the government offset this threat of unaffordable pharmaceutical imports by increasing health budgets between 2007 and 2009 — from 380,000 krona per person to 453,000. Patients did not lose access to care. Iceland also maintained its social protection system programs to help people maintain food, jobs, and housing.

The health of the Icelandic people actually improved during the economic collapse. From 2007 to 2010, the worst years of the crisis, death rates continued to fall steadily throughout the country. There was a slight rise in suicides after the market crash, but not a statistically significant one. There was no increase in heart attacks, as might be predicted for a banking crisis. Mental health indicators were stable.[5] In terms of "gross national happiness" Iceland remained number one in the world. Iceland survived the IMF's austerity program by rejecting it.

The Greek Odyssey on the Way to Tragedy

The Greek Odyssey left the same station as the Icelandic disaster but ended up at a different destination, a Greek tragedy. Greece's

---

[4] Stuckler and Basu, *op. cit.*, p. 65.
[5] *Ibid.*, pp. 67–68.

financial sector was caught in a storm when U.S. banks blew through their cash positions in 2008. Greece was hit by a series of financial earthquakes. First came a demand shock or loss of demand for Greek goods and services, as well as less construction. Then, it was discovered that the government had been cooking the books on Greece's budget deficits. Then, came the "austerity crisis" from the IMF and European Central Bank measures imposed on Greece in return for financial bailouts. These were neither necessary nor helpful for economic recovery or preventing a public health disaster.

The demand shock came from the U.S. mortgage-backed securities crisis. Between May 2008 and May 2009, the Athens Stock Exchange fell by 60%. When Europe's investors lost their fortunes, lavish trips to Greek islands stopped, imports of Greece's fruits and vegetables declined, and construction projects came to a halt; cranes were left dangling in mid-air. Meanwhile, Europe's and North American's bankers were bailed out; this did little to shore up the ripple effect on the Greek economy. Average Greek household income fell by 0.2% in 2008 and another 3.3% in 2009, in Greece's slow descent into financial despair.

The demand shock was followed by a financial earthquake — the discovery that Greek authorities had wrongly classified certain debts as being outside the government budget. This greatly altered national budget deficits in real numbers. As noted, Goldman Sachs hid hundreds of billions of dollars of real borrowing costs from public view (for handsome fees). In reality, Greece's debt levels had grown from 105% in 2007 to 143% of GDP in 2010.

When the truth was revealed in 2010, panic ensued. Greece's bonds were downgraded to "junk" status in April 2010. Interest rates on Greek government bonds spiraled out of control as investors fled the country. Greek interest rates jumped from 2% in 2009 to 10% in 2010. The real numbers shock was followed by even more suffering.

Greek GDP sank further, falling by 3.4% in 2010. Ordinary people paid the piper, since the super-rich had stashed funds in offshore bank accounts. Unemployment rates rose from 7% in May 2008 to 17% in May 2011. Among young people employment rose from 19%

to 40%. A generation of newly educated people was starting adult life out of work. Greek society stood at the brink of collapse.

With the Greek currency tied to the euro, Greece turned to the IMF for help. In May 2010, the IMF offered loans with the usual strings attached — privatize state-owned companies and infrastructure and cut social protection programs. In turn, the IMF and the European Central Bank would provide 110 billion euros in loans as part of a three-year bailout plan that would help to pay off Greek debt. Greece's creditors — including the French and German banks that helped fuel Greece's construction bubbles — took a haircut, agreeing to write off half their debts and to lower interest rates on their loans to the country.

Greece's leaders, unlike those of Iceland, saw no alternative except to accept the IMF package. There was no public referendum. Prime Minister George Papandreou said upon approving the plan: "With our decision today our citizens will have to make great sacrifices."[6] This ranks right up there in the top 10 of historical understatements.

The IMF's aim was to make cuts totaling 23 billion euros in three years, about 10% of the entire economy, and sell off state enterprises for 50 billion euros to reduce Greece's deficit from 14% to less than 3% of GDP by 2014. It was an ambitious, Draconian plan. Public sector workers would face mass layoffs, wage cuts and pension reductions. The bailout also included conditions to raise taxes on fuel and related commodities by 10%, further emptying people' pockets and reducing their buying power. Apparently, fuel was considered a luxury.

Led by the Direct Democracy Now! movement, peaceful protests against the IMF plan began in May 2010. Soon the protests turned violent. Tear gas, riot gear, and tanks were bought in for use by the police and military. As in Iceland, the Greek protestors called for a nationwide referendum on the agreement, to no avail. The first IMF austerity package went into effect in May 2010, without a vote.

---

[6]H. Smith, "Greece's George Papandreou Announced 140 billion euro Bailout Deal," *The Guardian*, May 2, 2010.

What about public health? The IMF's "recovery" plan had as a goal "to keep public health expenditure at or below 6% of GDP, while maintaining universal access and improving the quality of care delivery. In the short-term, the main focus should be on macro-level discipline and cost-control." No one knows where the 6% came from. For example, Germany, an advocate of the austerity plan in Greece, spends more than 10% of a much larger GDP on healthcare. As it turned out, the IMF in practice caused people to lose access to healthcare. The Greek government reduced public spending on outpatient pharmaceuticals from 1.9 to 1 and 1/3% of GDP. This in the face of rising healthcare costs. Further, the IMF cut hospital budgets, preventing hospitals from obtaining medicines and medical supplies. Waiting lines doubled and then tripled. The pharmaceutical company Novo Nordisk pulled out of Greece because it was no longer being adequately paid (the Greek state owed the company $36 million), a pull out that deprived 50,000 Greek diabetics of insulin.

Meanwhile, Greeks were reporting that their health was worsening. In 2009, compared to 2007, they were 15% more likely to report that their health was "bad" or "very bad." In 2009, people were 15% less likely to go to a doctor or dentist for treatment, compared with 2007 (before the crisis).[7] People were losing access because of long waiting lines and excessive treatment costs. People turned to public hospitals and clinics. Doctors took to taking bribes from desperate patients trying to jump the queues, leading to more inefficiency and making it more difficult for impoverished Greeks to access healthcare.

Recession and austerity created a perfect storm of miserable budget cuts, clinic closures, and more "hidden" costs. Overall, an estimated 50,000 people over the age of 65 had forgone necessary medical care during the period of recession and austerity. The elderly, who needed the care the most, was getting it the least.[8]

---

[7] Stuckler and Basu, *The Body Economic: Why Austerity Kills, op. cit.*, p. 85.
[8] *Ibid.*

Mental health was also worsening. Suicide rates were rising by 20% between 2007 and 2009. Besides, there were disguised suicide causes of death. Moreover, with public health programs collapsing in the face of austerity, the incidence of infectious disease skyrocketed. An outbreak of East Nile Virus killed 60 people in August 2010. Then there was a malaria outbreak. Special warning previously reserved for travelers to sub-Sahara Africa and tropical parts of Asia were issued. Greece was becoming a third-world country. An HIV outbreak — the only one to occur in Europe in decades — emerged in the center of Athens. Drug use was a major factor in the outbreak.

Greece's Health Ministry had few options. Its health budget had been cut by 40%. At last, in November 2011, at the time of the HIV outbreak, Prime Minister Papandreou tried the Icelandic solution. He announced a referendum on a second round of austerity measures from the IMF and the European Central Bank. After all, austerity was not working. In the face of all the budget cuts, government debt continued to rise — to 165% of GNP in 2011. Under pressure from German and other European leaders, Papandreou was forced to call the referendum off. A vote was vetoed in the birthplace of democracy.

Austerity was wreaking havoc on the health of the Greek people. Trying to cut health spending from 10.5 billion euros in 2009 to 7 billion in 2012 — in the middle of an HIV outbreak, a massive increase in homelessness, and a rise in suicides, among other problems — Athens was doing the best it could. Chaos prevailed in the healthcare system. With austerity came 28 billion euros in bailouts, yet Greece was not recovering. Government debt continued to rise, reaching more than 160% of GDP in 2012. And there was no stimulus for the economy. Much of the money was being funneled back to the U.K., France, the U.S., and Germany, to creditors who had contributed to Greece's disastrous bubble. Greece's bailout funds were being used to rescue the world's banking elite. Austerity was not simply a mistake, it was the worst possible kind of mistake. Greek's tragedy was that austerity will not save a failing economy. Moreover, the irony of Germany's insistence on austerity in Greece even though Germany had been "bailed out" by the U.S. and the rest of Europe after World War II (under the Marshall Plan) was not lost on the Greeks. Still, history will probably forget about the fate of Dimitris Christoulas, among others.

Death in Italy

In Italy, we now have the *vedove bianche*, the White Widows. After Italy's austerity drive in response to the Great Recession, the menfolk had not been able to find enough work to pay their tax debts. These men chose to end it all by taking their lives. Saddled with debt, and left to pick up the pieces, their widows were angry and frustrated that the government was not helping them. On May 4, 2012, a crowd of them waving white flags marched to the entrance of the Italian government's Equitalia tax office in Bologna. "*Non ci suiciderete!*" they chanted. "Don't suicide us." The leader of the protest, Tiziana Marrone, said, "The government must do something. It is not right what is happening in Italy." After all, the government had turned a blind eye to tax evasion by Italy's super-rich, but done virtually nothing to support those who had lost everything in the Great Recession. "My battle is not just mine," she continued, "it is of all Italians who find themselves in my condition, and most of all of the widows of those families who don't know where to turn to pay all these debts."[9]

This had been the second protest at the Equitalia building. Five weeks earlier, Giuseppe Campaniello, a self-employed bricklayer, and the husband of Tiziana Marrone, went to the same office. He had received a final note doubling a fine he reportedly could not pay. So in front of the tax offices, he doused himself with gasoline and set himself on fire. He left a love note for Tiziana. He died nine days later.

There were other victims of the Great Recession. In April 2013, there was a triple suicide in the seaside town of Civitanova Marche. A married older couple, Anna Maria Sopranzi and Romeao Dionisi had been struggling to live on her monthly pension of around 500 euros (about $650), and had fallen behind on rent. Because the

---

[9] A. Vogt, "Italian Women Whose Husbands Killed Themselves in Recession Stage March," *The Guardian*, April 30, 2012.

Italian government's austerity budget had raised the retirement age, Mr. Dionisi, a former construction worker, became one of Italy's exiled ones — older workers plunged into poverty without a safety net. On April 5, the two hanged themselves in a storage closet at home. When Ms. Sopranzi's brother, Giuseppe Sopranzi, 73, heard the news, he drowned himself in the Adriatic.[10]

Between 2007 and 2010, during the Great Recession unemployment jumped by 39% in Italy. During this time, there was a large rise in suicide death certificates labeled "due to economic reasons." Overall, Italy suffered an estimated 500 new cases of suicide and attempted suicides beyond what would have been expected if pre-recession suicide trends had continued. Figure 8.3 shows the jump

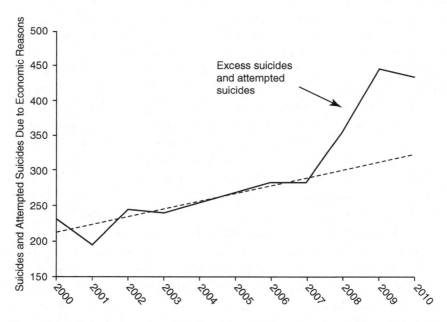

Figure 8.3: Recession and austerity increase Italy's economic suicides and suicide attempts.

Source: David Stuckler and Sonjay Basu, *The Body Economic* (New York: Basic Books, 2013), p. 111.

---

[10]David Stuckler and Sanjay Basu, "How Austerity Kills," www.nytimes.com, May 12, 2013.

in excess suicides and suicide attempts due to the lethal combination of the Great Recession and the Italian government's austerity response. The White Widows were not alone.

U.S. Healthcare during the Great Recession

Diane was 47 years old when a splinter ruined her life. She had been a teacher at a charter school in California. Because of $8 billion in education budget cuts the state enacted in 2009, she lost her job. With the job loss, she also lost her health insurance. She had to purchase an individual coverage plan with a $5000 deductible. This made her think twice about whether to seek medical help. Because Diane has diabetes, her minor wound of a splinter in her foot became a large gash, then an ulcer that would not heal. She felt that she could not afford a doctor's visit and prescription antibiotics.

Self-help did not work and she ended up in the hospital. Her leg was so badly infected, it had to be amputated. Many complications later, she had a stroke. Now Diane lives in a nursing home. She is unable to speak or walk or move the right side of her body. Her initial preventative medical treatment would have cost little; her care now will cost the state of California tens of thousands of dollars a year. If the accident had happened a few years later, she might have been covered under the Affordable Care Act.

Diane's case was not the only one not covered by health insurance. Before the Great Recession, the U.S. healthcare system failed to provide coverage for many of its people. Although two-thirds of Americans received health insurance through their employer, the rest — whose employers would not cover them, part-time workers, and the self-employed — were on their own, if they could not qualify for Federal insurance programs. These Americans had to buy health insurance on the private market, though many could not afford the monthly premium and high deductibles. Moreover, companies could restrict coverage on the basis of pre-existing health conditions, like diabetes or high blood pressure. The U.S. system left about 40 million Americans — almost 13% of the population — without health insurance.

Illus. 8.1:   Man standing on chair in empty building ready to hang himself.
Source: http_//www.inmagine.com-photo.

The Great Recession turned this bad healthcare situation into a
full-blown crisis. When Americans lost their jobs, they lost their
health insurance. A 2009 study found that people who lacked insurance were 40% more likely to die prematurely. During the Great
Recession, there were about 35,000 avoidable deaths due to the
lack of healthcare insurance.[11]

Just as in Greece, recession and austerity in the U.S. resulted in
people having to wait longer to see doctors and access necessary
treatment. Patients increasingly used emergency rooms more than
outpatient clinics as they ended up in situations like Diane's —
avoiding preventive care when they could no longer afford it. In

---

[11]A. Wilper *et al.*, "Health Insurance and Mortality in US Adults," *American Journal
of Public Health* 99(12) (2009), pp. 2289–2295.

short, the U.S. healthcare system failed to protect its people during the Great Recession.

One group benefited. Heath insurance company profits soared during the Great Recession. In 2009, the top five U.S. health insurance companies reported $12.2 billion in profits, a staggering increase of 56% over the figures for 2008. That same year 2.9 million people lost coverage. These profits came at the expense of patients. The rich got richer, and the sick got sicker. When it comes to healthcare, free markets are inefficient.

Other countries were more resilient during the Great Recession. Canada, Japan, Australia, and most European countries rejected market-based approaches to healthcare, providing state-sponsored care for all. While millions of Americans were losing access to healthcare during the Great Recession, there were fewer signs of people skipping doctor's visits or preventive care in the U.K., Canada, France, and Germany. There people were not forced to choose between bankruptcy and their health when the Great Recession struck.

Worse in the USA, the suicide rate went up sharply during the Great Recession. As noted earlier, there were an estimated 4750 excess deaths during the decline. This did not have to happen. In other countries, such as Sweden and Finland, ways were found to prevent a crashing economy from taking a toll on people's mental health.

Conclusions

The evidence is hard to ignore; the consequences painful to observe. Yet austerity's advocates have ignored evidence of the health and economic consequences of their recommendations. The worst offender, the IMF has to ignore its own data, if not its economists. Austerity's proponents, such as British Prime Minister David Cameron, continue to write prescriptions of austerity for the body economic, in spite of evidence that it has failed. It succeeds only as economic ideology, which comes from the belief that small government and free markets are always better than state intervention. It is a convenient belief among politicians to take advantage of the weakest citizens. It does great harm; it punishes those most vulnerable, and bails out those who caused the recession.

In prior crises, people chose to respond to recessions with programs like FDR's New Deal. The New Deal prevented public health disasters at a vulnerable time and helped to save capitalism. It also generated some of the most vital social protection programs that continue today, such as Food Stamps and Social Security. After World War II, when Britain's debt was over 400% of its GDP, the U.K. did not cut its budget to reduce its deficits. It instead attacked what Sir William Beveridge called the "five Giants" — Want, Disease, Ignorance, Squalor, and Idleness. When, in 1948, the British economy was in shambles, the Labour Party launched hugely successful social protection programs, including the National Health Service, and in so doing ended its debt crisis.

In Iceland, the public rejected austerity. History has vindicated the people's choice. Iceland's economy is stronger than ever before, and in the face of a massive recession, public health actually improved during the Great Recession. It took courage; Iceland had to tell the IMF to go to hell. If the little nation of Iceland can do it, why not the mighty United States?

9

The Austerity Lobby

Since the early 1990s, an expanding network of Washington and Wall Street notables has warned that the nation is overspending and over-promising, putting the solvency of the Republic and the prosperity of the next generation at risk. With the money and banking panic of 2008, these groups deliberately blurred the long-term need for adjustments in Social Security and Medicare with the unrelated and urgent question of how to recover from a prolonged deflationary downturn. As it turned out, the budget hawks found a receptive audience among media and political elites. Key commentators have embraced the story line of the need for shared sacrifice and grander fiscal compromise and the premise that we can somehow deflate our way to prosperity.

The Rise of Peter G. Peterson

What is instructive is the career of Peter G. Peterson, a billionaire investment banker and leading spokesman for belt-tightening.[1] Along with him, Koch Industries has bankrolled the austerity-oriented Tea Party. In 1982, Peterson began writing articles and books warning that "unfunded liabilities" of the government, most notably Social security, would lead to an economic collapse. Peterson warned that explicit and tacit government debts would crowd out

---

[1] Most of the details on Peter Peterson and his Foundation are gleaned from Robert Kuttner, *Debtors' Prison: The Politics of Austerity Versus Possibility* (New York: Alfred A. Knopf, 2013), pp. 51–62. All of Kuttner's book is worth reading.

Illus. 9.1:   U.S. Sen. Jim DeMint (R-SC) (L) and Sen. Rand Paul (R-KY) (R) join
Tea Party supporters at the first U.S. Senate Tea Party Caucus, January 27, 2011 on
Capitol Hill.

Source: Photo by Win McNamee.

productive private investment, increase interest rates, and reduce
confidence in the dollar. He insisted that this generation of elders
was living too well at the expense of their children and grandchil-
dren. He had the support of neoliberal economists, who saw savings
causing investment rather than the other way round. Left in the
lurch were the Keynesians.

For sure, a crash was coming. But when it came, it had everything
to do with lax financial regulation promoted by lobbyists such as
Peterson and Koch and had nothing to do with budget deficits
crowding out productive investment. In fact, interest rate and capital
costs were low and falling in the run-up to the 2008–2009 collapse.

Through the many pages of four books and myriad articles
and interviews, Peterson's jeremiads never mentioned the risks of
financial speculation. This is not surprising, since he was CEO of
Lehman Brothers and later made most of his billions as chairman

of the Blackstone Group, a private equity company, one of the most lightly regulated categories of financial firms. Peterson is emblematic of a creditor class that has become increasingly dominant — hegemonic — in American fiscal politics. He is not only well-connected, but he is also charming.

The dominance of Peterson has come with the dominance of unregulated finance. Finance has grown rapidly, especially its profits, as a share of the GDP. Financiers like Peterson are averse to deficits and phobic of Social Security. First, they have a genuine, though grossly exaggerated worry that very high levels of public debt could raise interest rates and trigger higher inflation. Neither of these variables are anywhere near such a danger point. Indeed, short-term interest rates in the USA have been near zero for many years. Overall, monetary policy remains amazingly easy. Public debt has gone up with the collapse of finance. Second, a large-scale social retirement system demonstrates the government's efficiency and reliability in providing pensions and reinforces public support for government in general. Third, Social Security means fewer retirement dollars invested through the financial industry. This is especially a sticking point. About $800 billion a year flows from payroll taxes to social Security payouts. Imagine how good it would be for Wall Street if those funds were invested privately. Private pensions have been a bonanza for Wall Street. So "saving" Social Security by privatizing it has long been high on Wall Street's wish list; likewise turning Medicare into a voucher program for a similar reason. To say that both are unsustainable is to erode political support for these immensely popular programs, especially among the young.

Peterson cashed out his stake in Blackstone in 2007, on the eve of the collapse and when stocks were near their peak. He then committed more than a third of his total fortune or a billion dollars to the newly created Peter G. Peterson Foundation to promote budget austerity and reduced social insurance levels. By 2012, the foundation had already spent $458 million. David Walter was hired as the foundation's president. He is the former Head of the government's General Accounting Office (now the Government

Accountability Office), and a crusader for balanced budgets. As Vice President, Peterson hired a mainstream economist from the Urban Institute, Eugene Steuerle. Both have since departed. Now the foundation is run day to day by the benefactor's son Michael, and Peter Peterson retains the title of chairman. It is a family business with the entire board of directors being Peterson, his wife, and his son. Walker is still an adviser to the foundation. Walker is free to lobby on his own.

A former commerce secretary under Richard Nixon, Peterson is personally close to Democratic economic eminence Robert Rubin. Both have promoted the idea of a radical fiscal bargain in which Democrats agree to cut social insurance and Republicans agree to higher taxes. Peterson served as chairman of the Council of Foreign Relations, and in 2002, led the search committee that recommended Rubin protégé Timothy Geithner as president of the Federal Reserve Bank of New York. Geithner, later Obama's Treasury secretary, doubtlessly returned Peterson's phone calls. In short, Peterson is part of a tight inner circle of financial and fiscal experts.

This is not to say that Peterson does not spread his money around. He funded the influential Institute for International Economics, long headed by centrist Democrat C. Fred Bergsten. Recently, this Institute was renamed the Peterson Institute for International Economics, separate from the Peterson Foundation.

The Crusade for Fiscal Austerity

There have been three phases to the crusade for fiscal austerity. During the mid-1980s, deficits became a big public issue with the famous or notorious "supply-side" tax cuts of the first Reagan term. They failed to deliver the promised revenue increases, as most economists predicted. They reduced government income. Deficits were disguised by the huge increase in payroll taxes of 1983, which were then borrowed by the rest of government, lowering the consolidated government deficit. The Reagan deficits were worsened by a military buildup. Deficits averaged about 4% of

GDP throughout the Reagan and George H. W. Bush presidencies, increasing the debt ratio from under 30% before Reagan to over 50% at the time of the 1992 election. While there were several attempts to bring the deficit down, they all failed. By the time of the election, the rising debt and political deadlock over how to address it had already become an emblem of dysfunctional government. In early 1992, Peterson founded the Concord Coalition to lobby for a balanced budget. The coalition was substantially underwritten by Peterson.

A subsequent economic boom and President Clinton's brave anti-austerity tax increase for the richest 2% of Americans nearly put the austerity lobby out of business. In a famous deal with the chairman of the Federal Reserve, Alan Greenspan, Clinton traded smaller deficits for lower interest rates. This was remarkable, given that Greenspan was the most independent of Fed chairmen.[2] There was no logical connection, except (luckily) in Alan Greenspan's ideology. Deficits, in real time and projected were having no effect on interest rates, which were under the control of the Federal Reserve. Cutting the deficit was a political imperative for Greenspan, not an economic one. After the 1993 budget raised taxes, cut spending, and reduced the deficit, Greenspan delivered on his part of the deal. Lower interest rates led to a rebounded growth of GDP throughout the 1990s. It was an agreement only the devil could appreciate.

Faster economic growth has many benefits. Among them, the budget was balanced in 1999 and endless surpluses were forecast. The Concord Coalition took down its clock in Times Square that displayed the escalating national debt. While Peterson's book *Facing Up* had in 1993 predicted a $300 billion deficit by 2000, the actual budget was in surplus by $236 billion. Greenspan had done what Peterson and the Concord Coalition had failed to do.

Since Social Security is financed out of wage and salary income, the date of Social Security's projected shortfall was pushed back by

---

[2]For the complete story of the Clinton–Greenspan alliance, see E. Ray Canterbery, *Alan Greenspan: The Oracle Behind the Curtain* (Singapore, New Jersey, London: World Scientific, 2006), pp. 45–68.

eight years — from 2029 to 2037. High employment meant more payroll taxes coming into the Social Security trust funds. At the rate of improving solvency, Social Security would soon be in perpetual surplus. It simply took decent economic growth with fruits shared by wage earners. Budget deficit hysteria lost its credibility, and the austerity crusaders went into temporary eclipse.

A Goldilocks' outcome could not last forever. Next came some gratuitous deficits. Tax cuts and wars of the George W. Bush administration, combined then by a financial collapse on Wall Street, sent the budget moderately back into deficit in 2002. The deficit had increased to 3.3% of GDP, enough to give Peterson and company a breather.

In 2007, David Walker, still head of the Government Accountability Office (GAO), and Robert Bixby, executive director of the Concord Coalition, set out on a Fiscal Wake-Up Tour, which was underwritten by, of course, the Peterson Foundation. In 2008, the foundation paid PBS to air I.O.U.S.A., a film covering the tour. In short, the Foundation paid public TV to treat its own event as news. Walter warns in the film, "We suffer from a fiscal cancer. It is growing within us, and if we do not treat it, it could have catastrophic consequences for our country." The movie was also shown in some four hundred theaters and broadcast as part of a CNN special on the fiscal crisis that Peterson's people co-produced! The austerity lobby was back in business.

In a depressed economy, fiscal tightening creates more and deeper deficits. Worse, as the economy went into a debt deflation, the austerity lobby did not alter its message. It treated the economy's new woes as an ideological windfall, showing the urgency of deeper cuts in a now-larger deficit. The financial collapse predictably caused a sharp deterioration in the nation's fiscal picture. The Federal deficit swelled from 3.3% in fiscal year 2008 to 10.1% in 2009, then declined slightly in 2010 to 9% and to 8.7% in 2011. Of projected increases in the deficit, only about 9% is the result of deliberate federal stimulus spending.

Despite the facts, the growing deficit was seized upon by the austerity lobby as vindication of its claims. Progress on long-term deficit reduction, it was supposed, would restore business confidence and thus economic growth. They were relying on what entrepreneurs might do under expected deficit reductions, or really a confidence fairy.

Beyond the Concord Coalition

Peterson bankrolled more than simply the Concord Coalition. That Coalition now has been joined by the Committee for a Responsible Federal Budget, the Peterson–Pew Commission on Budget Reform, the Policy Center, the Moment of Truth Project, Fix the Debt, several campus initiatives, and a fiscal seminar of deficit hawks spanning think tanks from the centrist Brookings Institution to the far-right Heritage Foundation (funded by Koch Industries). They all warn of fiscal Armageddon.

Peterson also underwrites the *Fiscal Times*, a conservative publication to which *The Washington Post* outsources its coverage of budget issues. The first article in *The Fiscal Times* contended that support was growing across the political spectrum for a bipartisan fiscal commission charged with specifying mandatory budget triggers. At the end of the piece, it said: "This article was produced by the *Fiscal Times*, an independent digital news publication reporting on fiscal, budgetary, healthcare and international economics issues." There was no acknowledgment that Peterson was paying for the publication.

The money for the right thought just keeps coming from Peterson. The Foundation gave $2.45 million between 2009 and 2012 to Columbia University Teachers College to develop a curriculum friendly to ending budget deficits. Furthermore, Peterson's foundation gave a group called America's Promise Alliance a million dollars to educate young people on the fiscal crisis, which included the film I.O.U.S.A. The National Academy of Public Administration received a grant of $783,000 for developing a fiscal learning tool, budget ball, to bring fiscal awareness to college students and others. In short, Peterson is aiming at the young and impressionable. In November 2010, the Foundation launched a $6 million media campaign called "Owe No!" using television spots to educate the public about the evil consequence of running large deficits and increasing the national debt.

Spend enough money, purchase enough allies, throw enough propaganda at the wall — and some of it will stick — this seems to be the mantra of the Peterson Foundation. Well, it has worked. Most Washington opinion leaders have bought the basic story that debt is a bigger menace than another Great Depression. Money talks in Washington. They ignore the inconvenient fact that there would be no fiscal problem but for the Reagan and Bush tax cuts.

Peterson's austerity bandwagon is not without critics. Look no further than the works of Nobel laureates Paul Krugman, Joseph Stiglitz, and Robert Solow. There is also the editorial page of *The New York Times*. Further, there are the efforts of advocacy groups such as the Center on Economic and Policy Research and the Economic Policy Institute, as well as Demos, and Robert Kuttner, and other think tanks. Many mainstream economists share Krugman's skepticism that the confidence fairy will somehow restore growth if only Congress would slash the deficit. Still, the austerity story has dominated the media. Dissenters are ignored.

Ironically, Peterson Opposes Government Shutdowns

Politics sometimes makes strange bedfellows. A report, prepared by Macroeconomic Advisers for the Peter G. Peterson Foundation, examines the cost of crisis-driven fiscal policy by looking at indicators including GDP growth, the employment rate and the corporate credit spread.[3] The main findings are as follows. First, since late 2009, fiscal policy uncertainty has raised the Baa corporate bond spread by 38 basis points,[4] lowered GDP growth by 0.3 percentage points per year, and raised the unemployment rate in 2013 by 0.6 percentage points, equivalent to 900,000 lost jobs.

---

[3] Peter G. Peterson Foundation Website, "The Cost of Crisis-Driven Fiscal Policy," October 14, 2013.
[4] As noted earlier, a basis point is 0.01%.

Second, a two-week partial government shutdown would directly trim about 0.3 percentage points from 4th-quarter growth. Third, on the debt ceiling, the paper considers two scenarios. The first assumes a brief, technical default that is quickly resolved, and the second assumes an extended, two-month stalemate. In scenario one, risk aversion rises, financing costs rise, prices of risky assets fall, and the economy enters a recession. Exacerbated by the Fed's inability to lower short-term interest rates, growth only begins to rebound at the end of 2014 and the unemployment rate rises to a peak of 8.5% before starting to decline. At its peak, 2.5 million jobs would be lost. Scenario two implies a longer and deeper recession than in the first scenario, but one characterized by extreme volatility. Annualized GDP growth fluctuates rapidly between ±8% until the oscillations diminish in 2015. Unemployment rises to a peak of 8.9% bringing with it 3.1 million lost jobs, before trending down.

The paper also addresses the adverse effects of cuts in discretionary spending. Such reductions have reduced annual GDP growth by 0.7 percentage points since 2010 and raised the unemployment rate 0.8 percentage points, representing a cost of 1.2 million jobs.

Is the Peterson Foundation contradicting itself on its austerity program? The short answer is, no. The Peterson Foundation is pro-growth; it is simply confused regarding the causes of economic growth. As their paid-for study shows, the government shutdown and playing chicken with the national debt are anti-growth policies. As it turned out, the Republicans backed down on both issues, and an unemployment crisis was avoided. The Peterson Foundation might have been influential in that decision. The austerity lobby is small but has a huge multiplier effect.

Free Corporate Speech and Deregulation

The National Labor Relations Board (NLRB), released in summer 2011, a new rule requiring businesses to put an 11-by-17-inch black-and-white poster notifying employees of their rights under Federal law. Beneath the official NLRB seal and above the phrase "This is an official government poster," it informed employees that they have the right to join or not join a union, and that they cannot be coerced into doing either. As messages go, it was rather bland.

The business community was incensed. The new rule was described as yet another government intrusion that would do nothing more than "create unemployment," "weaken the economy," and cause "immediate, irreparable harm for which no adequate remedy at law exists." A firestorm of litigation was launched by a coalition of industry groups led by the U.S. Chamber of Commerce and the National Association of Manufacturers (NAM), eventually suing the agency in two Federal appellate courts. The NAM, the biggest trade group in the nation, was arguing that by forcing companies to "engage in speech they would not otherwise issue," the government was "in violation of their rights under the First Amendment." The First Amendment dictates that "Congress shall not make a law ... abridging the freedom of speech." It makes no mention of corporations, commercial transactions, or advertising, nor does it name dissidents, or anarchists, or seditious radicals of any stripe, and for a long time, justices, judges, lawyers, and jurists were more or less in agreement that the First Amendment did not protect any of those things.

Still, conservatives like William Rehnquist saw the writing on the wall. "The logical consequences of the Court's decision in this case (*Virginia Pharmacy*), a decision which elevates commercial intercourse ... to the same place as had been previously reserved for the free marketplace of ideas, are far reaching indeed," he wrote in a dissenting opinion. Thereafter, a "doctrine of commercial speech" emerged, which attempted to set down criteria under which the government can regulate commercial speech — for instance, if the regulation is "narrowly tailored" to address a "substantial" government interest — and under which companies have the right "not to divulge accurate information." These criteria and definitions have been Silly Putty in the hands of clever industry lawyers, stretched and molded over the years to fit their needs. Commercial speech has been stretched to include basically anything whatsoever that involves information — a very, very broad umbrella in today's information economy — including the act of accessing or transferring digital data.

The mother of all corporate First Amendment cases is *Citizens United,* in which the Supreme Court held in 2010 that any law constraining corporate political expenditures was a violation of companies' rights to free speech. The corporation was given the same free speech rights as the individual. Dozens of cases have crafted innovative new First Amendment defenses to parry all sorts of "government intrusions," from antitrust suits to false advertising. In the summer of 2012, the U.S. Chamber of Commerce attacked two new Securities and Exchange Commission rules mandated by the Dodd–Frank Wall Street Reform and Consumer Protection Act that required publicly traded international corporations, including Exxon and Chevron, to disclose certain information to the public such as how much they were paying host countries for extraction rights. Forcing those companies to speak, the Chamber argued, was a violation of their First Amendment-protected commercial speech. The Chamber and Business Roundtable have appealed one of those cases to the D.C. Court of Appeals, which will hear it in January 2014. Doubtless, the corporations will win the cases.

Illus. 9.2:   Corporate free speech.

Source: From the web.

The same court will also hear another case from the American Meat Institute, representing Tyson and Cargill, among other giants, which is taking a similar tack in an attempt to kill a Department of Agriculture rule mandated by consumer protection requirements in the 2002 Farm Bill. It requires meat packers to label their products indicating in which country the animal, or animals, in their meat had been born, raised, and slaughtered. Forcing companies to use those labels, the meat-packers say, is equivalent to making them engage in speech they would not otherwise issue and is therefore a violation of their First Amendment-protected commercial speech. It would only be a short step to extend this free speech right to the animals. The trend is one of First Amendment opportunism.

If the trend continues, then corporation's First Amendment-protected speech cannot reasonably be fettered by economic regulation. There will be no corporate transparency whatsoever. No way to enforce workers' rights. No way to compel companies to protect investors or shareholders. And all regulations that require corporate disclosure, including most financial regulations, will cease to exist in any meaningful way. We will descend into an era like the period from the Gilded Age to the Great Depression characterized by unchecked corporate power, untouchable monopolists, very few worker or consumer rights, rampant environmental degradation, and extreme inequality. All this for the right of a corporation, merely a legal shell, to speak as freely as a person.

We have witnessed what began during the 1970s. The Pacific Legal Foundation, the Heritage Foundation, and what later became the CATO Institute, funded by the Koch brothers, formed alliances with the U.S. Chamber of Commerce and other powerful trade groups, in an effort to push an anti-regulatory, pro-business agenda, with expanded corporate free speech rights as a key weapon. The free speech of corporations combined with the pro-business lobby is fast-forwarding the austerity agenda of deregulation.

10

Monetary Remedies

The Federal Reserve System's building is not unique in Washington DC. Architect Howard Roark of Ayn Rand's *The Fountainhead* would have designed it differently. The clean, classical exterior of white marble looks very much like the neighboring Federal buildings that went up during the New Deal era. An American eagle in white marble, perched over huge bronze doors, is the only thing pretentious or forbidding about it. The doorway leads to a lobby displaying portraits of Woodrow Wilson, the Fed's founding President, and Senator Carter Glass of Virginia, who shepherded the Federal Reserve Act through Congress in 1913. The lobby's ceiling is decorated with a plaster relief of Greek coins surrounding the goddess Cybelle, symbol of abundance and stability. Everyone, from clerks to governors, enter the Fed through the back door on the C Street side of the building.

Perhaps Howard Roark *should* have designed the Fed building, for the Federal Reserve is unique among government (really, quasi-public) agencies. Moreover, it has more power than all the others, with the occasional exception of the White House. Why do we say "quasi-public"? The 12 Federal Reserve banks that make up part of the System are owned and controlled by private commercial banks, which hold stock in the Reserve Banks as a condition of membership in the System. In truth, the Federal Reserve building is owned privately. In this sense, it could have been built by Howard Roark. The Federal Reserve maintains its independence of the Federal government with great energy and urgency. When it is convenient, the Federal Reserve considers itself government. Otherwise, it is not. The Federal Reserve enjoys its ambiguity.

Purposes and Organization of the Fed

The original purpose of the Federal Reserve was to protect the banking system from periodic liquidity crises, temporary shortages of money that led to bank failures. Through the discount window, the Fed provides short-term loans to banks that are temporarily strained, helping them through the tight spots. With one spectacular exception, the Crash of 1929 and the banking panic that closed nearly half of the banks in America, the Fed's protection was extraordinarily successful. Until the 20th century the main macroeconomic problems were bank and financial panics. The purposes of the Fed have since been broadened. Today the objectives include (1) maintaining price stability, (2) fostering a high rate of economic growth, and (3) promoting a high level of employment. By law, the Fed has specific targets. It is required to attempt to reach goals of no more than 4% unemployment and no more than 3% inflation. The specific law is the Full Employment and Balanced Growth Act of 1978,

Illus. 10.1:   The Federal Reserve Board building — Marriner S. Eccles Federal Reserve Board building.

Source: *Wikipedia*, the free encyclopedia.

also known as the Humphrey–Hawkins Act. In practice, the historical focus of the Fed has been to restrain inflation at all costs. This focus has been lost in recent years as deflation has become the central macroeconomic problem.

That the Fed has ignored its duty to prevent unemployment in favor of fighting inflation reveals an embarrassing secret. It reveals the interests and background of its members, because few, if any, governors represent ordinary workers and prevention of unemployment was not as important to them. That many represent the interests of the bankers is highlighted by their compulsive interest in the prevention of inflation, which is of great concern to bankers and to Wall Street.

The organization of the Fed is quite tidy. At the top of the System are the seven governors of the Federal Reserve Board, appointed by the President for 14-year terms and confirmed by the Senate. These seven share power with the presidents of the 12 Reserve Banks, each serving the private banks in its region, from Boston to Atlanta and Dallas to San Francisco. The Reserve Bank presidents are elected by each district's board of directors. Six of the nine directors in each case are, in turn, elected by the commercial banks, the member banks of the Federal Reserve System.

From the standpoint of the making of monetary policy, the most powerful group in the System is the Federal Open Market Committee (FOMC). In FOMC decisions, the governors have seven votes and the Reserve Bank presidents have five votes, rotated annually among the districts. Only the president of the New York Fed, more important than all the others, votes at all meetings. The New York Fed is unique since it is located next to Wall Street, the nation's financial district. As in George Orwell's *Animal Farm*, the New York Fed is more equal than the others.

The commercial banks hold stock shares in each of the twelve Federal Reserve Banks. This, however, does not give commercial bankers preferred access and influence at the Fed. The internal power relationships give the Board of Governors, appointed by Washington, more authority than the presidents of the 12 Federal Reserve Banks. Moreover, the chairman of the Board of Governors has unique authority. When a regional board of directors selects a new president, the chairman at the Fed's home office can veto the choice. Still, the perception that the private banks have undue influence remains. It is a vestige of the original arrangement. Suspicion and mystery endures.

The 12 Federal Reserve banks have considerable autonomy. They each have a large research staff of economists and publish a monthly *Review*. They also occasionally publish other pamphlets. I once served as the Assistant Office Manager for the research Department of the Federal Reserve Bank of St. Louis, under the legendary Homer Jones. Jones would meticulously rewrite each monthly *Review* after it was published. The banks have distinct points of view; the Federal Reserve Bank of St. Louis has traditionally emphasized the role of the money supply in monetary policy. This was the consequence of Homer Jones' tutelage at the feet of Milton Friedman, long a professor at the University of Chicago.

There is a mystique to central banking and indeed the confidential fraternity that economists enter into when they join the Fed staff is called "taking the veil," the expression that describes nuns entering a convent. The senior economists are sometimes referred to as "monks." Some have suggested that the institutional temperament and structure is similar to the Catholic Church. It has a pope (the chairman), a college of cardinals (the governors and bank presidents), and a curia (the senior staff). A laity is comprised of the commercial banks. If you are a naughty banker, you come to the discount window for a loan, instead of for confession. The Fed's official secrecy naturally enhances the mystique.

The powerful FOMC meets to deliberate on the money supply and interest rates 8 to 10 times a year, but its decisions are made in secrecy. Some six or eight weeks after the FOMC meetings, the Fed releases the edited minutes of the meeting. Internal reports and memos, the economic analysis behind the decisions are kept confidential for five years. No other agency of government, not even the Central Intelligence Agency, enjoys such privacy.

Conventional Monetary Policy

What does the Federal Reserve control? When economists speak of money, they mean that which can be used immediately to buy things, such as cash (coins and bills) or demand deposits in checking accounts at private banks. When they talk of the "money supply," however, it is something quite different. This is the principal monetary aggregate known as M-1; it is the sum of all currency and demand deposits held by every consumer and business in the country. This is what is also usually meant by money. But there are other monetary aggregates with varying degrees of liquidity, or convertibility into M-1. The aggregate M-2 includes M-1 plus small savings accounts and time deposits at banks, credit unions or S&L's plus whatever people have invested in money-market mutual funds. Then, M-3 includes M-2 plus large-denomination financial instruments such as $100,000 certificates of deposit that only corporations, financial institutions or wealthy investors can afford to hold. A final measure of money, known simply as L, for total liquidity includes all the financial assets that can be sold and converted into spending money — Treasury bills, commercial paper, U.S. savings bonds and a few others.

While all these M's are studied by economists like tea leaves, only M-1 can be controlled by the FOMC. To be exact, only demand deposits or about 70% of M-1 can be controlled by the FOMC. Because of the way this is done, the Federal Reserve at the same time controls interest rates. Well, they control directly one interest rate which is the benchmark for all other interest rates.

The way this is accomplished requires some explaining. The Federal Reserve System is the largest holder of U.S. government bonds, holding the bonds as assets on its balance sheets. As liabilities, it holds in reserve large quantities of the demand deposits of private member banks. The private banks operate a fractional reserve system whereby, a fixed percentage of its deposits are held as bank reserves on the balance sheets of the Federal Reserve Banks. These reserves are used to buy and sell government bonds. Thus, if the FOMC wants to increase M-1, it buys bonds. It credits the private banks reserve account for the amount of the purchase. This increase in reserves enables the banks to issue more credit. Private banks cannot be forced to make loans; so sometimes during economic recession, the FOMC is pushing on a string. If loans are made, private business investment increases, increasing the GDP.

During inflation, the FOMC is a net seller of bonds to the private banks. Checks are written for the bonds by the banks and their bank reserves are reduced. Out of less bank reserves, fewer loans are made and the money supply contracts. So too does private business investment. The contraction of credit and the money supply is pretty much guaranteed, so central banks are more effective in fighting inflation than recession. Perhaps they like doing what they do best.

How are interest rates affected? The private bank can lend its excess reserves to other banks (usually overnight). These are bank reserves in excess of those required by the Fed's reserve requirement. The rate charged for the use of such surplus funds is called the Federal funds rate. When the FOMC buys bonds and increases excess reserves in the banks, it also lowers the Federal funds rate. When the FOMC sells bonds and reduces excess reserves, it raises the Federal funds rate. When the Great Recession began in 2007, the FOMC decided to lower interest rates. The Federal funds rate was reduced by buying bonds from banks to give them more reserves. The rate eventually fell to close to 0% in the recession. Since other interest rates are related to the Federal funds rate by a mark-up, other interest rates fell as well. Rates have stayed low for several years because recovery from the Great Recession has been slow.

As luck would have it, the lower Federal funds rate seemed to have only a small effect on the economy. Low levels of private investment have persisted. This despite the fall in the prime rate (the interest rate banks charge their best corporate customers) to 3.25% — the lowest rate since the early 1950s. Other factors influence investment decisions. When these factors cause the profit outlook to look gloomy, losses are predicted for any investment; then, the interest rate, low though it may be, is irrelevant. Free money does not necessarily result in surging investment spending.

There are other monetary policy tools. If the required reserve ratio is 10%, the private banks can lend only 90% of their deposits.

This reserve ratio is set by the Board of Governors. Raising the reserve ratio would limit the ability of the banks to lend. But it is a blunt instrument and is seldom changed. The last change was made in 1992.

The discount window is used for overnight loans to private member banks. The discount rate or the interest charged the bankers generally follows the Federal funds rate, after a lag. Sometimes the discount rate is used to signal a shift in FOMC policy. It does represent the ability of the Federal Reserve banks to be lenders of last resort. The Federal Reserve can lend directly to banks that are facing bankruptcy. Whereas typical loans by the Fed to banks averaged $50 million a week between 2003 and 2005, beginning in the fall of 2008 and by the end of October 2008, the Fed had lent out over $100 billion. These loans were made at a very low discount rate. This was in reaction to the money and banking panic. The Fed was doing what it had originally been established to do.

Finally, the Federal Reserve can set margin requirements on stocks. Margin requirements force the buyer of stock to use a certain amount of cash. A buyer cannot purchase all of the stock on credit. Margin requirements have been set at 50% since 1974. Stock market bubbles could be restricted by the raising of the margin requirement. For whatever reasons, margin requirements have not been used to burst market bubbles. The Fed had an excellent chance to do so in the 2000–2002 Nasdaq bubble. It blew another chance with the housing bubble of 2005–2008.

Unconventional Monetary Policy

The persistence of the Great Recession and the absence of an expansionary fiscal policy led to several policy innovations. Thereon, began a series of non-traditional monetary policies. From November 2008 to March 2009, credit lines amounting to $7.8 *trillion* were established. Most of this was not used, but actual loans to stop the financial crisis did amount to over $2 trillion. Over the period from August 2007 to April 2010, the Fed's loans to banks were at interest rates as low as 0.01%. These rates permitted banks to make riskless investments in U.S. Treasury bonds (at rates ranging from 1% to 4%

for 2009 and 2010, netting a total estimated at $13 billion profits. This kept the banks in business without having to make risky loans to private industry.

The Fed also flooded the banking system with even more money. It was thought that the banks would be willing to make loans at lower long-term interest rates. This was done though the new tool of quantitative easing, an innovation of Ben Bernanke's making. Quantitative easing means buying various assets from banks and paying cash for them. To combat the Great Recession the Fed bought Treasury notes from banks, bank loans from banks, and so-called mortgage-backed securities from banks. Many of these mortgages were no longer being paid by the poorer homeowners. Thus, the Fed gave the banks an enormous amount of cash for worthless loans.

Of course, the Fed hoped that the banks would make loans to private business. Instead, the cash holdings of banks reached a peak of $2.1 trillion in June 2010. In November of 2010, the Fed announced a second round of quantitative easing (QE2). It would buy $600 billion of U.S. Treasury securities by the end of the second

Illus. 10.2:   Ben Bernanke official portrait.
Source: *Wikipedia*, the free encyclopedia.

quarter of 2011. These bold actions did not succeed in jump-starting the economy because investment was not stimulated. One positive result: despite rising budget deficits, long-term interest rates and the servicing costs of the national debt remained low.

Financial Regulation

The regulations created in the 1930s as part of the New Deal lasted into the 1970s. By that time, people had forgotten about the wild excesses of the financial corporations that worsened the Great Depression. The neoliberals argued that economic institutions were self-regulating. Government regulation unnecessarily tied the hands of private businesses, thus slowing economic growth. Government regulation simply prevented the self-adjusting mechanisms of the markets from working.

After 1970, one U.S. president after another, with the help of a willing Congress, reduced financial regulations. By 2007, there were no regulations left in place to stop unscrupulous and unsustainable schemes for making money. These included the large, legally passable schemes of giant firms such as Citicorp and AIG to make money in very risky and unsustainable ventures. These ventures temporarily produced very high rates of return in the financial sector and large profits. Lax regulations, however, also made the financial sector fragile and vulnerable to crisis if the economy were to falter. The economy, including a housing collapse faltered in 2007 and 2008, so the financial system crashed in 2008 and almost collapsed. It was saved by the innovations of the Federal Reserve plus some government help.

The Obama administration proposed extensive financial regulations in an attempt to curb the worst abuses of the financial firms. After a year of struggle in Congress, with many attempts to soften its regulations, the Dodd–Frank Bill was finally passed in mid-2010. The Dodd–Frank provisions include the following measures. First, it established a system of government monitoring and regulation of all financial corporations, not just the banks. The monitors decide if a corporation is getting into trouble by taking unjustified risks. If the monitors find trouble, the Federal Reserve System would then move in to demand that the firm secure more capital assets before it made more loans. Second, Dodd–Frank attempts to create a situation where no institution is ever "too-big-to-fail" by creating a structure for the "orderly liquidation" of even the largest institutions. Third, to reduce the possibility that taxpayers will have to pay for the losses of large institutions, Federal Deposit Insurance Corporation (FDIC) insurance for the creditors of large financial institutions is limited. If you lend a lot of money to a large financial institution, not all of your assets will be covered. This regulation prevents banks from lending huge amounts of money to each other, as they did before the 2008 crisis. Fourth, the bill also created a Consumer Protection Agency that forces banks and all other financial corporations to take many consumer-friendly actions. Banks would actually have to tell lenders — in plain English — their terms of every loan they took from the bank. The Consumer Protection Agency would be particularly stringent in forcing credit card companies and what are called "payday lenders" to accurately describe to their customers, in simple language, the cost and terms of borrowing. When the bill finally passed the Senate, all Democrats (except one) voted for it and all Republicans (except three) voted against it. The Republicans were the party of austerity, and corporate free speech continues to erode its powers. It remains to be seen whether this bill will reduce the dangers of runaway financial speculation in the future.

What more can be done to regulate finance? Long-term capital gains — taking place over several years — within an industrial firm have long been considered the flywheel of capitalism. Rare is the economist who suggests that long-term capital gains are undesirable. I am with the majority on the blessing of strong long-term capital gains. Quick capital gains on secondary financial instruments are of a different character; generally, the purpose of such sudden sales is to make money out of money, something accomplished in a time too brief and too indirect to produce goods and services. If we prefer lasting to fleeting capitalism, we would discourage speculative gains. Such speculation led to the · recent banking and money panic.

A long time ago Nobelist James Tobin recommended a small transactions tax on foreign exchange and stocks to dampen speculation in such markets. I endorse the Tobin tax but suggest it be substantially greater than half a percent. A transactions tax also recommends itself for other kinds of domestic financial transfers. The purpose would not be to punish manufacturers for earning profits or stockholders for unearned dividends. The 30-year bond, for example, was not designed to change hands daily. It and 10-year bonds were intended to provide funds for long-term real investment. Mortgages for financing housing is another example that comes easily to mind. Even equities were originally considered "long-term capital investments" both because perpetual corporations used them to provide finance for new factories and because households held them such a long time.[1]

A properly designed financial transactions tax would discourage speculation in securities. I recommended a transactions tax, not as a levy on productivity, which it is not, but as a penalty for pure speculation. It is intended to punish people for the misuse of money and wealth. Such a tax, sufficient to sting but not so great as to eliminate all gains, would be directed at the new leisure class of wealthholders, who have increased financial market volatility and made speculation more lucrative, moving from bonds into stocks and back again, and sometimes into derivatives.

Any person or institution buying and selling General Motors or any other stock in less than a year has either been improvident in his purchasing decision or is speculating. A transactions tax, graduating from a high percentage near term and vaporizing at the end of a two-year holding period, would discourage short-term speculation

---

[1] I first proposed a transactions tax on wealth in E. Ray Canterbery, *The Global Great Recession* (Singapore, New Jersey, London: World Scientific, 2011), pp. 306–308. In an important new book, Thomas Piketty has recommended a wealth tax on "capital" which he defines as comprised mostly of personal net worth today. See Thomas Piketty, Translation by Arthur Goldhammer, *Capital in the Twenty-first Century* (Cambridge, MA. & London, England: The Belknap Press of Harvard University Press) 2014, especially pp. 530–534. While his focus is on France, his take on the wealth distribution in the U.S. is similar to mine. For many reasons, his entire book is worth a good read.

in the stock markets. The design of the tax itself should be the subject to long-term study.

Still, as a starting point for discussion, I would recommend a transactions tax of 12% on the value of the spot purchase or sale (in the case of short-position) for all stocks held for less than 30 days. Thereafter, the transactions tax would be reduced by a half percentage point for each month that shares are continually held. The tax would be introduced gradually but would eventually apply to all stock holdings. The same tax would be applied to financial derivatives based upon stocks and bonds.

The purpose of a transactions tax penalty is not to discourage the buying and selling of securities. If speculators can gain more than 12% (after other fees) during the first holding month, they will still make a profit, though a smaller one. Moreover, the government will have additional revenue going toward deficit reduction (and reduced interest) or toward particular programs.

Because most mature in less than a year, U.S. Treasury bills are not a speculative threat. However, U.S. Treasury bonds and corporate bonds are intended to be long-term investments. Federal, state, and municipal bonds have a variety of maturities. The same 12% transactions tax could be levied on bonds maturing in one year and held for less than 30 days with a downward-sliding penalty equaling a full percentage point less every 30 days thereafter. If then bonds are held to maturity, no transactions tax would apply. For bonds maturing in two years, the 12% transactions tax would be phased out by a half percentage point every 30 days. The same kind of structure would apply to the transactions tax on bonds maturing in three or four years. Further, a tax good enough for standard financial instruments should be applied, perhaps with even greater enthusiasm, to financial derivatives based upon bonds.

After four years, we are looking at truly significant holding periods, and we do not wish to discourage individuals and institutions from buying such long-term bonds. The 12% transactions tax could be phased out at zero after holding a bond for five years, whatever its final maturity date. Thus, a bond maturing in 10 years or 30 years would be subject to no transactions tax if sold at the end of five years. A transactions tax structured to encourage the buying of long-term bonds would have a surprising benefit. By encouraging the purchase of long-term bonds, that part of the bond market would be deepened and would enjoy greater liquidity, making it less subject to sudden collapse.

Still, some will say that a transactions tax on financial debt instruments and equities will take some excitement off the markets. They justifiably indict such a tax. However, the gaming tables and slot machines will still be open for business in Las Vegas, Reno, New Orleans, Atlantic City, and even Biloxi. Leisure-class speculators lusting after fast gains or losses can enjoy them in the same manner as the working class. Of course, to the extent that a transactions tax subdues financial speculation, real returns in industry would tend to supersede the paper profits from paper.

International Financial Reform

There is also a need to reform the international financial system. For one thing, there is too much speculation in foreign exchange. This can be mitigated by the extension of the financial transactions tax to foreign exchange. It can be structured the same way as for domestic transactions. This, however, is not enough.

It is important to make Special Drawing Rights (SDRs) more important as global reserves and by giving the IMF more power over exchange rates. Many years ago, I recommended a wide gold band that moves as a delayed peg.[2] The widening of the gold bank would have required a minor modification in the IMF Articles of Agreement. At the time exchange rates were calibrated in terms of the price of gold. This has changed with nations divided between those with completely flexible exchange rates such as the U.S. and those with managed exchange rates such as China. Many exchange rates are tied to the U.S. dollar or the British pound. Today, I recommend that the exchange rate be calibrated in terms of the SDR. The

---

[2]See E. Ray Canterbery, *Economics on a New Frontier* (Belmont, CA: Wadsworth, 1968), pp. 212–216.

combination of a wide SDR band and delayed peg would be a good compromise between flexible and fixed exchange rates. The band would be 6%, a fluctuation of 3% either side of the SDR par value.

The wide SDR bank and the allowance of rates to move freely within it would have several distinct advantages: (1) There would be considerable uncertainty for potential currency speculators and thus, tend to lessen speculation based on too narrow a fluctuation. (2) Purchasers of foreign securities who did not always "cover" exchange risks under the narrower band would now be virtually compelled to enter forward exchange markets and "cover" their exchange position. This would broaden the forward exchange market in several maturities, providing a wider market for export–import covering against the risk of exchange rate fluctuations. (3) With smaller "hot money" flows from anticipated devaluation, short-term capital flows would probably be more stable. (4) Moderated short-term capital flows would eliminate one excuse for a monetary policy geared to "international considerations." (5) World liquidity needs would be lessened because balance-of-payments adjustments within a wide band would reduce the frequency of intervention and hence, the level of required international monetary reserves.

The second step would be to move to even more exchange rate flexibility under the IMF. Because exchange prices would still have upper and lower limits, there would be an "early warning system" for identifying a par value level that differed greatly from the natural market exchange rate. If the U.S. exchange rate, for example, had to be supported near the lower end of its 6% range (losing foreign exchange reserves) for several months, that necessity would be a signal for reducing — not devaluing — the par value of the dollar in terms of SDRs. The SDR band would be lowered with the old lower limit as the new par value. The announcement of the new band would come several weeks after its adoption in order to deter speculators. Because the exchange rate can be pegged until the economy catches its breath, this delayed peg would allow for some domestic adjustments. This new parity would be precisely supported to give those traders not covered against exchange risks an opportunity to scurry for cover in the forward exchange markets. Moreover, the maintenance of this level for an indefinite period plus a slow rate of depreciation would further deter heavy speculation in the appreciating currency. In order to prevent the lower limit from becoming a "fixed-for-all-times" rate, the IMF would be empowered to alter currency par values under a semi-automatic market rule. This new role for the IMF would insulate exchange rate adjustments from political stress. Nations would have already agreed to the IMF rules.

The objections voiced by opponents to more flexible exchange rates are clearly modified under the delayed peg. But would uncertainty about rates still disrupt trade and capital flows? Quite the opposite would be true. The forward markets which cover against exchange risks would be even more viable than they are today. The necessity of trade covering would generate heavier markets in very long maturities, so that every reasonable exchange risk could be offset.[3]

The adoption of a wide SDR bank with a delayed peg can be briefly summarized.

(1) The implementation of 6% SDR bank would cause short-term capital flows to stabilize. This width would be sufficient for substantial adjustments in trade accounts.

(2) When, and if, the exchange rate of any nation rises or falls toward the new exchange rate limits for a prolonged period of reserve losses, the band can be moved with the new par value centered on the violated limit.

(3) The new par value would be sustained for an indefinite period. Speculators could not be certain whether the rate would then appreciate or depreciate.

(4) Under the delayed peg and wide SDR band, monetary policy would be free to perform its domestic duties. At the same time

---

[3]Short-term capital flows are self-limiting when exchange rates are sufficiently flexible. With forward covering, interest-rate parity occurs and the cost of covering rises to equal the interest-rate differential. For theory that explains the consequences for speculation, see E. Ray Canterbery, "A Theory of Foreign-Exchange Speculation Under Alternative Systems," *Journal of Political Economy*, May–June 1971. Among systems explained is the wide band with a delayed peg.

the delayed peg could be used to stimulate exports during an economic recession without the use of monetary policy.

(5) The timing and moving the peg would be determined by the IMF. Rules for such changes should, however, be made explicit, but sufficiently vague in actual implementation to fool most speculators.

The advantages to the adoption of this reform plan are several and can be briefly summarized.

(1) The powers of the IMF would be enhanced as well as the role of the SDR in international finance.
(2) Fixed exchange regimes would be relics of the past.
(3) The role of the IMF would be strengthened in the global community.
(4) The old Triffin dilemma of the reserve-currency nation whereby deficits are required to supply foreign exchange but the accumulation of reserves abroad threatens devaluation would be ended.
(5) Currency wars could be avoided.
(6) Small nations such as Greece would be freed to follow expansionary fiscal and monetary policies.

China's currency was overvalued by about 40% against the dollar in the fall of 2010. The yuan, the Chinese currency, is presently tied to the dollar. Under a wide SDR band with a delayed peg, the yuan could be brought down gently, thereby stimulating U.S. exports and dampening U.S. imports from China. China is a problem because it holds a substantial volume of U.S. dollars as official foreign currency reserves. A fall in the value of the dollar might lead to a shift by the Chinese into Japanese yen or even South Koran won.

The ultimate goal would be to eventually move to a world currency in which the SDR served such a role. The wide gold band system tied to the SDR would be a way of strengthening the role of the SDR in the world system, especially since more reserves would have to be held in SDRs. The common interest of all nations in one financial system might even be a force promoting world peace. It would shift the current focus of the IMF away from austerity programs in such nations as Greece, Spain, and Portugal.

Janet Yellen: Good News for the Unemployed

Janet Yellen's *vita* was so strong that she could not be turned down by the Senate, and was easily confirmed as the first women to head the Federal Reserve System. She began her career with groundbreaking research about things like how lower wages can lead to higher unemployment, contrary to classical microeconomics. She taught at the University of California, Berkeley, ran the President's Council of Economic Advisers and steered the Fed's San Francisco bank successfully through the subprime crisis, about which she raised concerns as early as 2005. "She's an economist of great intellect, with a strong ability to forge consensus," says Nobel laureate Joseph Stiglitz. Stiglitz says further that she was one of

Illus. 10.3:   Janet Yellen official portrait, Federal Reserve Board of Governors.
Source: *Wikipedia*, the free encyclopedia.

his brightest students when he taught at Yale. She has a keen understanding of financial markets and their imperfections and has a strong belief that human suffering was more related to unemployment than anything else.

Some worry that she will ignore inflation at the nation's peril. With wages still relatively flat and the unemployment rate above 6%, wage and price inflation appear remote. Deflation is more likely a matter of concern. Either way, whether the choice is inflation or unemployment, she will have to walk a fine line on timing the taper — the plan to slowly wean markets of the stimulus Yellen helped design. It must be steady enough to deflate bubbles and bring markets back down to earth but not so quick that it creates another credit crunch. History is on her side. Periods of asset-buying need not be painful, as long as the central bank effectively and clearly communicates its goals — something Yellen is especially good at.

While much of Yellen's tenure is likely to be dominated by managing tapering, she will also have a unique opportunity to shape post-crisis efforts to regulate the financial industry and rebalance the relationship between finance and the economy. While her priority will be making sure that the Dodd–Frank banking reforms are properly implemented, she's already indicated her support for new ideas like cutting the interest rates that banks are paid to park spare cash with the Fed, boosting margin requirements on riskier derivatives trades and requiring big banks to hold more capital. During her November 2013 hearing, Yellen addressed the too-big-to-fail issue: it "has to be among the most important goals of the post-crisis period."

Unlike Greenspan, and (to a lesser extent) Benanke before her, she is not going to buy the finance industry's argument that it should be left alone to regulate itself. Princeton Professor Alan Blinder, who was the Fed Vice Chair in the 1990s, remembers speaking many times with Yellen "about how the Fed was being too lax on regulation of finance. And since then," says Blinder, "it's only gotten worse." First on her agenda, however, is getting the unemployment rate below 6%, stabilizing markets and making sure the recovery is more inclusive and robust. Generally, she is expected to be a friend of labor while being wary of Wall Street. The austerity lobby has every reason to fear her policies.

Conclusion

For the past two decades, monetary policy has been the only macroeconomic policy available. Under the chairmanship of Ben Benanke, conventional and unconventional monetary policy was deployed in a way that prevented the Great Recession from becoming a second Great Depression. Still, there is the need to once again free fiscal policy for stabilization purposes as well as developing an incomes policy. To these matters, we next turn. While Janet Yellen has a goal of pushing unemployment below 6%, getting to full employment (4%) will require more than traditional monetary policy.

11

Fiscal Remedies

For if effective demand is deficient, not only is the public scandal of wasted resources intolerable, but the individual enterpriser who seeks to bring these resources into action is operating with the odds loaded against him.

> — John Maynard Keynes, *The General Theory of Employment Interest and Money* (New York: Harcourt, Brace and Company, 1936), p. 329

The debate between the stimulus view and the austerity view becomes very clear when we turn to fiscal policy. John Maynard Keynes and his *General Theory* are the most famous proponents of the stimulus perspective. Keynes says that government must stimulate the whole economy by giving millions of public jobs to people in fields like teaching, nursing, engineering, and construction work. This can be done indirectly by government deficit spending or by tax reduction. Beyond the initial stimulus, each of those hired will spend new income and this leads to the hiring of many more. There is a Keynesian multiplier effect.

The austerity view holds that there is too much government intervention in the economy. Specifically, there is too much government employment. The government is said to use resources inefficiently. Reducing taxes and the size of the government will unleash incentives in the private economy. Reduced government spending will permit the private sector to run most of the economy, even in areas traditionally thought of as the purview of the public sector (schools and prisons, for instance). While the austerians are radicals in their thinking, it is fair to say that there are political limitations on using government spending to stimulate the economy. We will recognize this when it comes to the Obama stimulus of 2009.

The austerians argue that government spending always does more harm than good. As to fiscal policy, the argument is somewhat sophisticated. They say that government spending "crowds out" private investment. It is said to work this way. Budget deficits lead to higher long-term interest rates. The higher interest rates raise the cost of borrowing for private business investment. Private business investment is "crowded out" by the government spending. Actually that does not sound all that sophisticated.

The presidential campaign of 2012, illustrates the debate between the stimulus view and the austerity view. The Republican candidate, Governor Mitt Romney, argued that those Republican governors who cut public-sector jobs were perfectly correct in doing so. Cutting government jobs, such as teaching positions, would reduce the size of government. The austerity policy of lower government spending would free private business to invest and expand the economy. Romney also endorsed the budget plan of Congressman Paul Ryan (R. Wisconsin), which drastically cut all civilian government spending, including infrastructure, which happened to be crumbling. Infrastructure includes roads and bridges, airports and harbors. Romney chose Representative Ryan as his running mate for Vice President. Romney was very popular for his plan of immodest austerity, no matter what people thought of other Republican proposals. In almost every poll, most people say they support less government spending, not more.

Barack Obama, on the other hand, argued that the government should stimulate the economy through jobs for millions of teachers, nurses, firefighters, and police. The Democratic candidate pointed out that 630,000 jobs in these categories had been lost by the states since the beginning of the Great Recession. If the Federal government gave enough money to the states to hire back all of these highly productive workers, the rehired workers would have more money to spend on food, clothing, and shelter, as the whole economy is stimulated. There is an employment multiplier.

Illus. 11.1:   Oval Office, White House.

Obama also made the case for infrastructure spending. This would lead to the hiring of hundreds of thousands of construction workers to build bridges and roads. They too would spend their money and stimulate the private sector. Those roads and bridges would be built through the use of private contractors getting government money, so there would be a direct stimulus of the private sector.

The Tools of Conventional Fiscal Policy

Fiscal policy begins with net government spending, spending more than tax revenues. The spending includes that for goods and services, but also for transfer payments from governments to individuals or businesses. Purchases of goods and services increases aggregate demand. Also, if $1 billion is spent in transfer payments in the way of unemployment compensation, this newly created income is soon spent, adding indirectly to aggregate demand.

Illus. 11.2:   Budget policies.

How is spending financed? There are two ways — taxation and by bond issuance. If government spending exceeds current tax revenue, a budget deficit is incurred. The budget deficit can be financed by the issuance of government bonds, mostly long-term bonds. In turn, interest on the bonds add to the deficits. Hence, lower interest rates are beneficial in the conduct of fiscal policy. (There is a small amount of government revenue from government enterprises such as the Tennessee Valley Authority.) If revenue exceeds spending, there is a fiscal surplus. The national debt, or accumulated deficits, are *reduced* by government surpluses.

The use of tax cuts to stimulate the economy is only slightly more complex. Since some income is saved, every dollar of a tax cut does not lead to spending of an equal amount. The extra spending amount depends on the marginal propensity to consume (MPC), that is, the share of extra income that is spent. The MPC varies across the income distribution, falling as income rises. We have a mildly progressive income tax structure in which tax rates rise with income. The reasoning is that higher income at the margin goes to satisfy less urgent needs and wants. The pain for taxation at the upper income levels is less than at lower income levels. This progressiveness provides some automatic stabilization for the economy. As incomes fall, so do tax revenues, more so for the rich than for the poor. And vice-versa. When the economy is expanding, tax revenues rise more than in proportion to the rise in incomes. This automatically dampens the expansion of the economy. Politically, tax cuts are easy to implement; tax increases seldom happen. This makes tax policy lopsided for the business cycle.

We should reserve three cheers for the rich in one respect. Most government bonds are held by the very rich or by institutions; it is about 50:50. Thus, the rich are the lenders to the government and help to finance budget deficits. At the same time this has created a bondholding class with substantial power over public policy, far more than in proportion to its small population.[1]

The government can do what the public is forbidden to do; it can print money. Thus, when the government runs deficits, it writes checks at the Treasury for the amount of the bonds purchased. The fiscal power of the government is virtually unlimited. It is constrained only by the willingness of the public, corporations, banks, and the Federal Reserve to hold government bonds. In this way, the budget habits of the government can vary from that of the household. Austerians try to draw an analogy between the private household and the U.S. Treasury, but the world does not work that way. Still, from about 1800 to 1945, the dominant classical view that maintained that fiscal policy was not needed for a market-based economy prevailed. No fiscal policy tools were required.

The Keynesians came into view during the 1950s and 1960s. The Keynesian use of fiscal tools was taught in almost every classroom and influenced most governments in the U.S. and Europe as well as much of Asia. When there is unemployment, governments should stimulate the economy by increasing government spending and reducing taxes became the mantra. During economic booms with inflation, government should shift into reverse and reduce spending and raise taxes to lower aggregate demand. American and European governments were all influenced by the Keynesian fiscal proposals.

The consequence of Maynard Keynes combined with other forces has been very low levels of British unemployment during the

---

[1] For much more on the bondholding class, and how it influences public policy, see E. Ray Canterbery, *Wall Street Capitalism: The Theory of the Bondholding Class* (Singapore, New Jersey, London: World Scientific, 2000).

post-World War II years up to Thatcherism. In the U.S., this new ethic led to the Employment Act of 1946, which committed the Federal government to follow policies that would provide employment opportunities for those able, willing and seeking work. Keynesian economic policies were vigorously pursued by the Truman administration, then a modified Keynesian program was perhaps most successfully followed by the Kennedy and Johnson administrations prior to the escalation of the Vietnam War in 1968.[2]

Keynes did not write the *General Theory* in order to solve puzzles about hypothetical conditions but out of an urgent concern that governments would fail to end the massive unemployment and deprivation of the 1920s and 1930s in Britain and of the 1930s in the U.S. After the Vietnam War, U.S. economists shifted their focus to the "equilibrium" tendencies used by Keynes as academic argument, thus obscuring his stress on uncertainty of the future on economic fluctuations. If we rush unthinkingly into the arms of equilibria every chance we get, we are simply substituting a mechanical analogy for history. At equilibrium nothing can be done — because we are already there. This is exactly the way the neoliberals and the austerians wanted it. They have prevailed since sometime during the 1970s. The conventional wisdom became — it was best to meet any recession or unemployment not with government spending but with cuts to government spending. Along with these cuts came the elimination of government regulations.

There was an attempt to revive Keynesian economics during the Great Recession. When President Barack Obama took office in January 2009, the economy was in a shambles. More than 700,000 were losing their jobs every month, millions of houses were sliding towards foreclosure, and the largest industrial corporations were threatened with bankruptcy, as were the largest banks. There was a

---

[2]For Keynes and Truman, see E. Ray Canterbery, *Harry S. Truman: The Economics of a Populist President* (Singapore, New Jersey, London: World Scientific, 2014). For the details of Keynesian policy as applied theory during the Kennedy years, see E. Ray Canterbery, *Economics on a New Frontier* (Belmont, California: Wadsworth Publishing Co. 1968).

gap between actual aggregate demand and potential output of $1.2 trillion. Obama proposed that the economy should be stimulated by government projects, increased transfer payments, and tax cuts. In February of 2009, Congress passed the American Recovery and Reinvestment Act, the largest stimulus bill ever. The Congressional Budget Office found that between the time that law was passed and the end of 2011, the total spending increases and revenue reductions resulting from the bill had been $739 billion. This fell short of the $1.2 trillion needed to fill the demand gap. Conservative Democrats and Republicans prevented the bill from being any larger. As it was, all Republican senators except three voted "no" on the stimulus act. The spending bill should have been 60% more than the legislated amount.

In any case, of the $739 billion, only $224 billion in government purchases directly filled part of the $1.2 trillion spending gap. The tax cuts and transfer payment increases cushioned the falls in consumption, but did not have as great a multiplier or stimulus effect. Still, the Recovery Act was a traditional Keynesian attempt to counter a dramatic fall in aggregate demand and rise in unemployment. It was in the right direction but of insufficient magnitude, especially on the spending side.

These Keynesian policies went global. Nations around the world adopted comparable though mostly less ambitious fiscal stimulus policies. The European Economic Recovery Plan, adopted in the fall of 2008, provided some 20 billion euros to a variety of projects; nations such as Germany and France followed with their own smaller stimulus plans. Japan initially planned a massive stimulus package, but the government ultimately instituted a much more modest mix of tax cuts and new spending measures. China's more ambitious plan totaled US$586 billion, the bulk of which went to public works, rail lines, roads, irrigation, and airports. Smaller economies such as South Korea and Australia also initiated Keynesian policies.

These orthodox Keynesian policies did much to slow the global decline. The deficits led to growing debt relative to GDPs: This problem was postponed until recovery set in, also a Keynesian strategy. The U.S. issued more Treasury bills and bonds, most of which were bought by the Federal Reserve and added massively to the Fed's assets. The policies did not work perfectly. For example, the tax cuts and tax rebates led to increased savings in 2008 and 2009. Consumers spent only 25 cents or 30 cents on every dollar they received from the government; the balance was used to repair balance sheets.

Unconventional Fiscal Policies

Other policies were ground in the mill of conventionality. Among unconventional policies is the use of guarantees of other people's money. This is a kind of fiscal policy because the guarantees often end up costing taxpayers money. A typical guarantee is that the government will protect money that people have deposited in a bank from a run. During the Great Depression the U.S. adopted deposit insurance through the Federal Deposit Insurance Corporation (FDIC). The FDIC normally does not depend on taxpayer dollars; it assesses fees on the commercial banks. Also, the Federal Savings and Loan Insurance Corporation (FSLIC), was founded in 1934 to protect deposits and savings and loans institutions.

These bank deposit guarantees became an issue in 2008. The FDIC had been insuring deposits up to $100,000. (Similar insurance existed in other countries, though the ceiling varied by country.) In the U.S. alone, some 40% of deposits remained uninsured, a problem underscored by the bank runs on Countrywide, IndyMac, and Washington Mutual. The threat of still more runs triggered a round of new government guarantees. In September 2008, Ireland had to increase its deposit insurance to €100,000, then fully guarantee all the deposits of its six largest banks. In the U.S., the FDIC raised the ceiling for insured bank deposits to $250,000. A few days later Germany guaranteed all of its private bank accounts; the next day Sweden extended insurance to all deposits to the sum of 500,000 krona (about US$75,000). Then, a week later Italy announced that none of its banks would be allowed to fail and that no depositor would suffer any loss. The next month Switzerland increased its ceiling on deposit insurance. The European Union guaranteed its banks' bonded debt in October 2008. The same month the FDIC guaranteed the principal and interest payments on debt issued by banks and bank holding companies up to a total of $1.5 trillion. Other countries followed with similar deposit and debt guarantees.

Ultimately it is the taxpayer that makes these guarantees good. This is highlighted by the FDIC funds dipping into negative territory in the third quarter of 2009. The taxpayer would need to shoulder part of the burden in the form of an FDIC bailout, much as it did in the wake of the savings and loan crisis.

Another kind of unconventional fiscal policy is the bailout. The big bailouts of the Great recession in the U.S. began with Fannie Mac and Freddie Mac in September 2008. When the two mortgage giants came under government conservatorship, the Bush Treasury pledged $400 billion to underwrite the takeover. This made explicit the Federal government's guarantee of their debt. The Treasury is on the line to cover some $5 trillion worth of obligations insured by the the two institutions, along with another $1.5 trillion worth of debt that they issued. If housing prices continue to fall and many more mortgages go into foreclosure, the Treasury could end up sustaining considerable losses. Prior to the Fannie and Freddie bailout, the Housing and Economic recovery Act of July 2008 pledged some $320 billion to help struggling homeowners refinance into mortgages that were insured by the Federal housing Administration.

This was part of a cluster of bailouts and guarantees funded by the Troubled Assets Relief Program (TARP). As noted earlier, the legislation initially allocated $700 billion to purchase toxic assets. The money has been used to prop up banks and the automakers General Motors and Chrysler and their financial arms, GMAC and Chrysler Financial. This auto bailout amounted to $80 billion. This was just the beginning, as a sizable share of the TARP funds — some $340 billion — was given at nearly 700 different financial institutions, including giants like Citigroup, Bank of America, JPMorgan Chase, Goldman Sachs, and AIG, as well as a host of smaller banks. Most of the funds comprised capital injections, from which the government purchased preferred shares in the institutions. Besides a steady dividend payment, these shares provided a partial ownership stake in the companies. This marked a radical departure for fiscal policy; American taxpayers became owners of large swaths of the financial system, not to mention the automotive industry.

The government formed a kind of insurance partnership with two giant ailing banks. The Treasury guaranteed several hundred billion dollars' worth of impaired assets held by Bank of America and Citigroup. The pool of troubled assets totaled $118 billion in Bank of America's case, with a "deductible" of $10 billion. This kind of partnership was adopted widely in the U.K.

All of these measures combined managed to stabilize the global financial system. In turn, they helped to prevent (along with a super-easy monetary policy) the Great Recession from becoming another Great Depression at a time when aggregate demand was in free fall.

Keynes originally intended to save capitalism from its worst offenses and weaknesses. He never intended for the government to attain ownership of corporations. Moreover, he never envisaged the use of government funds to bailout entire industries such as the financial system and the auto industry. All these policies were courageous and unconventional. TARP itself was an excursion into unexplored waters.

12

Incomes Policy Remedies

K eynes, writes John Kenneth Galbraith, was long held suspect by his colleagues because of the clarity of his writing. But "in *The General Theory* ... [he] redeemed his academic reputation. It is a work of profound obscurity, badly written and prematurely published."[1] Perhaps fog is to be expected when one sails into uncharted waters. Keynes struggled to avoid comparison of the *General Theory* with his earlier literary efforts such as *The Economic Consequences of the Peace*. In the struggle, Keynes succeeded all too well, and Keynes's classic beget a host of interpretations.

Several loosely chartered schools of "Keynesians" can be discerned in the mists. These include the neo-Keynesians and the more diverse Post Keynesians. The neo-Keynesians have an orthodox following whereas the Post Keynesians are considered left and radical. There nonetheless is some overlap in their policy recommendations. The Post Keynesians are the founders of incomes policy, so we will mostly be interested in their thinking. To clarify, the conventional fiscal policy that we discussed in the previous chapter is a product of the fiscal Keynesians.

The Post Keynesians

It often takes adversity to bring diverse strands of economic thought together or, even to bring diverse people together. In the opening

---

[1]John Kenneth Galbraith, *Money: Whence It Came, Where It Went* (Boston: Houghton Mifflin, 1975), pp. 217–218.

scene of George Bernard Shaw's *Pygmalion* (later a musical, *My Fair Lady*), sundry people are brought together by the common necessity of protecting themselves from a sudden downpour. There we encounter the impoverished middle-class Clara Eynsford-Hill, with her genteel pretensions and disdain; a wealthy-Indian gentleman (Colonel Pickering), who seems tolerant enough, an egotistical professor of phonetics (Henry Higgins), who seems exceptionally intolerant; and a pushy, notably rude flower girl (Eliza Doolittle) from the lower class, embodying the essence of vulgarity. These characters never would have been found together except for something like a sudden rain shower.

The same could be said for the diverse Post Keynesians. A number of economists sympathetic to Keynes but also to Keynesianism have long disparaged the vulgarization of the great man's theories and the zealous monetarism that thereby arose. This dissenter movement spent several decades in the economic catacombs. The "sudden rain shower" that brought together diversity extending across oceans and continents was simultaneous high inflation and high unemployment of the 1970s. This stagflation caused a widespread crisis of faith among "orthodox" neo-Keynesians, those Keynesians classed as "vulgar" by the Post Keynesians.

Post Keynesians have flourished not only in America but also in Cambridge (England) and in Italy.[2] On both sides of the ocean they have returned to the classicals' concern with the income distribution. The Americans, however, have focused more on a monetary economy and the Europeans more on a classical real economy.[3]

---

[2] Two periodicals devoted to Post Keynesian economics, the *Cambridge Journal of Economics* in England and the *Journal of Post Keynesian Economics* in the United States, bear witness to these developments. The founding co-editors of the latter were Paul Davidson and the late Sidney Weintraub of the University of Pennsylvania. John Kenneth Galbraith, one of the founding patrons of the *JPKE*, was chairman of the honorary board of directors. The late Joan Robinson and Lord Nicholas Kaldor were among the founding patrons of the *Cambridge Journal*. The Italian Post Keynesians publish in both journals.

[3] Much of this discussion of Post Keynesians follows E. Ray Canterbery, *A Brief History of Economics* (Singapore, New Jersey, London: World Scientific, 2011), pp. 250–261.

By their works ye shall know them. The Post Keynesians have done at least the following things that distinguish them from the hyphenated Keynesians.

(1) They have extended Keynes's doctrine by demonstrating how income distribution helps to determine national income and growth over time.
(2) They have combined the notion of imperfect competition with classical pricing theory to explain simultaneous stagnation and inflation (stagflation).
(3) They have used these two concepts — income distribution theory and price markup theory — to forge a new incomes policy.
(4) They have conducted a revival of Keynes's ideas on uncertainty, specifically in regard to liquidity preference and business investment, and they have also resurrected Keynes's notion that money is primarily created by the banking system's inside money. As a result, they have redefined what monetary policy can and cannot do.

The Income Distribution

With regard to income classes, John Maynard Keynes seemed to be of two minds: His *General Theory* showed how great income and wealth inequalities led to dysfunctional capitalism, whereas his personal comfort was found within his own upper class and the ruling elite. This, even though George Bernard Shaw — converted to Fabian socialism by reading Marx — was only down the street, so to speak, from Keynes and the Bloomsbury group. Clara Eynsford-Hill, one of Shaw's characters and superficially without a trace of vulgarity, nonetheless represents aspects of the middle class (bourgeoisie) which Shaw and Eliza Doolittle reject — that is, Clara is disdainful of people whom she considers beneath her. Keynes too disdained the bourgeois workers surrounding Queen Victoria, but they were beneath *him*.

In his concluding notes in the *General Theory*, Keynes had the British opposing the further removal of great disparities of wealth and income for the mistaken belief that a great proportion of the growth of capital is "dependent on the savings of the rich out of their superfluity."[4] As his theory shows, "the growth of capital depends not at all on a low propensity to consume but is, in the contrary, held back by it." Indeed, he proceeds to the conclusion that "in contemporary conditions the growth of wealth, so far from being dependent on the abstinence of the rich, as it commonly supposed, is more likely to be impeded by it. One of the chief social justifications of great inequality of wealth is, therefore, removed."[5]

Unemployment is caused by great wealth and income inequalities; this, an economist could easily surmise, is the central idea of the *General Theory*. After all, investment determines saving, not the other way round. Just when the progressive economist is about to proclaim, "by George, I think he's got it," however, Keynes undoes him; he reopens the closet door to conservatism. "I believe that there is social and psychological justification for significant inequalities of income and wealth, but not for such large disparities as exist today."[6] To the conservative, "large disparities" exist only in the dream world of the liberal.

It is not then simply a matter of "Why can't the Keynesians be more like Keynes?" There remains the question: Why wasn't Keynes more like a Post Keynesian? Once again, the shorter our answer, the better. Keynes had the Great Depression on his mind; there was precious little time for pursuing every avenue opened by his *General Theory*. Keynes's ultimately conservative mission was to save capitalism by relying on the intellectual elite in Britain to implement his social program. Besides, class consciousness was not one of Keynes's traits. In an attack on *Das Kapital*, Keynes wrote, "How can I adopt a creed [Marxism] which, preferring the mud to the fish, exalts the boorish proletariat above the bourgeoisie and the intelligentsia, who with all their faults, are the quality of life and surely carry the

---

[4]John Maynard Keynes, *The General Theory of Employment Interest and Money* (New York: Harcourt, Brace & World, 1965), p. 372.

[5]*Ibid.*, p. 373.

[6]*Ibid.*, p. 374.

seeds of all human achievement?"[7] There is no contradiction: Keynes relied on the elite — especially the intellectual elite in Britain — to implement his social program. Eliza Doolittle and the income distribution were left to the Post Keynesians to ponder.

Sraffa's Attempted Purge of Marginalism

The Cambridge, England Post Keynesians for sure have attempted to overthrow the marginalist explanation for income distributions. For this, they begin with a critique of marginalism that reaches back to the ideas of David Ricardo.

The classical system of fixed input proportions was swept away by the marginalists. In classical production in which equal amounts of, say, labor are always combined with a unit of capital, the marginal product of capital is not simply invisible — it is not there! The real wage cannot be decided by the marginal physical product of labor or the extra units of output from each additional worker. The theory of value or price of the marginalists vanishes with the margin.

Piero Sraffa (1898–1983), Keynes's pupil, was a brilliant and lovable Italian economist who much preferred leisure to publishing. He managed to edit the many volumes of David Ricardo works during a few minutes or a few hours of daily effort only because he lived so long. Moreover, he finally published in 1960 a slim volume he had *written in the 1920s,* an enigmatic book with a curious title, *Production of Commodities by Means of Commodities: Prelude to a Critique of Economic Theory,* putting Ricardo in modern dress while providing a devastating critique of marginalism.

Capital goods, contends Sraffa, are diverse, and any measure of the "quantities" of capital in terms of a common denominator (such as another good or money) will vary as the prices of the machines themselves vary. And these prices will fluctuate with wage and profit rates. Therefore, the value of capital (its price times its quantity) is not decided by capital's marginal product, nor is the income distribution decided by the markets for land, labor, and capital.

---

[7] Quoted in Charles Hession, *John Maynard Keynes* (New York: Macmillan, 1984), p. 224.

This book was physicality produced, for example, using three machines: a computer, a printing press, and a binder. The money values of capital, however, depend on the price times quantity of all these capital goods (and others) combined. The computer, the press, and the binder all sell at varying prices. Profits can no longer be a return on capital for these prices, or the "rentals" for the services from these capital goods, which themselves depend on the distribution of income between workers and capitalists.

The reincarnation of Ricardo is not as remarkable as the interpretation. No economic explanation for the income distribution emerges, and that is its central message. Wages and profits are social and political matters. Like John Stuart Mill, Sraffa thus separates issues of production and economic efficiency from income distribution concerns. Sharing of income among classes is determined not by the impersonal forces of the economy but by class struggle, administered wages, and relative bargaining power. The vita theory, presented in Chapter 13, is an income distribution theory aimed at filling the gap left by Sraffa (and Kalecki, below).

Kalecki's Income Classes

Another contributor to Cambridge Post Keynesianism was the Marxist economist Michal Kalecki (1899–1970). While at Cambridge in 1935 in self-imposed exile from Poland, Kalecki was befriended by John Kenneth Galbraith. "A small, often irritable, independent, intense man," Galbraith relates, "Kalecki was the most innovative figure in economics I have known, not excluding Keynes."[8] Like Sraffa, Kalecki seldom put pen to paper. But when he did, the clarity and depth of his thoughts were powerful.

In 1933, Kalecki had developed a Keynes-style theory of the level of employment, prior to and independent of Keynes's *General Theory*. Kalecki's income distribution views, however, were more in tune with the Ricardian and Marxian chorus about income classes.

---

[8]John Kenneth Galbraith, *A Life in Our Times: Memoirs* (Boston: Houghton Mifflin, 1981), p. 75.

In fact, Kalecki's theory can be summed up in the adage, "The workers spend what they get; the capitalists get what they spend." It would have made a marvelous line for one of George Bernard Shaw's plays.

The national income or product can be measured from either the income side or the expenditures side, so:

Income

> Profits (capitalists' income) + wages (workers' income)
> = National Income.

Expenditures

> Investment + capitalists' consumption
> + workers' consumption = National Product.

In this scheme, all workers' wages are spent entirely on necessary goods, so wages must equal the workers' expenditures on consumption goods — the food, shelter, clothing, and transportation required for life and for work. (In reality, of course, today's workers spend income on some goods and services that are not strictly necessities, but Kalecki is using Marx's and Mill's notion of cultural subsistence.) Sraffa's system reveals the inputs necessary to produce particular outputs; Kalecki's defines the amounts of necessary consumption goods. Together, they comprise the necessary economy.[9]

If we further simplify by saying that all profits are diligently plowed back into business to purchase new investment goods, savings as well as investments are equal to profits. The capitalist is the lone saver in this simple economy.

The first surprise? Capitalists can add to their current share of the national income (profits) by having increased their investment

---

[9]The author has created this bridge in E. Ray Canterbery, "Galbraith, Sraffa, Kalecki and Supra-Surplus Capitalism," *Journal of Post Keynesian Economics* 7 (Fall 1984), pp. 77–90. This article contains more detail on how the ideas of Galbraith, Sraffa, and Kalecki can be synthesized. See also Canterbery, "A Theory of Supra-Surplus Capitalism," Presidential address, *Eastern Economic Journal* (Winter 1988).

spending in a prior period. Investment, Keynes-like is multiplied in terms of total output. Out of a larger output come greater profits.

More shockingly, even if the capitalists consume their profits in the style of the savings and loan executives of the 1980s — buying yachts, building vacation homes, supporting lovers — they experience no decrease in profits income. Capitalists' income is not vulnerable to how it is spent because increases in the purchase of goods lead to higher levels of production. Capitalist profits are like the water of the artesian well: No matter how much water is taken out, the well never empties.

The accumulation of capital is both the rainbow and the pot of gold! If a greater share of national output is devoted to investment goods, the level of employment in the investment sector will be greater and (since investment equals profits) a greater share of the national income will go to the capitalists. Conversely, if a greater share of output is devoted to consumer necessities, the workers snatch a larger piece of the national income pie.

Although the capitalists are masters of their own universe in this sense, Kalecki saw outside elements, such as uncertainties regarding profitable investments, causing unavoidable fluctuations in profits.

The Price Markup

The struggle between the working and capitalist classes shapes not only the income distribution but also classical-style pricing. In turn, the combination of these forces provides one explanation for stagflation — that dreaded combo of stagnation and inflation.

Kalecki was very much into the world of imperfect competition in which production was a business of only a few firms in each industry or oligopoly. A firm can raise its own price right along with its production costs if other firms in the industry do likewise. When General Motors signs a union contract with United Auto Workers of America for higher wages, the corporation also raises prices more or less in proportion to the wage hike. Chrysler and Ford and the others then follow suit.

The "degree of monopoly" was the outcome not only of industrial concentration but also of tacit agreements, selling agents and advertising. In one of his last published papers, Kalecki explained how high markups (of price over costs) would encourage strong trade unions to bargain for higher wages, since oligopolistic firms had the ability to pay them. There is a wee bit of Galbraith in that paper.

The introduction of imperfect competition into macroeconomic theory is due not only to Kalecki, John Kenneth Galbraith, and Joan Robinson, but also to Sidney Weintraub (1914–1983) at the University of Pennsylvania. Kalecki's and Weintraub's vision of pricing in the manufacturing sector can be dramatized in Kalecki's cryptic style — markup.[10]

An example will clarify the role of the markup. If the wage cost per personal computer is $700 and the markup is 10%, the profits flow per unit of production is $70. If one million PCs are sold yearly, industry profits are $70 million. If wage costs rise to $800 per unit, the unchanged markup of 10% over current cost will now generate an earnings flow of $80 million, given the same number of units sold. The markup is a powerful thing, and happens to be the way prices are set.

If money wages are administered by union-management agreements, the balance of income is provided by the markup over wages, most of which will be retained profits (profits plus depreciation) and dividend payouts. Capacity utilization may move up and down with demand, but the firm usually will stick with the markup that achieves its target level of retained profits. This target depends on its dividend payout ratio to stockholders, its amount of debt relative to its equity, and (according to some Post Keynesians such as the

---

[10]Whereas Kalecki's markup applies only to manufacturing, Weintraub's is more general and applies to all industries, including those that are nearly competitive. A markup pricing rule is now widely used in orthodox economic modeling. See *The Econometrics of Price Determination*, ed. O. Eckstein (Washington DC: Board of Governors of the Federal Reserve System, 1974).

late Alfred Eichner) its' perceived investment needs. According to Weintraub, even highly competitive firms price according to a markup rule.[11] Although the margin of prices over current costs already reflects the market power of the firm in a concentrated industry, even a fixed markup allows for a higher price when the unit cost of production goes up.

Income in excess of cultural subsistence leaves a demand wedge and breathing space for producers. The price markup is the breath of fresh air that fills the void. Although the stylized income division between workers and capitalists creates the Marxian drama of a "class struggle," Kalecki understood that such a razor-sharp division cannot fully explain the income distribution effects in an "affluent society" (Galbraith's term). The new upper middle-class consumer, once satisfied with a black Model T, must now be motivated to buy a streamlined, racy, colorful machine designed for maximum road comfort and perhaps fulfilling exotic fantasies. In the affluent society there is room for marketing and advertising.

Incomes Policy

The Post Keynesian explanation of the income distribution and the price level leads to a third kind of economic policy to supplement Keynesian fiscal and monetary policy. If the tenacious advocacy of deficit spending characterizes the fiscal Keynesians, the relentless pursuit of an incomes policy distinguishes the Post Keynesians.

Some fiscal Keynesians, such as James Tobin, nonetheless joined hands with the Post Keynesians to endorse an incomes policy. An incomes policy blatantly requires that wages be "controlled" in some

---

[11]According to Canterbery in "A Theory of Supra-Surplus Capitalism," *op. cit.*, and "An Evolutionary Model of Technical Change with Markup Pricing," in William Milberg, *The Megacorp and Macrodynamics* (Armonk, New York and London: M.E. Sharp, 1992), pp. 85–100, the target's highest limit is determined by the current number of firms in the industry and by the firm's perceived price elasticity of demand or consumers' sensitivity to price changes. Generally, the fewer the firms in the industry and the lower the price elasticity of demand, the higher the upper limit to the price markup.

sense. The profit margin will be whatever it will be because of the relative consistency of the price markup. However, as time goes by, wages go up and the price level with them.

The age-old question: What do we control, wages or profits? Firms prefer, if anything be controlled, it be wages: Unions favor the control of profits. Equity and political problems quickly emerge with the control of wages alone. A variable markup can be a source of profits-push inflation so that the part of profits not retained by corporations for financing investment also would require regulation. Dividends and corporate salaries might be taxed at a rate that keeps them in line with the growth of wages income. Irrespective of whose ox is gored, all incomes polices have the same theme. Money income changes are to be geared to the pace of productivity.

Real-world incomes policies have ranged from voluntary wage and price guidelines to the mandatory wage and price controls long advocated by John Kenneth Galbraith. Such measures were utilized in different forms with varying vigor by the Truman, Kennedy, Johnson, Nixon, Ford, and Carter Administrations.

An alternative to wage and price guidelines or controls is tax incentives, smart-targeted to modify the behavior of labor unions and concentrated industry. Incentives and deterrents of the price mechanism are used ju-jitsu style against itself. One tax-based incomes policy (TIP) was developed by Weintraub and by Henry Wallich (1914–1989), once a governor of the Federal Reserve Board.

TIP works this way. Whenever a corporation grants a pay increase in excess of an established norm — say 6% — the firm granting the pay raise would be penalized by an increase in its income tax. If a firm increased the wage pay of its workers by, say, 10% rather than 6%, the firm might be required to pay 10% more in taxes on its profits. The wage–salary norms would be the average increase in wages and salaries of the firm, so that above-average wage stipends could be awarded to meritorious workers. The goal would be to confine *average* money wages increases to the gains in average labor productivity in the economy.

What is the premise underlying TIP? Individual businesses will be encouraged to resist unreasonable wage demands only when they are convinced that resistance also will come from other firms and industries. TIP tilts the individual firm in the direction of yielding only non-inflationary average wage increases. The laborers would benefit from real wage gains as inflation subsides.

A TIP is a very flexible policy: It can provide a penalty for a wage increase above the norm, a reward for wages below the norm, or both. The neo-Keynesian Arthur Okun (1928–1980), once economic adviser to President Johnson and later associated with the Brookings institution, preferred carrots to sticks. If a firm holds its average yearly rate of wage increase below 6% and its average rate of price increase below 4%, Okun's plan would give the employees of the firm a tax rebate (carrot I) and the firm would receive a break (carrot II) on its income tax liabilities. A TIP of the carrot persuasion was proposed by President Jimmy Carter in October 1979. However, the incentive was indirect, a kind of diced carrot. It would have provided tax relief for those workers who stayed below the wage norm if the annual inflation rate ended up above 7%. Congress rejected the initiative.

Illus. 12.1:   Relative incomes policies, carrot versus stick.

Conditions have changed since the original TIP proposal; for one thing, the effective average corporate income tax rate, the original tax penalty base for TIP, has been approaching zero. For another, net interest income as a share of national income increased 14-fold between the end of World War II and 1990. Therefore, it appears essential to obtain a new federal revenue source to exert downward pressure on interest rates as well as a TIP that acknowledges monetary interest as a new, increasingly important source of rising production costs.

To deal with the problems associated with the original TIP, in 1983 I proposed: (a) an equitable value-added tax (VAT) as a new revenue source and as the ideal tax base for the immediate implementation of TIP; and (b) a simplified personal income tax program that would satisfy those critics of VAT who viewed it as inequitable. Several features of the simplified personal income tax plan have been implemented by Congress: VAT remains in limbo, though it has been suggested many times.[12]

Minsky and Financial Fragility

Hyman Minsky (1919–1996), a laconic but persistent American Post Keynesian with Italian connections, connected the dots between Kalecki's markup, retained earnings, and inside money to financial volatility. Minsky emphasized how the retained earnings from the markup levered by debt could finance the acquisition of additional capital assets. The capital assets acquired by the non-financial firm may be purchased out of the existing plant and equipment

---

[12]See E. Ray Canterbery, "Tax Reform and Incomes Policy: A VATIP Proposal," *Journal of Post Keynesian Economics* 5 (Spring 1983), pp. 430–439. A later, more detailed version appears in E. Ray Canterbery, Eric W. Cook and Bernard A. Schmitt, "The Flat Tax, Negative Tax, and VAT: Gaining Progressivity and Revenue," *Cato Journal* (Fall 1985), pp. 521–536.

(corporate takeovers, etc.) or through the production of new investment goods. Only in the latter case will new increments and industrial capacity be added to the economy's productive potential.[13]

Minsky's theory of investment focuses on how Keynesian uncertainty, speculation, and an increasingly complex financial system lead to business cycles. Any sustained "good times" stagger off into a speculative, inflationary binge and a fragility of financial institutions. Minsky's ideas are no longer orphans; events have overtaken his explanation.

Since business debt has to be serviced (scheduled payments on principal and interest made), Minsky suggests that such cash flows (and debt servicing commitments) determine the course of investment and thus, output and employment. In this manner, Minsky has extended Post Keynesian monetary theory to include not only credit, but the special problems connected with financial speculation in a capitalistic system.

The monetary system still is at the core of the debt creation and repayment process. Money is created as banks make loans, mostly to business, in response to profits expectations. Minsky emphasizes, however, that this "inside money" is destroyed as profits are realized and loans are repaid to the banks. The monetary system's stability depends on profit flows to borrowers sufficient to service the loans. Thus, the central problems of capitalism are connected to the ownership, creation, and financing of capital assets that, in turn, contribute to business cycles.

The prelude to a financial crisis is some "outside" shock to the system, such as war (Vietnam), crop failure, OPEC, a Schumpeterian basic innovation such as the automobile, or some massive debt disturbance. Whatever the origin of the shock, it significantly changes profit opportunities in at least one important branch of industry. If new profit opportunities arise, increased investment and

---

[13]Much of what follows is based on E. Ray Canterbery, *The Making of Economics, Vol. III The Radical Assault* (Singapore, New Jersey, London: World Scientific, 2010), pp. 157–161.

production generate a boom — a boom fueled by the expansion of bank and other forms of credit. Since profit opportunities create lending opportunities, booms ordinarily are financed at some interest rate. Moreover, financial innovations emerge in the form of new financial institutions and new credit instruments such as CDs, junk bond (bonds rated BB or lower), and even financial derivatives, instruments based upon existing credit instruments. This evolution of credit explains why financial institutions are among the first to be regulated.

Rising wage costs during an economic expansion at a constant markup elevate production costs. Since the amount of markup is not unlimited (price elasticity of demand for products is not zero), only generalized inflation can ensure full employment. In this process a rising share of investment is financed by debt. Bankers and businesspeople go along with the rising ratio of debt to internal financing so long as they are reasonably convinced of the continuance of inflation.

Speculation in financial assets eventually spills over into enhanced Keynesian effective demand for goods. Pressure on the capacity for goods production elevate prices still more. Rising prices of both goods and financial assets provide still more profit opportunities. Thus, a round robin of new investment increases ready income, motivating still more investment and still more income. The prices of goods or financial assets now include a speculative "markup" or what I have called a "casino effect."[14] Many market participants will become pure speculators who buy goods for resale rather than for use. In the U.S. pure speculation characterized much of the housing and commercial real estate markets during the 1970s, early 1980s, and the early 2000s. This culminated in financial asset inflation in 2008 and a subsequent bursting of bubbles.

---

[14] "Casino effect" is the term I use in "Reaganomics, Saving, and the Casino Effect," in James Gapinski, editor, *The Economics of Saving* (New York: Kluwer Academic Publishers, 1992). In this essay, I identify a "speculative multiplier" that plays a role quite different from the investment or employment multiplier credited to Keynes and Kahn. It is an asset multiplier rather than an income or employment multiplier.

Eventually, the number of firms and households buying strictly for resale rather than for further production begin to dominate the economic environment. What normally characterizes the bond and stock markets, where only about 1% of all transactions directly lead to real investment, becomes more and more characteristic of goods markets. A large share of the economic actors are now placing bets rather than making real investments. A continuation of the boom means higher prices, interest rates, and velocity of money. Policy issues emerge when knowledgeable people begin to talk about the need to control the explosion of credit.

The boom may end because of price resistance by consumers. After all, it is because the price elasticity of demand for products is nonzero that the amount of markup is limited. The boom may end because the central bank begins to contract credit. The hope, eventually, is that wages and thus costs and inflation will slow.

Any slowdown in wage rates, however, does not alter contractual debt commitments so that the burden of debt rises during disinflation or deflation. Debt-financed investment decreases, and purchases of investment goods financed by money supply increments decline. Business firms will begin to pay off debt instead of buying a new plant and equipment. As in Keynes, employment falls with the decline in use of the existing capital stock. Once again, business conditions are at the mercy of uncertainty and financial market behavior.

The leveling-off of prices brings financial distress for certain participants and industries. They all have been betting that prices will rise forever. Firms, including farms, have counted on a particular inflation rate for their products in order to service their mounting debt. (The same could be said for middle-class homeowners, who since World War II have counted on the appreciation of houses as a source of net worth.) Yet, those most in the know in the financial markets, the insiders, take their profits and run. This is the start of a race toward liquidity as financial assets are cashed in.

As Keynes had it, the holding of money "lulls their disquietude." Outright financial panic can be avoided only if (1) prices fall so low that people move back into real assets; (2) the government sets limits to price declines (e.g., agricultural price supports), closes banks (e.g., the "bank holiday" of 1933), and shuts the exchange; or (3) a lender of last resort steps in, as the Federal Reserve did in the financial turbulence following the Penn–Central collapse (1969–1970), the Franklin National Bank bankruptcy (1974–1975), the Hunt–Bache silver speculation (1980), and the stock market crash of 1987, and as the Federal Deposit Insurance Fund (FDIC) did in nationalizing Illinois Continental Bank (1984) or banks since. More recently, in 2008–2009 the Fed directly bought assets of failing banks at home and abroad. Such interventions prevent the complete collapse of the value of assets. In short, performing in the lender of last resort role, the Fed can prevent the collapse of the financial system.

The Federal Reserve did not function as lender of last resort during the Great depression and massive unemployment followed. Ben Bernanke at the Fed learned a lesson from studying this experience. As Minsky tells the story, however, what the government and the Federal Reserve (as its agent) do to shore up values to avoid depressions sets the stage for still higher inflation. Since debt inflation also means profits deflation in the casino economy, the otherwise stabilizing effect of government deficits and last-resort lending has its dark side.

Liabilities such as junk bonds and other financial innovations of the boom are validated as the central bank refinances the holdings of financial institutions. This propping up of capitalism creates the base for still further expansion of credit during the economic recovery, a process that helps to explain the inflation following the financial crises of 1959–1970, 1974–1975, and 1980. Goods inflation, but not financial speculation, was tamed by the near-depression of 1981–1982 and the Great Recession of 2007–2010. Contrary to Minsky, goods inflation has not accompanied the "recovery" from the Great Recession. Still, the completion of a Minsky cycle could culminate in a massive meltdown again in the value of financial assets. Thus far, goods inflation has been prevented by high levels of unemployment, much as Keynes would have predicted. The 2008–2009 episode was what Paul Krugman and Canterbery have called a Minsky moment.

Monetary and fiscal policy may not be adequate during a Minsky cycle. Financial speculation calls for a graduated transactions tax discussed earlier. It also calls for more financial regulation, as already discussed. Wages inflation calls for the use of an incomes policy, such as TIP or VATIP. At the extreme, hyperinflation, wage and price controls may be needed, as they were in World War II and the Korean War. Fiscal contraction will cause more unemployment; monetary contraction may cause a collapse in financial asset prices. Luckily, zero interest rates and quantitative easing remain the foreseeable wave of the future.

13

The Importance of Economic Growth and Full Employment

The outstanding faults of the economic society in which we live are its failure to provide for full employment and its arbitrary and inequitable distribution of wealth and incomes.

— John Maynard Keynes, *The General Theory of Employment Interest and Money* (New York: Harcourt, Brace and Company, 1936), p. 321

What John Maynard Keynes wrote in 1936 rings with truth even today. The lack of full employment is well understood because its ills are so visible. Not so the problems of an arbitrary and inequitable distribution of wealth and incomes. These are measured less frequently and are for the most part invisible. The Forbes 400 are well-known and widely publicized but are thought to comprise the exceptional. True, they are exceptional, being the wealthiest of them all, a small slice of the top 1% of the wealth distribution, the tip of the top. We hear references to the top 1%, but that is all. Like the poor, it is presumed that they will always be with us.

The arguments favoring full employment are about the same as they were in 1945 when the Full Employment Act was first drafted. It was considered such a radical document, however, that it was greatly modified and a compromise (watered down) bill was passed as the Employment Act of 1946.[1] The Full Employment bill was drafted in the shadow of World War II. It was widely feared by economists and politicians that a depression would follow the war, much like what followed the end of World War I. This did not happen, partly because of the use of modern fiscal policy, under the Harry S. Truman administration.

What unemployment rate would constitute full employment today? There are always some workers between jobs that are not really permanently unemployed. These are the frictionally unemployed and are thought to comprise about 2% of the labor forces. Besides these, there are youth between the ages of 18 and 21 that are enrolled in colleges and universities and are temporarily out of the labor force. It is difficult to know what effect these have on the unemployment rate. Recent history provides a clue. Figure 13.1 shows the unemployment rate for 2003–2013. There are a couple of surprises in the data. For one thing, the unemployment rate has been very high during much of this period. The era includes the years of the Great Recession, in which the unemployment rate

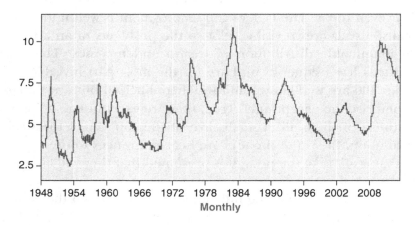

Figure 13.1:   U.S. unemployment rate.

Source: Bureau of Labor Statistics.

---

[1]The full story of the thinking that went into the Full Employment bill is told in E. Ray Canterbery, *Harry S. Truman: The Economics of a Populist President* (Singapore, New Jersey, London: World Scientific, 2014), Chapter 5.

Illus. 13.1:   Unemployment line in the United States.
Source: The Web.

peaked at about 10%. The most recent low unemployment rate was achieved around January of 2007. It did not quite reach 4%.

To be exact, the unemployment rate for all of 2007 was 4.5, but the rate for men 20 years and over was 4.1%. Other rates, for minorities and part-time workers were higher. One might expect inflation, but the price level actually declined during the two mid-quarters of the year. In short, the economy can operate at near 4% unemployment with little or no inflation. There is little reason to suppose that today would be much different. After dipping during the Great Recession, prices have been amazingly stable since. Of course, unemployment has remained high. All in all, we can conclude that a 4% unemployment rate is a reasonable target and would constitute effective full employment. It should be sufficient to employ those youth who choose to enter the workforce and forgo higher education.

Illus. 13.2:   Full employment.
Source: Google Search, from the web.

There are many benefits from full employment, the most important of which is jobs. Crime rates fall and the health of the population improves. The costs of government fall as unemployment compensation, food stamp expenditures, and the negative income tax move to the black. Tax revenues rise. Federal budget deficits fall and may move into surplus. Suicide rates decline. All these indicators turn bleak during economic downturns. As we witnessed, during the Great Recession, crime rates rose, the health of persons worsened, suicides increased, the cost of social services rose, Federal budget deficits soared, and the public debt expanded. Austerity was bad for the economic health of the nation.

In April 2014, the unemployment rate had dropped to 6.3 % or 2.3 percentage points above full employment. But the rate fell because the number of people working or seeking work also fell sharply. People are not counted as unemployed if they are not looking for a job. This happens when the jobless are discouraged. In no other American economic recovery have there been so many discouraged workers. The true (unofficial) unemployment rate is around 8%.

In the third quarter of 2013, according to advance estimates, current dollar gross domestic (GDP) rose 4.8 percent (annual rate), real GDP in chained (2009) dollars rose 2.8 percent, and the chained price index rose 1.9 percent.

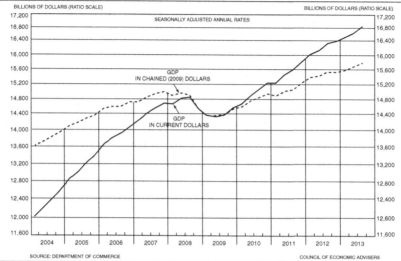

SOURCE: DEPARTMENT OF COMMERCE COUNCIL OF ECONOMIC ADVISERS

[Billions of current dollars; quarterly data at seasonally adjusted annual rates]

Period	Gross domestic product	Personal Consumption expenditures	Gross private domestic investment	Net exports	Exports	Imports	Total	Federal Total	National defense	Non-defense	State and local	Final sales of domestic product	Gross domestic purchase¹	Addendum: Gross national product
2003	11,512.2	7,764.4	2,027.9	-500.9	1,043.4	1,544.3	2,220.8	824.8	519.9	304.9	1,396.0	11,493.0	12,013.2	11,580.3
2004	12,277.0	8,257.8	2,276.7	-614.8	1,183.1	1,797.9	2,357.4	892.4	570.2	322.1	1,465.0	12,213.2	12,891.8	12,367.1
2005	13,095.4	8,790.3	2,527.1	-715.7	1,310.4	2,026.1	2,493.7	946.3	608.3	338.1	1,547.4	13,035.8	13,811.1	13,189.0
2006	13,857.9	9,297.5	2,680.6	-762.4	1,478.5	2,240.9	2,642.2	1,002.0	642.4	359.6	1,640.2	13,790.9	14,620.3	13,926.3
2007	14,480.3	9,744.4	2,643.7	-709.8	1,665.7	2,375.5	2,801.9	1,049.8	678.7	371.0	1,752.2	14,445.9	15,190.1	14,606.8
2008	14,720.3	10,005.5	2,424.8	-713.2	1,843.1	2,556.4	3,003.2	1,155.6	754.1	401.5	1,847.6	14,752.3	15,433.5	14,893.2
2009	14,417.9	9,842.9	1,878.1	-392.2	1,583.8	1,976.0	3,089.1	1,217.7	788.3	429.4	1,871.4	14,565.5	14,810.1	14,565.1
2010	14,958.3	10,201.9	2,100.8	-518.5	1,843.5	2,362.0	3,174.0	1,303.9	832.8	471.1	1,870.2	14,896.7	15,476.7	15,164.2
2011	15,533.8	10,711.8	2,232.1	-568.7	2,101.2	2,669.9	3,158.7	1,304.1	835.8	468.2	1,854.7	15,497.4	16,102.6	15,794.6
2012	16,244.6	11,149.6	2,475.2	-547.2	2,195.9	2,743.1	3,167.0	1,295.7	817.1	478.6	1,871.3	16,178.5	16,791.8	16,497.4
2010: I	14,672.5	10,042.3	1,989.5	-495.1	1,746.4	2,241.4	3,135.7	1,269.2	811.9	457.3	1,866.5	14,660.4	15,167.5	14,875.9
II	14,879.2	10,134.7	2,092.7	-529.7	1,807.0	2,336.7	3,181.5	1,304.6	829.3	475.2	1,878.9	14,829.0	15,408.9	15,084.3
III	15,049.8	10,234.3	2,164.6	-543.8	1,8603	2,404.0	3,194.7	1,321.6	346.3	475.3	1,873.1	14,928.2	15,593.5	15,249.5
IV	15,231.7	10,396.3	2,156.5	-505.3	1,960.4	2,465.7	3,184.2	1,320.1	843.5	476.6	1,864.2	15,169.3	15,737.0	15,447.2
2010: I	15,242.9	10,527.1	2,120.4	-554.7	2,029.5	2,584.1	3,150.0	1,297.4	822.0	475.4	1,852.6	15,221.4	15,797.6	15,491.2
II	15,461.9	10,662.6	2,199.9	-572.2	2,095.5	2,667.7	3,171.7	1,315.4	844.2	471.2	1,856.3	15,416.2	16,034.1	15,712.1
III	15,611.8	10,778.6	2,222.2	-553.7	2,143.4	2,697.1	3,164.6	1,308.5	851.6	456.9	1,856.1	15,625.3	16,165.5	15,884.0
IV	15,818.7	10,878.9	2,385.7	-594.4	2,136.2	2,730.7	3,148.5	1,294.9	825.6	469.3	1,653.6	15,726.8	16,413.1	16,091.0
2012: I	16,041.6	11,019.1	2,453.6	-590.8	2,173.4	2,764.2	3,159.7	1,291.8	815.3	475.5	1,867.9	15,938.7	16,632.4	16,289.6
II	16,160.4	11,100.2	2,454.0	-557.9	2,197.4	2,755.3	3,164.1	1,293.8	816.7	477.1	1,870.3	16,093.6	16,718.3	16,419.2
III	16,356.0	11,193.3	2,493.3	-524.4	2,199.2	2,723.6	3,193.5	1,322.1	841.9	480.2	1,871.4	16,274.4	16,880.4	16,603.7
IV	16,420.3	11,285.5	2,499.9	-515.8	2,213.7	2,729.5	3,150.7	1,275.2	793.7	481.5	1,675.4	16,407.3	16,936.1	16,677.3
2013: I	16,535.3	11,379.2	2,555.1	-623.1	2,214.2	2,737.3	3,124.1	1,255.0	775.8	479.2	1,869.1	16,471.9	17,058.4	16,772.7
II	16,661.0	11,427.1	2,621.0	-503.0	2,238.9	2,747.9	3,121.9	1,252.6	776.3	476.3	1,869.3	16,583.8	17,170.0	16,907.9
III^p	16,857.6	11,525.4	2,689.8	-493.1	2,238.8	2,761.9	3,135.6	1,251.0	777.2	473.9	1,884.5	16,747.3	17,350.8	....

¹GDP less exports of goods and services plus imports of goods and services.

Figure 13.2: Gross domestic product.

Source: Department of Commerce (Bureau of Economic Analysis).

Full employment requires that the economy operate at full-capacity output. This in turn requires a substantial growth rate in GDP. Figure 13.2 displays the U.S. GDP in current and real inflation-adjusted) dollars for 2003–2013. The Great Recession is clearly visible in the data. Employment rises and falls with GDP. Hence, it is important to understand what makes GDP tick. From the expenditures side, GDP is comprised of spending for personal consumption, Gross private domestic investment, government, and net exports. In recent years, net exports have subtracted about a half a billion dollars from GDP. Of the spending classes personal consumption has been growing the fastest, with private business investment lagging behind. Federal government expenditures have recently been falling, while state government expenditures have been rising moderately. As to government, we are in a period of austerity, thanks to ideology and the austerity lobby.

Private business investment is the drive wheel of capitalism. It is difficult to understand why investment is stagnant when interest rates are historically low. The Federal funds rate is averaging near zero: it can't go lower. Is the business environment that uncertain? In Keynes *General Theory*, full employment depends upon adequate business investment. When such investment falls short, it is to be supplemented by Federal government investment. This is not happening. We first need to explain the weakness in business spending.

First, business looks to consumption as the rationale for investing. At a given markup on unit wage costs, profits are generated. Profits provide the incentive for investment. Figure 13.3 shows the % changes in employee costs to business firms for 2003–2013. These costs were growing at a 3% to 4% clip prior to the Great Recession. Costs fell off a cliff during the downturn. They have remained at a fairly constant 2% per year since. Obviously, consumption would be rising faster if employee compensation were growing faster than 2% per year. In turn, the incentive for more investment would be enhanced. In any case, the markup applies to a fairly constant wages cost figure.

What about the "animal spirits" of the businessman as measured by stock prices? One might suppose that a robust stock market would be bullish for business investment. First of all, the corporation can issue new stock and raise funds cheaply for further investment. One might suppose this, but one would be wrong. Since

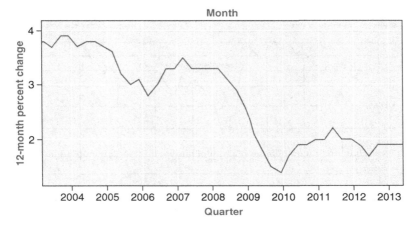

Figure 13.3:   Percentage change, employee costs.
Source: US Bureau of Labor Statistics.

the fall of 2011, the stock market has been soaring. A broad stock price index is shown for recent years in Figure 13.4. Moreover, thus far there is not a bubble in stock prices. The earnings/price ratio on stocks is at a steady 5%, which means that profits have been healthy. Indeed they have been, as shown in Figure 13.5. Moreover, corporate profits taxes have remained low and most of the profits have not been distributed. Undistributed corporate profits are available for business investment, but in that respect have remained idle. Since employee costs are stable, a rising markup would explain rising profits.

The "Angels' Share" of Savings

As a first approximation in Kalecki, profits equal investment, but that is only under the assumption that the capitalist reinvests all profits. Clearly this is not the case, and the markup is being used for other purposes. The corporation is engaging in savings. Since they did not become investment, the savings evaporate in the real economy. This naturally raises the question of where do they go? Elsewhere, I have called these evaporating savings the "angel's

Stock prices rose in October

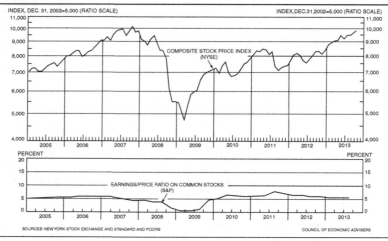

SOURCES: NEW YORK STOCK EXCHANGE AND STANDARD AND POORS   COUNCIL OF ECONOMIC ADVISERS

Period	Common stock prices[1]							Common stock yields (percent)[7]	
	New York Stock Exchange indexes (December 31, 2002=5,000)[2,3]				Dow Jonas Industrial average[4]	Standard & Poor's composite index (1941–1943=10)[5]	Nasdaq composite index (Feb. 5, 1971=100)[6]	Dividend/price ratio	Earnings/price ratio
	Composite	Financial	Energy	Health Care					
2003	5,547.46	5,583.00	5,273.90	5,288.67	8,993.59	965.23	1,647.17	1.77	3.84
2004	6,612.62	6,822.18	6,952.36	5,924.80	10,317.39	1,130.65	1,986.53	1.72	4.89
2005	7,349.00	7,333.70	9,377.84	6,283.96	10,547.67	1,207.23	2,099.32	1.83	5.36
2006	8,357.99	8,654.40	11,206.94	6,685.06	11,408.67	1,310.46	2,263.41	1.87	5.78
2007	9,648.82	9,321.39	13,339.99	7,191.79	13,169.98	1,477.19	2,578.47	1.86	5.29
2008	8,036.88	6,278.38	13,258.42	6,171.19	11,252.62	1,220.04	2,161.65	2.37	3.54
2009	6,091.02	3,987.04	10,020.30	5,456.63	8,876.15	948.05	1,845.38	2.40	1.86
2010	7,230.43	4,744.05	10,943.85	6,230.62	10,662.80	1,139.37	2,349.89	1.98	604
2011	7,871.41	4,641.01	12,880.35	6,847.80	11,966.36	1,267.64	2,677.44	2.05	6.77
2012	8,011.65	4,616.63	12,512.31	7,503.05	12,967.08	1,379.35	2,965.56	2.24	6.20
2012: Oct.	8,295.68	4,855.25	12,812.78	7,988.93	13,380.65	1,437.82	3,060.26	2.24	
Nct.	8,129.90	4,804.71	12,343.98	7,757.04	12,896.44	1,394.51	2,941.02	2.33	
Dec.	8,367.74	5,012.50	12,550.75	7,943.33	13,144.18	1,422.29	3,003.79	2.28	6.07
2013: Jan.	8,759.89	5,334.30	13,126.08	6,271.48	13,615.32	1,480.40	3,125.91	2.24	
Feb	8,896.97	5,428.85	13,172.85	8,466.93	13,967.33	1,512.31	3,169.21	2.21	
Mar	9,038.29	5.50012	13,168.60	8,665.01	14,418.26	1,550.83	3,236.17	2.19	6.59
Apr	9,092.21	5.526.59	12,917.17	9,090.44	14,675.91	1,570.70	3,251.35	2.16	
May	9,440.35	5,842.60	13,456.16	9,271.60	15,172.18	1,639.84	3,440.38	2.12	
June	9,204.10	5,697.29	13,064.60	3,199.64	15,035.75	1,618.77	3,416.74	2.18	6.66
July	9,463.58	5,908.95	13,394.54	9,394.52	15,390.21	1,668.68	3,559.71	2.14	
Aug	9,496.64	5,897.94	13,404.11	9,466.69	15,105.69	1,670.09	3,639.93	2.15	
Sept	9,639.34	5,988.45	13,715.91	9,473.99	15,269.84	1,687.17	3,731.26	2.13	6.65
Oct	9,840.99	6,124.54	13,990.65	9,647.71	15,289.29	1,720.03	3,848.20	2.10	
Week end:									
2013: Oct 12	9,606.69	5,984.40	13,664.57	9,438.94	14,975.79	1,676.75	3,739.12	2.17	
19	9,857.35	6,188.29	14,047.69	9,653.83	15,322.88	1,721.48	3,845.23	2.12	
26	10,022.53	6,237.85	14,198.39	9,791.36	15,470.54	1,751.51	3,925.80	2.05	
Nov 2	10,049.82	6,195.55	14,288.30	9,845.28	15,605.87	1,763.11	3,932.97	2.03	
9	10,018.40	6,129.53	14,236.92	9,844.49	15,672.00	1,763.83	3,916.54	2.04	

[1] Average of daily closing prices.
[2] Includes all the stocks (in 2012, over 2,900) listed on the NYSE.
[3] Effective January 9, 2003, the NYSE relaunched the composite index with changes in methodology, definitions, and based on DEC. 31,2002=5,000. Effective January 8, 2004 new indexes for Financial, Energy, and Health Care were introduced by the NYSE. Previous indexes shown for Industrial, Transportation, Utility, and Finance were discontinued.
[4] Includes 30 stocks.
[5] Includes 5DQ stocks.
[6] Includes over 2,400 stocks in 2012.
[7] Standard & Poor's series. Dividend/price ratios based on Wednesday closing prices. Earnings/price ratios based on prices at end of quarter.

Source: New York Stock Exchange, DCW Jones & Company, Inc., Standard & Poor's, and Nasdaq Stock Market.

Figure 13.4:   Common stock prices and yields.

Sources: New York Stock Exchange, Dow Jones & Company, Inc., Standard & Poor's, and Nasdaq Stock Market.

In the second quarter of 2013, according to revised estimates, corporate profits before tax rose $46.6 billion (annual rate) and profits after tax rose $36.6 billion.

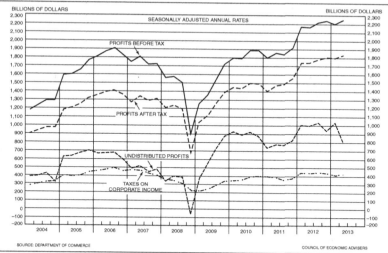

[Billions of dollars; quarterly data at seasonally adjusted annual rates]

Period	Profits (before tax) with inventory valuation adjustment[1]								Profits before tax	Taxes on corporate income	Profits after tax			Inventory valuation adjustment
	Total[2]	Domestic industries												
		Total	Financial	Nonfinancial							Total	Net dividends	Undistributed profits	
				Total[3]	Manufacturing	Utilities	Wholesale	Retail						
2003	959.9	793.3	306.5	486.7	125.3	13.5	59.3	90.5	969.4	243.8	725.7	434.0	291.7	−9.6
2004	1,215.2	1,010.1	349.4	660.7	182.7	20.5	74.7	93.2	1,254.6	306.1	948.5	564.1	384.4	−39.5
2005	1,621.2	1,382.1	409.7	972.4	277.7	30.8	96.2	121.7	1,653.3	412.4	1,240.9	580.5	660.4	−32.1
2006	1,815.7	1,559.6	415.1	1,144.4	349.7	55.1	105.9	132.5	1,851.4	473.4	1,378.1	726.0	652.1	−35.7
2007	1,708.9	1,355.5	301.5	1,054.0	321.9	49.5	103.2	119.0	1,748.4	445.5	1,302.9	818.9	484.0	−39.5
2008	1,345.5	938.8	95.4	843.4	240.6	30.1	90.6	80.3	1,382.4	309.1	1,073.3	808.6	264.7	−37.0
2009	1,474.8	1,122.0	362.9	759.2	171.4	23.8	89.3	108.7	1,468.2	269.4	1,198.7	568.7	630.0	6.7
2010	1,793.8	1,398.6	405.3	993.3	284.9	29.8	102.2	118.3	1,834.8	370.6	1,464.3	563.9	900.3	−41.0
2011	1,791.3	1,354.8	384.1	970.7	303.9	11.1	98.3	116.1	1,847.4	374.2	1,473.1	701.6	771.6	−56.0
2012	2,180.0	1,761.1	477.4	1,283.7	404.3	37.1	137.8	149.2	2,190.0	434.8	1,755.2	770.3	984.9	−10.0
2010: I	1,751.6	1,354.1	387.1	967.0	228.4	44.6	99.2	120.9	1,791.7	344.8	1,446.9	521.8	925.1	−40.1
II	1,762.2	1,367.8	362.6	1,005.2	283.9	14.5	118.0	119.0	1,782.8	351.7	1,431.2	542.8	883.4	−20.6
III	1,861.5	1,476.8	415.6	1,061.2	324.3	35.3	114.5	118.0	1,879.5	387.5	1,492.1	576.0	916.0	−18.1
IV	1,800.0	1,395.9	456.0	939.9	303.0	24.8	77.2	115.4	1,885.2	398.3	1,486.9	615.2	871.7	−85.3
2011: I	1,672.2	1,244.3	377.8	866.5	278.1	3.9	74.4	112.2	1,792.3	393.0	1,399.2	668.3	731.0	−120.1
II	1,782.3	1,354.9	334.6	990.3	291.5	29.7	94.7	109.1	1,850.4	384.3	1,466.1	692.9	773.2	−68.2
III	1,805.4	1,354.6	348.8	1,005.8	314.5	3.2	110.3	114.9	1,833.1	351.0	1,482.1	717.5	764.6	−27.7
IV	1,905.4	1,465.2	445.1	1,020.1	331.7	7.9	105.9	128.2	1,913.6	368.6	1,545.1	727.6	817.5	−8.2
2012: I	2,142.5	1,726.7	462.5	1,264.2	408.7	34.5	128.8	149.9	2,162.1	437.2	1,724.9	727.4	997.5	−19.5
II	2,169.8	1,740.5	447.7	1,292.8	410.5	39.4	146.5	145.3	2,160.0	429.7	1,730.3	739.6	990.7	9.8
III	2,186.6	1,774.0	507.2	1,266.8	387.8	40.8	131.6	142.5	2,238.5	439.1	1,769.4	746.7	1,022.7	−22.0
IV	2,221.1	1,803.0	492.1	1,310.9	410.1	33.6	144.4	159.0	2,229.5	433.2	1,796.4	867.6	928.7	−8.4
2013: I	2,180.0	1,781.5	486.9	1,294.6	389.7	38.3	150.2	148.9	2,193.1	408.2	1,784.8	763.8	1,021.0	−13.0
II	2,248.6	1,845.5	511.9	1,333.6	381.8	47.2	151.1	169.9	2,239.7	418.2	1,821.4	784.2		8.9
III	...	...	...	...	...	...	...	...	...	...		ᴾ858.0		

[1] See p. 4 for profits with inventory valuation and capital consumption adjustments.
[2] Includes rest of the world, not shown separately.
[3] Includes industries not shown separately.

Note: Data by industry are based on the North American Industry Classification System (NAICS).
Source: Department at Commerce [Bureau of Economic Analysis].

Figure 13.5:   Corporate profits.

Source: Council of Economic Advisers.

share" of savings.[2] In the vineyards of France, the angels' share of cognac is the amount necessarily evaporated to give cognac its celebrated quality. The winemakers think that the amount evaporated seasonally equals all the cognac consumed in France during the year, sufficient to keep many spirits high. In like fashion, most of the personal savings of the rich evaporate; we can call it the "angels' share" of savings. Since Wall Street is addicted to these personal savings, the normal amount evaporated must be sufficient — from the wealthholders perspective — to maintain the celebrated quality of Wall Street capitalism. In truth, Wall Street needs a rapidly expanding angels' share of savings for its prosperity.

Where the angels' share goes is the great unsolved mystery of Keynesian economics. Put differently, where do personal and business savings go when they die in Keynesian economics? Once we know the corporeal manifestation of these savings, we at last have a complete understanding of them and what can be done about them — and about the wealthholding class.

First, as Donald Rumsfeld might urge, consider what we do know. In today's macroeconomics, we correctly measure real saving as the value of real investment. Let us be clear; we are speaking here of saving, the singular. A society has not really saved unless it has a new factory, equipment or highway to show for it. If personal (household) and business savings do not lead to real investment, in the cloistered world of economists they play no further economic role. This turns out to be a mistake. During the 1980s, when money and bonds were thrown in giant bundles at rich people, net fixed investment (the *really* real part of investment because it excludes depreciation) declined from around 6.7% of net national product (GDP minus that depreciation) to less than 5%. Most important, the growth rate of capital services in the private business and manufacturing sectors had almost fallen through the factory floor by 1985–1988. During the 1980s, the one thing private business did

---

[2]See E. Ray Canterbery, *Wall Street Capitalism* (Singapore, New Jersey, London: World Scientific, 2000), Chapter 12.

best was depreciate — lose capital to wear, tear, obsolescence, and destruction. In this view, real savings stagnated.

Why — in the Gildered Age[3] when the idolatry of capital had never been greater and personal money savings were surely on the increase — did so many machines commit suicide? Total personal savings as commonly measured were nonetheless meager and continued to be anemic during the bullish 1990s. We can, therefore, ask the same question from the savings side. Where did all those exploding personal savings (money and bonds) of the rich go, if not into real investment? Did they simply evaporate? In the meaning ordinarily used by macroeconomists, savings *did* evaporate. It is a deep mystery, as if the savings were loaded aboard the Orient Express in Paris but disappear before the train pulls into Istanbul.

Why Savings and Saving are Unequal

Reading definitions can be boring. But, let us be clear; there is much at stake here. Besides, the consequences, once understood, turn out to be exciting. Savings (the plural) describes what individual households and firms do. Savings for the individual household or firm is different from saving (the singular) for the nation.

Individuals' savings accumulate from their spending less than their after-tax income. After paying income and social security taxes, consuming meals, gasoline, electricity, movie tickets, and so on, any dollars left over are savings. Initially, these savings are in the form of cash or demand deposits. The classical economists considered this consumption and savings activity to be a zero-sum game; that is, individuals could save more only by being stingy consumers, buying cheaper cars and living in smaller houses. This belief in the powers of thrift has a wonderfully Calvinistic edge to it and, therefore, considerable moral standing. Nevertheless, in the real world, individuals can increase their savings by simply earning more income. Savings, then is the difference between our net earnings and what we spend on hamburgers, denims, housing, and so on.

---

[3]Named for George Gilder, an unrestrained defender of Reaganomics.

A different view of savings comes from measuring income broadly. If income includes everything that contributes to wealth, then it includes capital gains from stocks and bonds plus wages and salaries. In this broader perspective, savings are the net additions to wealth or net worth. Therefore, if we have income from all sources (including realized capital gains from bonds of $10,000) of $70,000, pay taxes of $15,000, and spend $35,000 on consumption, we have savings of $20,000. If we began the year with wealth or a net worth of $250,000, our net worth at the end of the year will be $270,000, reflecting partly the $10,000 gain in bonds. The boost in net worth is our savings defined broadly. A broad view of income gives a broad view of savings.

Clearly, we need not hold our savings only in the form of cash and demand deposits which yield no return. "I just put $500 into my savings account," says Mother Jones (the mother, not the magazine). "The retained earnings of Ford Motor company increased $500 million this month, increasing the firm's savings by 30%," writes an editor of *Bloomsberg Businessweek*. Usually, firms hold these savings in interest or dividend-earning financial assets rather than in cash or checking accounts. In short, business firms hold their savings in a multitude of forms, much like rich households do.

Green-eye-shaded statisticians at the U.S. Department of Commerce calculate personal savings as any current income remaining after consumption. Such savings is a residual. The statisticians' estimate is very indirect: they do not go from door to door asking personal questions such as, "by how much did your personal savings change during the past years?" Instead, the statisticians measure disposable personal income (income after income taxes and government transfer payments) and consumption, then subtract consumption from disposable personal income to estimate savings. Gratefully, they make the calculations, sparing us the effort.

In 1996, for example, personal disposable income was $5589 billion and consumption expenditures were $5315 billion, leaving estimated personal savings at $274 billion. It is simply arithmetic. By this measure, personal savings as a % of disposable personal income had suffered a decline from 7.5% in 1981 to 4.9% in 1996. In most of the intervening years the savings rate was even lower: pundits and economists continue to wring their hands over this declining trend. This measure of savings, however, is much more important to a household than to the national economy. If an individual household saves too little, adults in the household may have insufficient funds for retirement, especially if they are long lived. If a nation saves too much, however, unemployment will result from inadequate total private demand in the economy. In this latter measure, the national saving must be measured as the total of all household and business savings. The distinction is important.[4]

This measure (PDI − C = SAVINGS) surely understates personal money savings, especially in recent decades. Since the Commerce Department uses the narrow definition of savings, it fails to account for changes in net worth, including that created by new credit or by capital gains. If Jenni Jones, Mother Jones' daughter owns assets such as securities that appreciate, which she sells at a comfortable profit, are those new savings any less real to Jenni than savings accumulated by thrift? Not all increases in a person's wealth are spent lavishly — spending depends upon one's income bracket and one's tastes, though rising disposable income would normally nourish some increase in both consumption and savings. Yet, if Jenni uses capital gains from the sale of her bonds and buys a new car, Commerce records an increase in consumption that *reduces* personal savings. Similarly, would not a depreciation of such assets diminish personal savings?

Returning to the Federal Reserve System, and considering its measure of savings, the plot thickens, as Agatha Christie's eccentric Belgian sleuth Hercule Poirot might say. Mysterious as it may seem, the Fed measures individual savings — indirectly but not covertly — using a flow-of-funds approach. "Flow of funds" means exactly what

---

[4]We recall that saving in the macroeconomy is measured after-the-fact as net business investment. This "saving" is created by net business investment, not the other way around. The classical economists are responsible for creating the confusion in which personal savings are equated with saving; only in this sense can saving create investment.

it says; these funds are identified according their uses, such as funds for automobile purchases, and their sources, such as bank loans. It is important to our story that the Fed's measure is a much closer approximation of change in net worth or wealth (savings). The Fed adds increases in financial assets to net investment in consumer durables (such as a new house purchase), and then subtracts the net increase in debts (such as new credit or charges) to arrive at savings. Now, by this broader measure, savings can decline because people are increasing their borrowing. Even so, the similarity in the two levels of savings — the Commerce Department's and the Fed's over two decades, 1961–1981 — tells us that they had once been measuring the same thing. However, during periods when the financial sector is growing relative to the manufacturing sector, the Fed's measure of personal savings is higher than that of the Commerce Department's. We have found the missing personal savings. They manifest themselves as increases in net worth in households. Thus, the two measures are no longer measuring the same things. Not surprisingly, the growth in net worth (savings increments) is highly correlated with the growth in the S&P 500.

We now can return to our main story, having learned that the wealthholding class possesses the bulk of these reported personal savings. The more that business and government parcels out payments of dividend and interest, the greater the increase in savings by the financial wealthholders. When 14 cents (net) of every new dollar of government spending goes to bondholders as interest, can anyone doubt that bondholder net worth is rising? The seven cents or so going to the super-rich amount to about $115 billion or an average of $105,000 annual risk-free yearly interest income from government bonds per family. When the S&P 500 soars more than a hundred points during a single year, can anyone doubt that the net worth of rich households has risen? Moreover, a corporation can increase its cash from equities only with new issues (which have been rare), Warren Buffet's family and other wealthy households can enjoy secondary market appreciation in its equities' holding without necessarily sharing any of those benefits with business. The net gain of the super-rich will have been about $1 trillion (equaling about an eighth of the national GDP) or roughly an average of half-a-million dollars per household during the past eight months. Since the wealthholding class at the top maintains its financial holdings tightly, can anyone doubt that the wealth distribution becomes more unequal as the bond and stock markets soar?

Wealthholdings are being resold daily so that capital gains are continuously being made. Moreover, the dramatic shift to debt finance during the 1980s assured the explosion in interest income; by 1991, Federal government interest payments to bondholders were exhausting half of all personal income tax revenue. Those unearned income gains essentially add only to the current savings of the wealthholding class, and do so without making any contact whatsoever with business firms other than brokerage houses. In truth, the middle class was borrowing more in an attempt to maintain its old standard of living. As to corporations, their savings actually turned negative during the late 1980s. During that decade, corporations were repurchasing their own stock thereby raising its price, to ward off takeovers during the outbreak of leveraged buyouts — evasive actions that probably explain the negative corporate saving. During 1990–1995, for similar reasons, corporations were again buying back great amounts of their own stock. The growth in net worth or wealth in the economy has switched from business firms to selected families, including those in the Forbes 400.

The convenient social myth that personal savings of the rich fuel real investment and growth of capitalism serves to protect and nurture Wall Street and the wealthholding class. It is hypocritical to tell the working class that their jobs depend upon the wealthholders becoming richer — at best, a twisted truth. Worse, the same workers are told that their jobs will only be safe if American multinationals increase their investment in new plants in foreign nations. That is, even when investments are made abroad, they somehow benefit workers at home.

The source of data on savings, saving and investment is provided by the Federal Reserve flow of funds matrix. That matrix for 2012 is given in Table 13.1. Looking first at the Keynesian measures: the values of gross investment and gross saving are approximately equal,

Table 13.1: Flow of Funds Matrix for 2012 (Billions of dollars: All Sectors — Flows)

	Households and non-profit organization		Non-financial business		State and local governments		Federal governments		Domestic non-financial sectors		Domestic financial sectors		Rest of the world		All sectors		Instrument discrepancy
	U	S	U	S	U	S	U	S	U	S	U	S	U	S	U	S	
	(1)	(2)	(3)	(4)	(5)	(6)	(7)	(8)	(9)	(10)	(11)	(12)	(13)	(14)	(15)	(16)	(17)
1 Gross saving less net cap. transfers	—	2224.5	—	2119.8	—	52.8	—	-930.5	—	3466.5	—	331.2	—	432.4	—	4230.1	—
2 Capital consumption	—	1373.0	—	1451.1	—	231.4	—	262.3	—	3317.7	—	188.3	—	—	—	3506.0	—
3 Net saving (1 less 2)	—	851.5	—	668.7	—	-178.6	—	-1192.8	—	148.8	—	142.9	—	432.4	—	724.2	—
4 Gross investment (5 plus 11)	2537.2	—	1967.6	—	91.7	—	-845.8	—	3750.7	—	256.9	—	446.3	—	4453.9	—	-223.8
5 Capital expenditures	1613.2	—	1777.9	—	345.1	—	282.7	—	4019.0	—	198.7	—	0.0	—	4217.7	—	12.4
6 Consumer durables	1123.5	—	—	—	—	—	—	—	1123.5	—	—	—	—	—	1123.5	—	—
7 Residential	354.3	—	79.5	—	5.3	—	0.9	—	440.1	—	5.3	—	—	—	445.4	—	—
8 Non-residential	143.8	—	1632.8	—	329.6	—	283.1	—	2389.3	—	193.4	—	—	—	2582.7	—	—
9 Inventory change	—	—	66.1	—	—	—	—	—	66.1	—	—	—	—	—	66.1	—	—

(Continued)

Table 13.1: (*Continued*)

	Households and non-profit organization		Non-financial business		State and local governments		Federal governments		Domestic non-financial sectors		Domestic financial sectors		Rest of the world		All sectors		Instrument discrepancy
	U (1)	S (2)	U (3)	S (4)	U (5)	S (6)	U (7)	S (8)	U (9)	S (10)	U (11)	S (12)	U (13)	S (14)	U (15)	S (16)	(17)
10 Non-produced non-financial assets	-8.4	—	-0.4	—	10.2	—	-1.4	—	0.0	—	—	—	0.0	—	—	—	—
1 Net lending (+) or net borrowing (−)	924.0	—	189.7	—	-253.4	—	-1128.45	—	-268.3	—	58.2	—	446.3	—	236.2	—	-236.3
2 Total financial assets	1018.4	—	957.3	—	-52.6	—	114.0	—	2037.1	—	1807.9	—	876.4	—	4721.5	—	—
3 Total liabilities	—	94.4	—	767.6	—	200.8	—	1242.5	—	2305.4	—	1749.7	—	430.1	—	4485.2	—
4 U.S. official reserve assets	—	—	—	—	—	—	4.3	0.0	4.3	0.0	0.2	—	0.0	4.5	4.5	4.5	—
5 SDR certificates	—	—	—	—	—	—	—	0.0	—	0.0	0.0	—	—	—	0.0	0.0	—
6 Treasury currency	—	—	—	—	—	—	—	0.0	—	0.0	0.6	—	—	—	0.6	0.0	-0.6
7 Foreign deposits	-1.8	—	21.5	—	—	—	—	—	-23.3	—	0.4	—	—	-30.2	-22.9	-30.2	-7.3

(*Continued*)

Table 13.1: (*Continued*)

	Households and non-profit organization		Non-financial business		State and local governments		Federal governments		Domestic non-financial sectors		Domestic financial sectors		Rest of the world		All sectors		Instrument discrepancy
	U	S	U	S	U	S	U	S	U	S	U	S	U	S	U	S	
	(1)	(2)	(3)	(4)	(5)	(6)	(7)	(8)	(9)	(10)	(11)	(12)	(13)	(14)	(15)	(16)	(17)
8 Interbank claims	—	—	—	—	—	—	—	—	—	—	-64.1	-208.8	-151.3	—	-215.4	-208.8	6.6
9 Checkable dep. and currency	82.0	—	108.0	—	-8.9	—	6.7	—	187.7	—	11.3	—	68.2	—	267.2	268.5	1.3
10 Time and savings deposits	409.6	—	26.2	—	20.3	—	0.2	—	456.2	—	13.4	516.1	46.4	—	516.1	516.1	—
1 Money market fund shares	-8.9	—	-3.2	—	-8.5	—	—	—	-20.5	—	-7.4	7.1	35.0	—	7.1	7.1	—
2 Fed. funds and security RPs	—	—	-2.2	—	-6.7	—	—	—	-8.9	—	96.2	-14.0	-39.9	—	47.4	-14.0	-61.4
3 Credit market instruments	-8.5	27.4	10.7	718.1	-66.1	-5.3	102.3	1140.2	38.4	1880.5	1111.1	-394.0	452.0	115.0	1601.5	1601.5	—
4 Open market paper	-0.3	—	-7.6	14.0	-5.1	—	—	—	-13.0	14.0	-7.3	-58.8	3.4	27.9	-16.9	-16.9	—

(*Continued*)

Table 13.1:   (*Continued*)

	Households and non-profit organization		Non-financial business		State and local governments		Federal governments		Domestic non-financial sectors		Domestic financial sectors		Rest of the world		All sectors		Instrument discrepancy
	U	S	U	S	U	S	U	S	U	S	U	S	U	S	U	S	
	(1)	(2)	(3)	(4)	(5)	(6)	(7)	(8)	(9)	(10)	(11)	(12)	(13)	(14)	(15)	(16)	(17)
5 Treasury securities	270.1	—	7.8	—	-11.8	—	—	1140.6	266.1	1140.6	284.9	—	589.5	—	1140.6	1140.6	—
6 Agency- and GSE-backed sec.	-141.9	—	-2.6	—	-28.2	—	-31.1	-0.4	-2088	-0.4	252.8	-22.4	-71.8	—	-22.8	-22.8	—
7 Municipal securities	-149.8	14.5	12.3	15.2	-0.7	-5.7	—	—	-138.2	-4.9	138.2	—	—	—	-4.9	-4.9	—
8 Corporate and fgn. bonds	41.3	—	—	579.6	-9.0	—	-0.2	—	32.1	579.6	416.2	-207.9	-14.4	62.2	433.9	433.9	—
9 Depository inst. Loans n.e.c	—	111.5	—	166.1	—	—	—	—	—	277.6	172.9	-124.0	19.2	—	172.9	172.9	—
10 Other loans and advances	-2.5	1.2	—	-20.9	—	0.4	2.5	—	0.0	-19.3	39.7	3.5	-49.9	5.7	-10.2	-10.2	—
1 Mortgages	-20.4	-240.0	0.7	-35.8	-11.2	—	1.7	0.0	-29.3	-275.8	-2309	15.6	—	—	-260.2	-260.2	—
2 Consumer credit	-4.9	169.1	0.0	—	—	—	129.4	—	124.5	169.1	44.6	—	—	—	169.1	169.1	—

(*Continued*)

Table 13.1: (Continued)

	Households and non-profit organization		Non-financial business		State and local governments		Federal governments		Domestic non-financial sectors		Domestic financial sectors		Rest of the world		All sectors		Instrument discrepancy
	U	S	U	S	U	S	U	S	U	S	U	S	U	S	U	S	
	(1)	(2)	(3)	(4)	(5)	(6)	(7)	(8)	(9)	(10)	(11)	(12)	(13)	(14)	(15)	(16)	(17)
3 Corporate equities	-363.0	—	—	-400.0	-4.8	—	-13.2	—	-381.0	-400.0	165.7	155.1	53.1	82.6	-162.3	-162.3	—
4 Mutual fund shares	419.2	—	-1.6	—	-2.5	—	—	—	415.1	—	66.5	625.7	144.0	—	625.7	625.7	—
5 Trade credit	—	1.5	95.9	123.2	8.5	39.1	2.9	8.3	107.3	172.2	-1.6	-0.0	11.5	6.3	117.2	178.5	61.3
6 Security credit	23.6	64.9	—	—	—	—	—	—	23.6	64.9	165.2	124.0	0.0	0.0	188.9	188.9	—
7 Life insurance reserves	-26.3	—	—	—	—	—	—	0.3	-26.3	0.3	14.7	-11.9	—	—	-11.6	-11.6	—
8 Pension entitlements	497.1	—	—	—	—	—	—	—	497.1	—	—	497.1	—	—	497.1	497.1	—
9 Taxes payable	—	—	—	6.6	1.3	—	11.9	—	13.2	6.6	—	6.5	—	—	13.2	13.1	-0.1
10 Equity in non-corp. business	1.1	—	—	-5.3	—	—	—	—	1.1	-5.3	—	6.5	—	—	1.1	—	—
11 Miscellaneous	-5.8	0.6	745.1	325.0	14.9	167.0	-1.0	93.7	753.1	586.2	235.7	171.9	257.5	252.0	1246.3	1010.2	-236.1
12 Sector discrepancies (1 less 4)	-312.7	—	152.2	—	-39.0	—	-84.7	—	-284.2	—	74.3	—	-13.9	—	-223.8	—	-223.8

General Notes: U = use of funds; S = source of funds. Domestic non-financial sectors (columns 9 and 10) are households and non-profit organizations, non-financial business, state and local governments, and Federal government.

Source: Board of Governors of the Federal Reserve system.

differing only by a statistical discrepancy. Gross investment consists mostly of capital expenditures and consumer durables expenditures. Inventory changes are sometimes important. We note that of $4721.5 billion in financial assets, about a fourth was held by households. A large share of these assets are comprised of Treasury securities and mutual fund shares. The domestic financial sector held about a half of all financial assets, which asserts its present dominance. This was about equal to one-half the value of capital expenditures by the non-financial sector. In other words, every dollar of real investment was represented by 50 cents of financial assets.

Another way of looking at financial asset holdings is as net worth or wealth. Table 13.2 shows family net worth by selected characteristics of families for 2001–2010. We find that the mean value of a family's net worth is $2,944,100 in the top 10%. In the bottom one-fifth of the distribution, the net worth of a family at the mean was only $116,800. The bottom one-fifth of the distribution hold only $6.2 billion in net worth. We see that the holdings of net worth are not only unequally distributed, but grossly so. A good part of the reason for the highly unequal distribution is found in the education level of the head of household. The greater the number of years of education, the higher the wealthholdings. A college degree yields a median of $195,200 in wealth while the absence of a high school diploma yields only $16,100, or roughly the value of that person's automobile. This reflects in great part the differences in income earned by the two sets of characteristics. It really pays to stay in school and pays even more to graduate with a college degree.

The pre-tax income shares of the top 1% of the income distribution are shown in Figure 13.6. In recent years, the top 1% "earned" about a quarter of all personal income. This is a high not reached since 1928, during the Roaring Twenties. There was a long period of decline for the top 1% from about 1933 to 1978. During much of this period, from the end of WWII to 1980, the economy experienced unprecedented economic growth and low rates of unemployment. In short, income need not be concentrated in a few hands to have prosperity and full employment. In the post-1980

Table 13.2: Family net worth, by selected characteristics of families, 2001–2010 surveys (in 000's).

Family characteristics	2001		2004		2007		2010	
	Median	Mean	Median	Mean	Median	Mean	Median	Mean
All families	106.1	487.0	107.2	517.1	126.4	584.6	77.3	498.8
	(3.7)	(8.2)	(4.9)	(11.2)	(5.7)	(9.7)	(2.8)	(12.7)
Percentile of income								
Less than 20	9.6	64.7	8.6	83.6	8.5	110.3	6.2	116.8
20–39.9	45.9	141.2	38.8	139.8	39.6	141.3	25.6	127.9
40–59.9	78.0	199.4	82.8	224.0	92.3	220.6	65.9	199.0
60–79.9	176.8	360.7	184.0	392.9	215.7	3939.9	128.6	293.9
80–89.9	322.4	560.3	360.9	563.7	373.2	638.1	286.6	567.2
90–100	1,021.5	2,777.1	1,069.7	2,925.2	1,172.3	3,474.7	1,194.3	2,944.1
Age of head (years)								
Less than 35	14.3	111.2	16.3	84.6	12.4	111.1	9.3	65.3
35–44	95.1	318.6	79.9	345.2	92.4	341.9	42.1	217.4
45–54	164.9	595.9	167.1	625.8	193.7	694.6	117.9	573.1
55–64	227.2	898.6	290.0	976.4	266.2	986.7	179.4	880.5
65–74	217.8	831.4	218.8	795.1	250.8	1,064.1	206.7	848.3
75 or more	190.3	574.8	187.7	607.7	223.7	668.8	216.8	677.8

(*Continued*)

Table 13.2: (*Continued*)

Family characteristics	2001 Median	2001 Mean	2004 Median	2004 Mean	2007 Median	2007 Mean	2010 Median	2010 Mean
Family structure								
Single with child(ren)	16.2	117.4	24.0	149.9	24.4	187.4	15.5	143.7
Single, no child, age less than 55	24.0	185.5	24.2	179.8	26.3	217.2	14.6	117.5
Single, no child, age 55 or more	111.9	355.8	134.0	405.8	150.7	408.9	102.0	391.6
Couple with child(ren)	139.3	540.0	140.6	580.5	147.5	629.1	86.7	555.7
Couple, no child	217.1	790.1	240.2	868.2	236.2	998.6	205.7	864.8
Education of head								
No high school diploma	31.3	127.5	23.7	157.1	34.8	149.7	16.1	110.7
High school diploma	71.1	222.0	79.1	227.2	84.3	263.8	56.7	218.1
Some college	89.8	352.1	79.8	355.7	88.8	384.5	50.9	272.2
College degree	262.2	976.6	260.2	982.3	298.6	1,154.5	195.2	977.7
Race or ethnicity of respondent								
White non-Hispanic	150.4	599.0	162.2	648.3	179.4	727.4	130.6	654.5
Non-white or Hispanic	22.0	144.1	28.5	176.2	29.7	240.3	20.4	175.9

Source: Board of Governors of the Federal Reserve System.

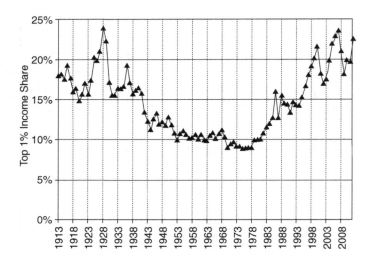

Figure 13.6:   Top 1% US pre-tax income share, 1913–2012.

Source: http://www.newyorker.com/online/blogs/johncassidy/2013/11.

era, the economy has become increasingly financialized and fewer households hold greater shares of the nation's wealth. At the same time, unemployment rates have remained very high.[5]

The distribution of wealth in a nation always is more lopsided than its income distribution. While some 1% of Americans are receiving a quarter of personal income of the nation, some 35% hold 1% of the wealth. Some 80% have just 11% of the wealth. The CEOs of the largest American companies make in one hour what their average employees make in a month. The CEOs on Wall Street make about twice that of other CEOs. One's occupation has a lot to do with whether you are in the top 1%, be it the income or the wealth distribution. Moreover, you are more likely to be among the super-rich if your earnings are from finance, making money with money.

Whether you read the book or saw the movie, you realize that the Wolf of Wall Street is likely to be richer than an elementary school teacher.

---

[5]For additional support for this view, see Thomas Piketty, *Capital in the Twenty-first Century, op. cit.*, pp. 294–296. He concludes that "... the increase in inequality in the United States contributed to the nation's financial instability" (p. 297). After analyzing hundreds of years of tax records from France, the U.K., the U.S., Germany and Japan,

The Vita Theory of the Personal Income Distribution

Since savings and wealth are derived from personal incomes, we need a theory of the personal income distribution. In the traditional world of economics wages and profits are factor payments to labor and capital. In the economy we have been describing, this is not so. Income payments are made to persons and therefore we are concerned with the *personal* income distribution.

Beyond his subsistence model wherein labor requires subsistence wages in order to meet basic physiological needs, Piero Sraffa provides no guide to the distribution of surpluses. What happens then with Sraffa's and Kalecki's theories when — as in the case of a modern economy — we find some "workers' with sufficient incomes to indulge in nonspending that is in line with wealth accumulation? If such persons purchase income producing financial assets they can then share (albeit indirectly) in total profits. The incomes of such persons then include labor earnings plus some capitalistic profits. In this case, of course, the "working class" receives a larger share of the national income than that derived from their labor efforts alone.

Because such earners also receive some non-wage income — interest on savings account, rents, or profits — more than two income classes exist, and the simple distinction between "workers" and "capitalists" dissolves. Such income intervals would identify the personal income distribution. However, this refinement of the income distribution does not alter Kalecki's general conclusions as long as there is one group that receives only profits income.[6] Such a group of income receivers does exist or coexist in modern capitalistic societies.

In short, the reliance on a stereotyped income division between workers and capitalists is an inadequate explanation for the income distribution of an affluent society. Moreover, it tells us little about the characteristics of the tabor receiving differential income payments beyond the color of their collars. We need to know more

---

he proves that the rich really are getting richer. And their wealth doesn't trickle down. It trickles up. This will not be news to the reader here and some of my other works.
[6] Seer Luigi I. Pasinetti, *Growth and Income Distribution* (Cambridge, England: Cambridge University Press, 1974).

about why different households occupy varied places in the income distribution. Our concerns go beyond the extremes of Tiger Woods' $110 million for playing golf, Jay Leno's $32 million as a talk show host, or Taylor Swift's $17.2 million for singing. A pharmacist in El Paso Texas earned $143,000 while a library director in Springfield, Illinois earned $35,000. The CEO of Xerox in Rochester, NY, earned $900,000 while the owner of a recycling company in Cadet, Missouri earned only $35,800. A real-estate appraiser in Vail, Colorado earned $215,000 while a copy editor in Corvallis, Oregon earned only $25,000. A family physician averages about $150,000 a year; a specialist averages $257,000. Generally, the more specialized the occupation, the higher the income. Incomes vary with a myriad of occupations, gender, and location. Unionized workers generally earn more than like-occupied non-union workers. The members of these diverse income classes end up spending their incomes in equally distinct stores, restaurants, and nightclubs. My vita theory provides a more eclectic explanation. Luckily, Sraffa and Kalecki leave open the possibility of a new theory of the personal income distribution.

A vita is a brief summary of the main attributes and event of one's life, a kind of autobiographic sketch. The vita theory is a way of saying that an individual's life history is important in deciding his or her income, and that income is important in deciding the person's life.[7]

The main thrust of a vita theory can be simply stated. Imagine that one labor market exists for each general class of labor, such as plumbers, medical doctors, electricians, or elementary school teachers. The individuals' quality as a productive member of the economic system determines which labor market that person enters. A person "qualifies" for a particular labor market by the state of his or her vita at the time. The vita begins with birth, when race, sex, religion, national origin, inherent or initial mental and physical capacities, inheritances, and family background (endowments) are duly noted.

---

[7]A detailed version of the theory (including the mathematics) appears in E. Ray Canterbery, "A Vita Theory of the Personal Income Distribution," *Southern Economic Journal* 46 (July 1979) pp. 12–48.

The birth vita suggests that considerable emphasis should be placed on childhood development. James Heckman, a Nobel economist, has proposed the Heckman equation. Poor families should have guaranteed access to education for their three- and four-years-old. Heckman grounds his argument in two long-term studies, one begun in the 1950s in Ypsilanti, Michigan, and another a decade later in Chapel Hill, NC. Both provided free preschool to children from lower-income families. In the decades since, researchers have been given periodic access to those children now adults. At age 40, the subjects from the Ypsilanti study were far more likely than their peers to have graduated from high school and have jobs. There were more likely to own homes and less likely to have needed social services. Children from the program in Chapel Hill had higher test scores than their peers through adolescence and were more likely to have gone to college. This initial investment provided what Heckman calls a "return to society" at an annual rate of 7% to 10%.

The autobiography is added to over the life span by education, other training, and experience. An individual does have some control over the length and depth of his autobiography. Mark Twain might have been content to write two books; instead, he wrote dozens and made a fortune. However, production "recipes" change in the long run. Today, unlike in Twain's day, some books are electronic e-books. Because labor demand is related to technology as well as to product and services demand, only the rarest of individuals can predict with any accuracy the amount of future demand for workers with his or her emerging or mature autobiography. Beyond this, specific labor supply conditions are a collective outcome that is beyond personal control.

Given his vita and the characteristics of the applicable labor market, the individual's basic wage rate depends upon the average wage for such services. Upon closer examination however, the individual's personal income exhibits differentials from potential labor market earnings. The differentials — occupational, geographic, inter-industry, union–non-union discriminatory, and so on — can often be traced back to the first vita stage, the birth vita. Second and third stages are the pre-career vita and the career or mature vita.

Speaking in terms of life stages highlights those events and times in which the individual often loses control over important choices. At birth the genetic code has already determined one's initial or innate IQ, sex, race, and initial state of health. The pre-career vita is the time for education when earnings qualities can be enhanced. For example, 35% of all white householders earned $30,000 or more in 1981 while 15% of black householders earned as much. Of these above-average whites, 63% were college graduates compared with 4% who had completed elementary school education. Of the above average blacks, 47% were college graduates whereas 7% had completed elementary school. Education adds substantially to the income of blacks though not nearly as much as to that of whites. Education beyond that which is mandatory and free normally depends heavily upon parental contributions. Individuals thus have only moderate control over their pre-career vitae because voluntary schooling and training is often directly related to inherited material endowments. By maturity the options of individuals are greatly narrowed; from the view of earning prospects, the autobiography is for the most part written although one new consideration enters at this life stage — years of experience.

The labor force is the supply side of the labor market and consists of those people who are of working age who wish to work and who have either pre-career or mature vitae, which identify the person's occupational characteristics. In the short run, individuals can enter only that labor market they "fit"; in the long run they potentially can change their characteristics and qualify for a different labor market, perhaps one with a higher wage rate. In general, however, the number of vitae directly applicable to the labor market decreases with increases in skill-specific aptitudes and required credentials. For example, the number of people who qualify as unskilled labor greatly exceeds the number who qualify as medical doctors; similarly the possibilities for substitution of different types of labor are greater among occupations with unskilled labor markets, the least labor substitution occurs within the most specialized occupation. At the higher skilled extremes in fact the professional occupation *is* the labor market.

There is no assurance that all vitae will be employed at any particular time, for employment levels depend upon demand. However, it is presumed that whatever involuntary unemployment exists, it involves those of lowest ranked employment vitae, including young people with pre-career vitae who lack job training or are being newly considered for on-the-job training.

During production and employment expansion, upward occupational mobility can occur. However, labor institutions — craft unions and industrial unions — are a major part of real-world conditions for mobility. Industrial unions for example organize entire industries; they consist of persons with diverse autobiographies and occupations, including both the unskilled and the semi-skilled. The main economic effect of the industrial union is the negotiation of a wage floor for its members. Moreover, the industrial union attempts to gain some of the advantages of the craft union through apprenticeship regulations, seniority practices, and (in some cases) discrimination.

Illus. 13.3:   The maze confronting the job-seeker.

Source: Graphicstock.com

These practices alter the mobility conditions for union workers as they attempt to change occupations within the unionized plant.

The vita theory points toward a structural view of labor demand. In the short run, employment and wages are not always determined by the same forces. In describing such a process, we lose the determinism of the neoclassical labor market but gain some realism.

In the short run, product, price, the state of technology, and industrial competition are givens. Employment is a fixed proportion of production, so the quantity of labor demanded is tied directly to the production level with fixed capital-to-labor combinations; employment levels are unrelated to the wage rate and therefore vary with output levels.

Technological progress can alter demand for a particular labor type in two ways. First is a change in labor quantity requirements. Though capital and labor complement each other in the short run or even the intermediate run (two workers may be needed for each new machine), they become substitutes for each other in the long run. In the long run, new capital equipment can be substituted for labor. The long-run trend of wages in the concentrated sector is known to be upward, and it is not surprising that the main purpose of new equipment in the industrialized economies is to reduce labor employment. Technological change also exerts a more indirect effect on labor demand. A new, more complex technology can cause a shift to labor of a different type altogether. Workers who once combined the ingredients for frozen cakes may be unqualified to monitor the automated machines that now perform this task, and unemployment of these workers results.

The labor markets dominated by industrial unions are akin to "administered" wages and prices. If the labor union is strong, industry ability to pay the demanded wage is enhanced by its ability to impose price markups upon the consumer. The industrial union's tool is the wage rate rather than the labor supply. This means that in the short run, employment is not related to the wage rate, and the wage rate is related to employment only if full employment extends across all labor, a rare event in recent years. (At full employment, wages can be bid up by Keynesian excess demand.) Therefore, a high wage can be associated with a high unemployment because employment is decided by the level of production.

Union labor sets the pace for the wage structure across the industrial economy. Moreover the price markup is not limited to concentrated industries. Competitive industries producing industrial or consumer necessities can pass along rising costs because the entity or consumer supplied does not have an alternative to the product.

The long-run labor supply is related to what individuals expect the wage rate to be, because the supply over time represents the maturing of vitae that have been directed along a career path designed years earlier. In the long run, increases in the expected market wage rate, for whatever reasons, are likely to attract new entrants, and the labor supply for that class of worker is increased. Even in this longer run, it is probable that the labor supply will be controlled in craft union areas. It is not mere historical accident that skilled workers were the ones to organize in craft unions and successfully raise wage rates.

The actual and expected wage rates may tend to converge for industrial labor, but this by no means assures a full employment equilibrium for such labor. The substitution of newer industrial processes that require less labor may have advanced to the point that long periods of idleness are traded for higher wages. Full employment under such conditions might require extraordinarily high production levels and a glut of goods. An unused supply of unskilled labor is a characteristic of recent experience in the U.S., England, and Western Europe.

The vita theory explains several kinds of wage differentials. If we impose the assumption of "rational man" or "super-rational man" with respect to income, these differentials represent an opportunity for a worker to move from a low-wage market to a high-wage market. Unfortunately, the mobility of labor is a complex, difficult, and cumbersome process. Studies attribute only 53–59% of migration to purely economic motives leaving considerable room for the motivations of regional preference, health, education, housing, marriage, lifestyle, and so on.

Vita Mobility and the Great Gatsby Curve

Still, according to the vita theory a higher wage rate for individuals depends upon their mobility. Significant upward mobility requires the acquisition of a "higher quality" set of skills, whether in response to changing technological requirements or because of the individual's desire to increase income and status. Despite the training and education that require a substantial amount of time and personal investment, this search for higher earnings may end with still another barricade. The individual may not receive the wage rate of the labor market and occupation of his choice because of genetic characteristics — race, sex, and nationality. Even age is a source of discrimination that can bar a worker from receiving the desired wage. Studies suggest that more than half of the earning differential is related to racial discrimination. In short, earnings and income differentials are wider than wage differences. Under such circumstances, the best advice is that children be very selective with regard to their parentage.

In states like Georgia, Mississippi, Arkansas, and South Carolina, poor white children tend to grow up into poor white adults. Moreover, regardless of race, the level of income inequality itself seems to play an important role in determining levels of social mobility. In places where income is divided very unequally, the poorer groups get only a small slice of the pie, very few people manage to start at the bottom and end up at the top. This is what the vita theory predicts. With a measure of inequality on the horizontal axis and level of social mobility on the vertical axis, Figure 13.7 shows the relationship for metro areas across the U.S. The negative slope indicates that high levels of parental inequality are associated with low levels of social mobility. Princeton's Alan Krueger, a former chairman of the Council of Economic Advisers, has dubbed this negative relationship, the Great Gatsby Curve, with a tip of the top hat to Fitzgerald's Jay Gatsby.[8]

---

[8]There is some irony is naming the curve after Gatsby, Fitzgerald's fictional character. Jay Gatsby came from poor origins and against great odds made a fortune, only to end in tragedy. See E. Ray Canterbery and Thomas Birch, *F. Scott Fitzgerald: Under the Influence* (St. Paul, MN: Paragon House, 2006), Chapter 7.

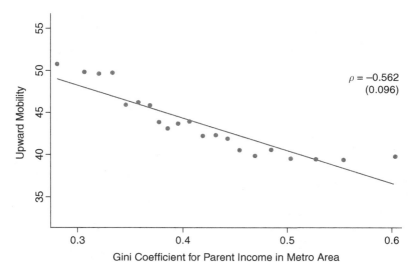

Figure 13.7:   Upward mobility versus inequality: The "Great Gatsby" Curve within the US.
Source: The White House, Council of Economic Advisers.

The relationship holds across several countries. Figure 13.8 shows the international relationship between parental income (vertical axis) and the income distribution. This is a slightly different way of looking at economic mobility. The upward slope illustrates that the higher goes parental income, the greater is income inequality. Inequality is transferred from one generation to the next. There is high social mobility in countries like Finland, Norway, Denmark, and Sweden. But mobility is low for Japan, France, U.K., and the U.S. The chances of moving up the income ladder are the least in the U.S., which brings us back to the Great Gatsby Curve for that country (Figure 13.7).

The vita theory also sheds some light on labor market conditions during the Great Recession in the U.S. By October 2010, the jobs crisis bought an unwelcome discovery for many of the unemployed. Job openings in their old fields existed. Yet they no longer qualified for them. Some companies asked staffers to take on a broader array of duties — duties that once were spread among multiple jobs. By

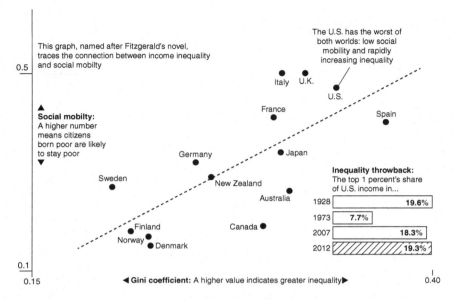

Figure 13.8:   The International Great Gatsby Curve.

Source: The White House, Council of Economic Advisers.

now, someone who hoped to get those jobs must meet the new requirements. The importance of the pre-career vita is highlighted by the distribution of employment in September 2010. For those with less than high school education, the unemployment rate was 15.4%; with high school completed, 20.0%; some college, 9.1%; and bachelor's degree or higher, 4.4%. Full employment existed only for the well-educated.

In light of the vita theory, an economy of workers demanding only minimal necessities cannot be described as robust. Only the austerians would opt for such a minimalist society. If we are looking for an "invariant" measure of value from the demand side, the quantity of necessities per worker seems a better candidate than Sraffa's composite standard commodity. Nevertheless, in the long run, just as the standard commodity must change with new technology, the quantity of "necessities" will change as workers redefine what is necessary. Whether necessities are a constant or a variable market basket of goods and services, their quantities and prices will determine their dollar value and the required dollar value of the wage bill. For example, in the autumn of 1980, the Bureau of Labor Statistics (BLS) estimated the annual cost of a "lower" consumption budget for a four-person family in the urban U.S. at $14,044. This household's budget included expenditures on food, shelter, furnishings, transportation, clothing, personal care, and medical care. If $14,044 represented the cultural subsistence requirements for an average family in the urban U.S., the wage bill paid to the household had to be at least $14,044. The current minimum wage would yield an income of $16,200.

Surpluses, a characteristic of the capitalistic economy, are production increments in excess of what is required merely to sustain life. Although it cannot be denied that there are American households at the biological subsistence level, ours is indisputably a supra-surplus economy, or Galbraith's affluent society.

The estimate for a "higher" consumption budget for a four-person family in the urban U.S. in 1980 was $34,409, nearly 2.5 times the lower budget. The "intermediate" budget was estimated at $23,134. Does this mean that the higher one's income goes, the greater the number of necessities the individual must meet? The answer, though not definitive is illuminating. In an economy such as ours, we need to distinguish between absolute physical necessities and "wants." The satisfaction of a greater number of wants is usually associated with higher standards of living. Leaving aside questions of whether people continue to be better-off at higher and higher income levels, we can say with certainty that the ratio of the dollar value of absolute biological necessities to the wage bill paid to the U.S. higher-income family is much less than one.

The vita theory also sheds light on the wealth distribution. Again the birth vita sets the upper and lower levels of wealth. It is difficult, though not by any means impossible to overcome disadvantages from sex, race, and meager household endowments. Women in 2010 had wages equal to about 87% of men's wages. Black people, especially women, had much lower wage levels than white people. Rich households tend to perpetuate themselves; again, there were notable exceptions. The stark reality is found in figures for the wealth distribution in the U.S. and worldwide.

The Waning of Austerity?

Even love affairs eventually end. The Republican's love affair with austerity is growing old and perhaps stale. There are some signs of a loosening in the belt cinching. After three years of belt tightening, governments from Washington to Madrid are easing up. Fiscal drag has been one of the forces tempering recoveries in the U.S. and Europe, so this may be good news. The term refers to the restraining effect budget chopping has on economic growth and employment. The bigger the chop, the more businesses and households rein in their own spending in response to less government hiring or curtailed public investment on things such as public works and education programs. Any softening of the fiscal drag is likely to play an important role in supporting a pickup in global growth.

Budget deficits are narrowing, leaving policymakers with more room to maneuver. Improving economies are helping to close the gap by bolstering tax revenue, just as the Keynesians forecast. The IMF forecasts that deficits of the Group of Seven countries will average 1.2% of gross domestic product in 2014, down from an average of 5.1% in 2010. Economists at Goldman Sachs and Deutsche Bank expect industrial economies almost to double their rate of expansion next year, to 2.2%, as policymakers relax spending controls. The U.S. budget that the Senate approved on December 18, 2013 restores $63 billion in spending over the next two years, effectively rolling back more than half of the automatic cuts known as sequestration, a by-product of the Republican austerians. Barring another embarrassing showdown over the debt ceiling in February, the budget deal should help spur the U.S. economy toward 2.8% growth next year, up from 1.7% in 2013. (However, the real GDP growth rate was −2.1% in the first quarter of 2014. This, in part, explains the great number of discouraged job seekers.)

The improving fiscal health of U.S. state and local governments also bodes well for the economy. Their $1.74 trillion (in real dollars) is 50% higher than the Federal sector, and they employ seven times more people. After declining for three consecutive years, state and local government spending jumped 1.5% in the third quarter of 2013, the most since the second quarter of 2009. There is a lot of catching up to do. This could raise the U.S. growth rate to 3.2% in 2014.

Austerity is also starting to give way in Europe, where it helped deepen the longest recession since the euro began trading in 1999. With countries under less pressure from the bondholding class to tackle excesses, fiscal policy across the continent will not be restrictive for the first time since 2009. Ireland, which is poised to be the first European economy to exit the region's bailout program, is scaling back the 3.1 billion euros ($4.2 billion) in cuts it originally sketched out for the next year to 2.5 billion euros. Spain's government is pledging no more tax increases and promises to cut taxes before the next election in 2015.

It may take until 2015 for the effect of all the cutbacks to diminish in Europe because policies implemented in 2013 have yet to take full effect. The euro area is likely to grow 0.8% next year, after shrinking 0.5% in 2013. This makes it all the more important that austerity ends. The love affair must be over.

Recent news in the USA is not all good. Some 1.3 million Americans were bracing for a harrowing post-Christmas jolt as extended Federal unemployment benefits come to a sudden halt on New Year's weekend. This has potentially significant implications for the recovering U.S. economy. A tense political battle likely looms when Congress reconvenes in the new, mid-term election year with the austerians running hard for re-election. Austerian Congressman Rand Paul says extending unemployment benefits would be a disservice to those receiving them, prompting poet Calvin Trillin to write[9]:

> You don't know how you'll ever feed the kids
> Without the benefits? You're getting nervous?
> Well, worry not, You heard what Rand Paul said:
> A cutoff's really doing you a service.

Contrary to Rand Paul, for families dependent on cash assistance, the end of the Federal government's "emergency unemployment

---

[9]Calvin Trillin, Deadline Poet, *The Nation*, January 6/13, 2014, p. 11.

compensation" will mean some difficult belt-tightening as an average monthly stipend of $1166 evaporates. Jobless rates could drop, but the economy may suffer with less money for consumers to spend on everything from clothes to cars. Having let the "emergency" program expire as part of a budget deal, it is unclear if Congress has the appetite to start it anew. Once again, the austerians may have played their Ebenezer Scrooge card, ignoring Dickens' lesson. Worse, another 1.9 million people across the country are expected to exhaust their state benefits before the end of June.

Without their unemployment checks, many will abandon what had been a futile search and will no longer look for a job. They are people like Stan Osnowitz, a 57-year old electrician in Baltimore who lost his state unemployment benefits of $430 a week. The money put gasoline in his car to help him look for work. He says that the continuation of his benefits would have enabled his job search to continue into spring, when construction activity usually increases and more electrical jobs become available. He had sought low-paid work at places like Lowe's and Home Depot. But he acknowledges that at his age, the prospect of a minimum-wage job is depressing. "I have two choices," Osonovitz said. "I can take a job at McDonald's or something and give up everything I've studied and everything I've worked for and all the experience that I have. Or I can go to retirement." Is the cut-off of unemployment benefits to people like Osnowitz really a disservice to them?

Conclusions

We have eliminated the main economic justifications for highly unequal income and wealth distributions. Business investment does not depend upon savings of the rich, but rather is impeded by income concentration at the top. The main purpose of the Angel's share of savings is to provide speculative funds and thus speculative excesses. Saving does not determine investment; it is the other way round. Business investment not only determines saving but also provides for employment (with a multiplier effect).

The vita theory leads to the Great Gatsby Curve. We find the mobility of persons in the income distribution impeded by elements in the Birth Vita. While persons have some choice regarding years of education, this choice is restricted by parental endowments for all except the rich. If we are to have more equal outcomes, more equal educational opportunities must be afforded to all pre-high-school children. This can only be guaranteed by Federal government aid. Beyond high school, a type of G.I. Bill could guarantee an equal chance for all to attain a college degree. It worked once before, after WWII, and it can succeed again.

The vita theory also highlights the limitations of conventional fiscal and monetary policies. To the contrary, an incomes policy would directly affect personal incomes. These blunt fiscal-monetary instruments can be used to elevate aggregate demand across all vitae. However, since employment by occupation is structural, fiscal, and monetary expansion cannot guarantee full employment — at least not full employment with modest inflation. Often, labor demand by occupational type and labor supply by required characteristics are mismatched. When this happens, there can be excess demands or supplies. This structural problem can be relieved by special training programs for shortage skills.

The social net can be smaller if the remedies prescribed in this book are applied. Still, there will be a need for progressive taxation, a negative income tax, a Federal minimum wage, and a minimal anti-poverty program. The minimum wage should be raised to $15 an hour with a cost-of-living provision. The affluent society can afford to pay everyone employed at least this subsistence wage. Moreover, this will help ensure that the next generation does not end up in the same low slot. As I have said before, most economic problems go away with full employment. It is time that the nation enforced its 4% full employment bill — one without reservations regarding minimum price inflation. An incomes policy is a safeguard against inflation (and does not add to employment). It is the least we can do for those willing and able to work full-time.

Index